Popular Antiques Yearbook

South Kensington picture director and auctioneer David Collins presides over a
crowded room during the studio sale of the artist Patrick Hennessy, R.H.A., in July

CHRISTIE'S SOUTH KENSINGTON

POPULAR ANTIQUES YEARBOOK

Volume 2

Trends and prices of everyday antiques for 1987

Edited by Huon Mallalieu

Phaidon · Christie's
Oxford

Phaidon · Christie's Limited, Littlegate House, St Ebbe's Street, Oxford, OX1 1SQ

First published 1986
© Phaidon · Christie's Limited 1986

British Library Cataloguing in Publication Data

Popular antiques yearbook : trends
  and prices of everyday antiques for 1987.
  Vol. 2
  1. Antiques——Periodicals
  745.1'075   NK1125

ISBN 0-7148-8035-3

Design, phototypesetting and origination by Gecko Limited, Bicester, Oxon.
Printed in Great Britain by Butler & Tanner Ltd, Frome, Somerset.

Contents

A note to the reader

The period under review in volume 2 of the *Popular Antiques Yearbook* is approximately June 1985 to May 1986. Unless otherwise stated, all the objects illustrated were sold at Christie's South Kensington on the date and at the price indicated in the caption. Where the photograph shows one of a pair or part of a set sold as one lot, the price indicated is the price paid for the whole lot. Prices of objects sold at Christie's King Street include the buyer's premium of 8 per cent, and at other houses the appropriate premium is included.

The measurement given in the captions is always the height of the object, unless it is indicated otherwise.

Overall responsibility for each chapter rests with the person who has written and signed its introduction. Queries and inquiries from users of this book will be welcomed, and should be addressed either to the author of the relevant article or to the author of the chapter introduction, at Christie's South Kensington, 85 Old Brompton Road, London SW7 3JS, telephone number (01) 581 7611.

Finally, a word of caution: each price recorded in the book is unique, and represents what one individual was prepared to pay at auction for a specific object on a particular date. We have made every effort to choose representative objects, to explain individual prices and to illuminate current trends, but the fact remains that prices do vary, particularly at auction, often in ways that defy prediction or explanation. Readers are therefore reminded that no price in this book should be taken as representing a fixed value for any object or type of object.

Foreword

On occasion, I, and no doubt every other auctioneer, have stepped down from the rostrum and made some generalized comment along the lines of, 'That was a fantastic (or terrible) sale', or, 'The bidding for that particular lot was very strong'. It is, however, frightening what forces can come into play to affect prices; forces over which the auctioneer often has no control. I remember a sale of Staffordshire ware many years ago, when one of the main collectors in what was then a very limited market thought the sale began at 2.30 p.m. and not 2.00 p.m. Once he had arrived, out of breath and flustered, prices picked up considerably. Of course, these individual market forces will come into play whether the market is 'up' or 'down', making the pricing of antiques an even more complex business and further justifying the publication of the Christie's South Kensington *Popular Antiques Yearbook*. It perhaps also helps to explain the success of the 1986 edition.

As I wrote in last year's Foreword, 'This yearbook is not a record of prices realized or just of "record prices"; it is a practical guide, explaining the differences in price for apparently similar objects. These can often be alarmingly different, and therefore price lists can be misleading. This is not only a price guide for the popular antiques market, therefore, but a price guide to the antiques and works of art which can be found daily in antique shops and markets, in provincial auction rooms, in your own attics and cellars and, above all, at Christie's South Kensington.'

In the second edition, we continue to be self-critical, comparing what we forecast with what has happened and making further predictions. We deal in depth with different topics and subjects within all the major fields, and have included three new chapter headings, for Transport Memorabilia, Tribal Art, and Books – the last two, in particular, being subjects full of pitfalls for the unwary.

I read last year's guide from cover to cover and was pleasantly surprised – and a little embarrassed, after years in the business – to realize how much I gleaned from its pages. I am proud to introduce this second volume and look forward to further embarrassment upon reading it.

Bill Brooks, Chairman

Introduction

by Huon Mallalieu

In the latter part of 1984, when the first *Popular Antiques Yearbook* was still more of an ocular gleam than an embryo, a number of hard-fought meetings took place between Bill Brooks, Christopher Elwes and Nicholas Pitcher of Christie's South Kensington, Roger Sears and Bernard Dod of Phaidon, and myself representing as best I could the likely reader of such a book. In general we were agreed as to the form that the book should take and roughly what it should contain. We felt we knew what the book should be, but we found it very hard to define and refine into a title. *Annual* against *Yearbook*, *Popular* versus *Everyday*, the struggles swayed back and forth, and as a sharp-eyed buyer of the first volume will note, we have been discussing the matter further over the last year.

As I say, we were fairly sure of our concept, and fairly sure that it was a good one. We wished to indicate the *why* of prices in the art and antiques market, rather than just list them. We would not concern ourselves overmuch with the great financial peaks, the million pound Old Masters and Impressionists and highly expensive masterpieces of furniture-making, but concentrate on the vast middle ground between them and the car boot or jumble sale. I think that we realized these intentions fairly well, and I hope that this year we shall have improved on our first performance.

That middle ground of the popular or everyday antique is indeed vast, and naturally we cannot cover it all in any one year. A favourite topic which merited an article last year may receive but passing mention in this volume. In no case has this been for some dramatic reason such as the collapse of a market, in most it is because we had as yet little to add to what had already been said, and we felt that the space could better be used by the discussion of new subjects.

There are three completely new chapters, Transport Memorabilia, Tribal Art and Books, and many new areas within the other chapters, such as Contemporary Ceramics. With a really vast subject like Books – which for our purposes also includes Maps – it must be re-emphasized that we are dealing with the middle ground, volumes worth perhaps £100 or £1,000 but not with Gutenberg Bibles at the one end nor Family Bibles at the other. This means that for the most part we are dealing with things that can be compared one with another. First editions of Ian Fleming's Bond books, for instance, can be assessed and evaluated on condition, since there are enough of them around to provide a track record, and yet there are not so many that there would be no market. Unique objects are always a problem to the auctioneer or antique dealer, since there is no form on which to base a realistic price. Perhaps the most difficult case to come up during the 1985/6 season was the manuscript of part of a play by Shakespeare's almost as great contemporary John Webster which was offered by Bloomsbury Book Auctions in June '86. In literary terms this was a highly important discovery, and since the proceeds of the sale were intended to safeguard the future of one of the more important gardens in Britain, everybody wished it well. However, the market can only exist if it is businesslike, and the manuscript was bought in at £170,000, rather than selling for the £400,000 or so that the auctioneers had hoped. In a way it would have been better to set no reserve and put about no estimate, because such a thing can only find its own level.

On the same day in June, Sotheby's took £143,000 for a manuscript of Edward Lear's drawings for his *Book of Nonsense*, 1845. This was not unique, since seven other such manuscripts are known, but they are all in libraries and collections in the United States, and this one contained a number of limericks which were not published in Lear's lifetime. In fact, it was so nearly unique that the saleroom estimate of from £40,000 to £60,000 was really an irrelevance, and the·market had to make up its own mind.

However, that sale did confirm the trend of increasing interest in illustrated books and the original illustrations for them. The buyer of the Lear manuscript, an American collector, also acquired a number of drawings for books by Charles Ricketts (see pp. 218–19), spending £12,650 on his frontispiece for the Vale Press edition of Milton's *Early Poems*, and £8,250 for another Vale Press frontispiece. In each case the price was roughly double the pre-sale estimate.

Just as the work of the twentieth-century illustrators is only now coming into its own in market terms, so too that in contemporary British ceramics provides some remarkable opportunities for a perceptive collector. Auction houses are not yet able to command the sort of prices that a good potter can expect when working through a regular dealer or agent, or even when selling direct, and such pieces that do appear in sales are still remarkably underpriced. In the first such sale held by Christie's South Kensington. I was very happy to be able to buy No.6 (centre) on page 119 for a mere £38, and subsequently I have been kicking myself for not seizing the bowls on p. 14 of this Introduction. In what department store could one buy a striking bowl together with' six soup bowls and saucers which had been mass-produced in a factory, let alone a set designed by one of the leading potters in the country, for a mere £22?

The subject of ceramics, although not up-to-the-minute contemporary ones, brings us to fakes. The 1985/6 season was a great one for fakes and forgers. About once a month the newspapers seemed to be dominated by headlines about the exposure of yet another fraud. There were Scottish Colourist painters in Edinburgh, Steiff Teddy Bears in York, marine paintings in Bristol, Clarice Cliff and Royal Worcester ceramics in the south, and examples of '17th-century' silver in Hackney. There were several more, including fakers of English watercolours, who have yet to appear in print, limelight or dock.

At first hearing, such stories cause much hilarity and considerable disquiet in the market place, especially among private collectors, but in one way they may be considered to be a positive and healthy sign. If all these things were not already in demand and expensive, there would be no point in faking them. Despite all the airy Robin Hoodishness with which he sought to gloss over his activities – 'doing belated justice to a poor and misunderstood artist', rather than lessening his reputation by passing off poor work as his – the late Tom Keating would certainly never have bothered to produce his 'Samuel Palmer' watercolours if a genuine example had not just been sold for some £14,000. Palmer was not particularly poor or particularly misunderstood in his own time. In Keating's he was financially worth faking.

At the time of writing nothing has been proved, but it seems possible that we shall soon be treated to the spectacle of newly emerged forgers claiming that their pastiches have only been intended to benefit the reputations of other

1. *Quentin Blake, 'Connoisseurship', pen and ink and watercolour.* Nov. '85 £380. This was the back cover of the dust jacket of a catalogue produced by Christie's South Kensington for a sale in aid of the Save the Children Fund. Together with the front drawing by Blake, showing a frenetic auctioneer, it was bought on behalf of the firm.

expensive British watercolourists such as John Sell Cotman and that poor murderous genius Richard Dadd.

The timing of the Clarice Cliff ceramic faker (see p. 117) was not so fortunate. The appearance of his or her efforts on the market happened to coincide with a temporary drop in prices for the real thing, and for once the operation may not have been financially worthwhile. I suspect that the spurious 'Royal Worcester' decorator, whose oeuvre was revealed to the public exactly a week after that of 'Cliff', has also made comparatively little money from the enterprise.

However, probably the best of this year's crop, Peter Ashley-Russell, a self-taught gold and silversmith from Hackney, seemed well on the way towards making serious money before he was caught. A spoon and fork by him were sold for £48,000, but before they were actually paid for the buyer insisted that the marks should be checked out at Goldsmiths' Hall, and instead of a cheque Ashley-Russell was rewarded with twenty-one months.

In Scotland the felicitously named Mr Conduct also earned a gaol sentence. This was largely because he had added theft to forgery, in removing the labels and old sale ledgers of a long-established and very reputable commercial gallery in Edinburgh, thus lending considerable authority and an impressive provenance to his versions of the works of Peploe, Cadell, Gillies and the rest (see p. 210–11). Luckily his painting was not quite up to the settings which he provided for it.

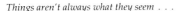

Things aren't always what they seem . . .

2 & 3. *Left: A Louis XV black and gold lacquer commode by Bernard van Risen Burgh,* sold by Christie's King Street at West Dean, Sussex, June '86, £58,320 – or was it? The previous lot (right) was a virtually indistinguishable copy by the James family's estate carpenter, and it was unsold at £4,500. Since on one occasion King Street were apparently confused enough to photograph the same thing twice, one must hope it was the right one which was delivered to the purchaser . . .

3. *The Carpenter's copy.*

By contrast the maker of 'Steiff' Teddy Bears in York got off with a fine of a paltry £500, little more than he had got for one of his creations. However, bear fanciers say that his work should not take in anyone who knows more about the subject than the mere name of Steiff, and the fact that genuine Steiffs are often marked with the maker's button in the left ear.

Before leaving the subject of fakes and forgeries, I would direct your attention to the 'Canaletto' on p. 209, and to the examples drawn from the field of scientific instruments on pp. 180.

Just as a successful forger will be hoping to do well in a new market where enthusiasm is higher than scholarly knowledge, so the wise collector will always be on the look out for subjects and areas where the standards of craftsmanship or artistic excellence are high, but which for some reason or none have not yet established a strong popular following. Two such areas have recently been transformed from eccentric hobbies to very serious markets, the first over the last five years or so, and the second in the last twelve months.

Sculpture seems never to have been a widespread British taste, with the exception of garden statuary. However, a few individuals have collected both antique and near-contemporary examples from the seventeenth century onwards. Others, although not particularly interested in classical figures, were happy to commission portrait busts rather than paintings to commemorate themselves. Such things have often been regarded as bulky and awkward

irritations by the descendants of the collectors or commissioners, but now the best of them are being studied and collected afresh. Even busts of relative nonentities by lesser-known or anonymous sculptors are now being sought after for their decorative qualities.

Even more recent is the serious attention which is beginning to be paid to Renaissance and later medals. Some of these are by very major artists indeed, but people who were prepared to pay vast sums for a drawing or a print by, say, Dürer, tended not to give a second glance to a medal from the same hand. However, a dealer-collector of my acquaintance now finds himself being made unrefusable offers for items which he had regarded as perhaps a pension for his children – and furthermore he is still able to buy other fine things by using only a part of the proceeds.

The textile market seems to me to be an area which offers several such opportunities for the future. For instance, early, that is to say before about 1820 or 1830, hand-made lace is distinctly undervalued. It is of far higher quality than its machine-made successor, and the skills needed to produce it have completely disappeared. While it is perfectly acceptable to recycle machine-made fragments, hand-made pieces should not be turned into flounces for cushion covers and wedding dresses, because they are quite literally irreplaceable. Some of the very best was made in Brussels in dark cellars where the conditions would induce heart attacks in the factory inspectors of today. A true expert is apparently able to tell if while working on a piece a lace maker was relocated on a better-lit upper floor. Venetian hand-made lace should be easy enough to identify – given a little patience. There are said to be 6,000 stitches per square inch.

One type of textile which has shown a marked increase in interest and price during 1986 is patchwork, in particular the English patchwork quilt which has been described as the true popular art of Britain. In a way this market interest is ironic, since in the words of a modern writer on the subject: 'Patchwork probably owes its existence to the fact

4. *Two underglaze blue and enamelled middle-sized cylindrical mugs with loop-strap handles and decorated with tree peonies.* Part of the Nanking Cargo. The most expensive of these pairs was £1,191 and the cheapest £502.

5. *One of twelve blue and white soup plates decorated with willow, peony, bamboo and rocks.* 9½ in. diam. Part of the Nanking cargo, this set sold for £4,438.

that it has never had any real commercial value . . . the time taken to make a true patchwork quilt which would show a reasonable profit to the worker has kept this traditional work entirely safe from the money-making business.' Now that the quilts have become antiques, however, prices no longer need to have any relationship to working hours.

In these undervalued areas the key is quality, and throughout this book, as in its predecessor, there is a repeated emphasis on the need to make a rigorous assessment of quality when buying or selling antiques. On rare occasions, however, quality, or the lack of it, is not the prime ingredient in the making of large and extraordinary prices. This year we have had one notable example of what can happen when a number of other important factors are combined together in the recipe of a sale.

The great sale of what was christened the 'Nanking Cargo', the porcelain and other goods raised from the wreck of the Dutch East Indiaman *Geldermalsen*, held by Christie's in Amsterdam in April 1986 was remarkable in many ways and instructive in several. There were approximately 160,000 pieces of eighteenth-century Chinese blue and white porcelain on offer, but to ceramic collectors and dealers there was very little that was intrinsically special. It was no doubt satisfying, but hardly vital, to learn that what had traditionally been termed 'childrens' chamber pots' – although too small for the outpourings of even the most modest of infants – were in fact feeding bowls or spittoons for the use of invalids. It was fascinating, but of little art historical moment, to see the effects of coral and some 230 years of immersion in salt water on underglaze blue and overglaze enamels.

In fact the pieces and patterns on offer were 'everday' in the context of the eighteenth century, and for the most part they were commonplace in modern market terms.

However, the auction itself became very special indeed for a variety of reasons, and this meant that the pieces acquired a 'value' that was far greater than their usual price range. The story was a romantic one – the loss: storm at sea, wreck on a coral reef, small boat of survivors bringing the ship's log safe to shore after a perilous voyage; the recovery: detective work in musty archives, intrepid team of divers, cargo largely intact, questions of international maritime law, and above all GOLD.

Then there was the very satisfying way in which the recovered porcelain could be matched up with the original lading documents of the Vereenigde Oostindesche Companie. The sale in Amsterdam was really a historical re-enactment of those regularly held on the quaysides there, in London and La Rochelle in the eighteenth century, when cargoes of 200,000 pieces were common.

All this was a perfect gift fo the publicity people. Video makers and television crews darted about like shoals of tropical fish, and magazine and newspaper articles sprouted like coral. I read a report of the sale in the local paper on a remote Greek island. There were natural doubts as to the ability of the market to absorb such a vast quantity of very similar wares, and it was hoped that the great department stores of Fifth Avenue, Knightsbridge and the Via Veneto could be persuaded to buy large lots as if they were modern dinner services.

However, in the event success far outran the most optimistic expectation. Porcelain dealers who had bought largely and often expensively as it seemed, were able to resell almost everything within the next few weeks. Only one month after the sale it was impossible to lay hands on one of the 120 gold ingots, some of which had gone for about twenty times the melt value of the gold. All that had not been bought to keep, had already been resold, presumably very profitably.

6. *A Chinese 'shoe'-shaped gold ingot from the Nanking Cargo, showing the marks.*

Incidentally, the ingots provide instructive reminders of the ways in which prices may vary for seemingly identical objects, due both to personal factors and tiny details. The most expensive, at DFl.197,200 or £53,297, was the very first to be offered. It was bought by one of the diving team who had decided that he wanted the first one whatever the cost.

Basically there were two types of ingot, the Chinese 'shoe' shape and the conventional rectangular bar. The first type contained rather more gold, but the second was of a slightly finer quality. There were seventeen shoes, other than that first lot. The second sold for DFl.150,800 (£40,757), but the rest then settled down in a range between DFl.87,000 and DFl.75,400. The range for the bars was from DFl.58,000 down to a mere DFl.19,720 (£15,676 to £5,330).

As I have said there was very little difference in size, quality or general appeal which would have been apparent to a casual observer. In fact, however, there were tiny variations. What some of the more astute buyers wanted – and in some cases got comparatively cheaply – were the ingots with the clearest Chinese characters stamped on them. It was the quality of the hallmarks, as it were, rather than the ingots themselves.

The prices for the European pottery jugs and jars with which the sale opened seemed to be dictated by the degree and quality of marine encrustation which they had attracted. Some had become splendidly sculptural *objets trouvés*, and the best of these were making up to ten times what had been expected by the auctioneers. Much the same was true of the glass wine bottles for the use of the crew; and even the stem of a broken wine glass, enclosing a single tear drop and faintly iridescent, which I had thought on viewing would be fun to own at perhaps £10, made DFl.186 or £50.

The interesting thing in future years will be to see whether objects from the 'Nanking Cargo' hold their value when the glare of publicity has faded and the romance dimmed with time. To some extent, I suppose, it will

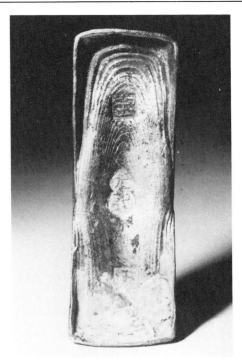

7. *A rectangular ingot showing the marks.*

depend on what Captain Hatcher and his rivals in the sunken treasure business come up with next. If it happens to be more of the same, then the market may well be saturated.

Amsterdam was the obvious and ideal place to hold this sale – after all it was the original port of destination for the cargo – and it is unlikely that many of the bidders and buyers were particularly concerned about exchange rates and currency fluctuations, although of course in normal sales these can be important.

During 1985 and 1986 the pound pulled back strongly against the dollar, having begun in such a weak state that parity was almost universally believed to be inevitable. This has naturally made things a little more difficult for Americans buying in London, although in fact even the new exchange rates are much more favourable to them than they were a few years ago. Also there are always two ways of looking at any fluctuation. It is now easier for British buyers to compete in New York, and the figures of British antique imports continue to rise.

The much bruited terrorist factor has had no discernible effect on auctions, or on the antiques trade fairs. While some antique dealers, especially in the prime tourist areas of the country, will undoubtedly have felt the lack of a seasonal passing trade of American visitors, serious dealers and collectors from the United States are not prevented from doing business by scares and rumours. In fact tourists have very little to do with auctions, and the people who mattered were still bidding, whether in person or by telephone or commission.

It is not impossible that the whole business may have had a good effect on business in Europe. So many statistics have been bandied about as a counter-blast to 'prove' that it is more likely that one would suffer from home-grown violence when visiting the United States than from any terrorist outrages in Europe, that surely some people will have been persuaded that they would be wiser to restrict their holidays and business trips to their own continent than they would be in venturing to the dangerous New World.

A little travel can be good for anybody in the antiques business, because markets do differ from place to place. This year as an example I would once again point to the textile section (p. 126). English collectors of high-quality Paisley shawls would be well advised to keep an eye on sales in Glasgow, where the best is often available, while Scots Paisley fanciers should look at London auctions, where there may be bargains to be found.

To return for a moment to the problems of terminology with which I began this Introduction: what is an antique? According to H.M. Customs and Excise and more importantly to the Export Licensing Board, it is anything that is 100 years old or more. This, in a bureaucratic and often illogical manner, cuts out many of the things with which this book attempts to deal. Edwardian furniture, Art Deco, lead soldiers, wrist-watches, modern first editions and paintings, none of these could be included were we to abide by the official decree.

One of the problems is that many people cannot think in terms of time and history. If something looks old or 'antique' to them, or if it was owned by Granny, then it must *be* old – even if Granny only died a year or two ago. Recently I bought a charming metalwork handbag as a present from a charity shop. The assistant (perhaps 70 years old, and thus not technically an antique) assured me that it was very old indeed. In fact it was probably half a century younger than herself. It was, as I had suspected, made in Turkey during the 1960s, and it is of a type that is now rather fashionable once again.

An even better example of taking age at face value – by both sellers and buyers, since I doubt that any dishonesty is intended – can be found in the street markets and tourist shops in Nigeria and probably other parts of West Africa. There you may be offered highly attractive bead necklaces and bracelets, which you will be assured are traditional local work. Only later might the thought strike you that they are made of glass beads, with threads of colour running through them as in sticks of rock, and that so far as is known there has never been a glass industry in West Africa.

There is an expression in those parts for when things go wrong, a sort of African Sod's Law. 'Wawa', they say with a shrug, which is an acronym for 'West Africa Wins Again.' In this case it is literally true.

These little pieces of glass originally came from the Venetian glasshouses on the Island of Murano, where the workmen turned the leftovers from larger jobs to decorative use. These are, in fact, the beads which our devious

8. *A truly splendid Bath chair.* May '86, £600. Surely a modest price to pay for being the envy of every Dowager at the Spa.

9. *A group of ear trumpets by F.C. Rein & Son of Charing Cross Road and The Strand. Left:* silver-plated, Jul. '85, £190. *Centre:* silver-plated and cased, Jul. '85, £340. *Right:* silver-plated brass, Jul. '85, £130. *Below:* silver-plated, Jul. '85, £240. These were by the leading maker of such things, and they all sold well above their pre-sale estimates.

ancestors used to pass off on 'the natives' in exchange for slaves, gold and ivory, and it is ironic, but far from unjust, that they should now have become 'beads for the tourists'.

Here for once it is not the instrinsic quality that counts, because in Venetian terms these were scraps and rejects, nor is it age, since both the African vendors and their unobservant buyers probably think the beads to have been made more recently than is actually the case. The things are sold at whatever is the going rate because they are attractive, and in the mistaken belief that they are 'ethnic'.

Something old and something new – and in both cases the prices seem remarkably modest . . .

Right, top row: Cypriot oenochoe decorated in red and black, with a similar bowl, jug and cup, *c*.8th century BC. 7 in. Nov. '85, £70. Cypriot terracotta two-horse chariot, 7th century BC. 6 in. long. Nov. '85, £200. Cypriot white-painted ware oenochoe decorated in red and black, *c*.8th century BC. 8 in. Nov. '85, £85. *Bottom row.* Cypriot red-polished ware deep bowl with bifurcated handles *c*.8th century BC. 6 in. Nov. '85, unsold at £110. Cypriot white-painted ware amphora decorated in red and black, *c*.8th century BC. 8 in. Nov. '85, £150. How can rather lovely things which are nearly three millennia old be so cheap?

Below: Tin-glazed earthenware bowl in white glaze and decorated with deep blue and green calligraphic motifs, by Alan Caiger-Smith, 15½ in. diam., with six matching soup bowls and saucers, all with the personal Aldermaston Pottery signature. June, '86, £22. This price was an insult to a fine potter, a bargain for the buyer, and will be a reproach to me, since I was sitting there and failed to raise a hand.

While on the subject of Africa, I would point to an instructive, and perhaps profitable, anomaly between our chapters on photographs and tribal arts. According to the first, collectors of nineteenth-century photographs show little interest in early African subjects, with the exception of Egypt. According to the second, collectors of tribal artefacts are keen to lay hands on such photographs because they often show interesting stools, clothes, weapons and regalia. Obviously such people should be viewing photographic sales as well as their own.

The 1985/6 season has seen considerable optimism in many branches of the antiques and art business. The most obvious sign has been the establishing of two major new international trade fairs in London. In June 1985 the first annual London Original Print Fair was held at Burlington House, and it did very well indeed. Then in January 1986 the first trade fair to be devoted exclusively to drawings and watercolours opened at the Park Lane Hotel. The doors had to be locked because of the crush twice within the first hour, and once more on the second morning, which is usually a dead period at fairs. This too proved to be a highly successful venture, and it is to be repeated in 1987.

However, antique dealers are rather like farmers; they are never happy to admit that they are happy. The current grouse, and it is a serious one, concerns the difficulty of finding new stock of high quality to replace what has been sold. This can only mean that prices for the best, and also for the second best, will continue to rise.

At the end of the season covered by this volume, financial and external pressures made it necessary for Christie's South Kensington to fall into line with many of their colleagues and competitors and introduce a 10 per cent buyers' premium at their sales. As a private individual I may express my sadness at this development; as editor of the *Popular Antiques Yearbook* I must point out that this premium will have to be taken into account in the future, when comparing the prices given in this volume and its predecessor to those which will appear in succeeding volumes. Where prices from other salerooms are quoted in this book, they are naturally given with the relevant premium included.

This book owes its being to many people. The continuing enthusiasm of Bill Brooks and Christopher Elwes, respectively Chairman and Managing Director of Christie's South Kensington, was obviously essential to the continuation of the series. Equally, without the skilled hands of Bernard Dod and Ruth Maccormac at Phaidon, our midwives as it were, we would never have seen our efforts in an acceptable printed form. The work of the many contributors needs no boost from me, as their articles are their own testimonial. However, there are a number of other people whose names do not appear, but who must be thanked for their aid in the task of compilation. Messrs. A.C. Cooper, Ted Holmes and Bob Masters have once again been responsible for the excellent photographs, and the drawing on this page has been especially produced by that fine cartoonist Hector Breeze. Nicholas Pitcher has again been the chief organizer and co-ordinator, and Jackie Lacey has performed a similar task in Glasgow, while John Gloyne was a civilized host in Amsterdam. The patience and support of Debbie Harman and Victoria Wolcough in the Press Office have been remarkable, extending even to the instruction of a notable Luddite in the basics of the new technology. Equally essential has been the patience and support, and in one case specialist advice, of my wife Fenella in the old-fashioned word factory of home.

"Someone's arrived with what he claims is a collection of original Beckett manuscripts"

1. *Furniture*

Introduction
by Hugh Edmeades

1

2

It is very satisfying to be able to report that the interest and awareness of antique furniture, which only really began on a large scale less than twenty years ago, is continuing unabated. For evidence of this, one has only to glance at the auction calendar page in any antiques journal to discover the number of sales that take place each week up and down the country, or drive through any town and count the number of antique shops. Or one can simply stay at home and witness the hordes of people who attend the BBC's 'Antiques Roadshow', not only to discover the value of their items, but also the history of them.

Over the last couple of years it has been apparent that a growing number of people from all walks of life are discovering the potential value of their possessions. Even if they are not interested in actually selling their furniture, they are keen to know about what they own and to make sure that it is properly insured. On the other hand, more and more people are realizing that they can afford to buy antique furniture to decorate their homes. Compared with modern designs and reproductions, buying 'antique' furniture, be it 18th-, 19th- or, indeed, early 20th-century, has to be a good investment, not only because it is usually of better quality and more durable, but also because should one ever want to sell it, one is likely not only to get one's money back, but usually, provided one has bought sensibly, actually receive more money than originally paid.

1985–6 saw only a slight increase in prices overall, and should be seen as a period of consolidation, rather than as a time of spectacular increase as was witnessed in the early 1980s. Bearing in mind the international nature of the art market, the relative strength of sterling against foreign currencies is an all important factor when considering any particular period. In 1984–5 when sterling was at its weakest, especially against the US dollar, foreign clients found it extremely attractive to buy in British salerooms and direct from the trade. However, over the last twelve months, with the increased value of sterling, the number of foreign buyers has decreased accordingly, and those that have been seen have been buying much more selectively both from the salerooms and from the trade. This in turn means that the British trade is having to buy more selectively.

However, regardless of the state of sterling, items always guaranteed to sell well are those that are of superior quality, and this all too bland generalization continues to apply to 1985–6, as can be seen in comparing No. 1 and No. 2. Both date from the early 19th century, and even though the former is in need of fairly extensive restoration, the overall attention to detail and quality of craftsmanship is of a far superior nature and this is reflected in its far superior price. In No. 3 the quality is again self-evident, but it is not for this reason that it is included here. Interest and desire for 'reproduction' furniture continues to grow. People who cannot afford to buy 'the real thing' are now more than happy to spend their money on later copies. This mahogany pedestal desk, loosely based on a Hepplewhite design and dating from the early part of this century, just goes to show that furniture does not necessarily have to be 'antique' to attract keen bidding.

3

4

5

Of course, copying or reproducing furniture styles is by no means a 20th-century phenomenon; perhaps the greatest exponents of reproducing earlier styles were the Victorians. The 19th-century Gothic Revival has long been considered a style in its own right and, as last year, has continued to be much sought after (No. 4). These chairs were part of a large consignment removed from a house in North Wales where they had been since they were made. Knowing the history or provenance of an item of furniture naturally makes that item more interesting and therefore more valuable. This fact is proved time and time again in the relatively higher prices achieved at sales that are held on the premises of houses, the classic example of which was the sale held at Elveden Hall in Norfolk in 1984.

In the same consignment as No. 4 was found the pair of bedside cabinets (No. 5). £900 for two bedside cabinets might seem a lot of money, but the fact that they are examples of the 19th-century Gothic Revival and that their provenance is beyond doubt contributed to the high price. There were also two other major factors: firstly, simply that they were a pair, and secondly, the size. Because many people can no longer afford to live in large houses, small pieces of furniture are increasing in value at a greater rate than large ones, especially if in pairs. This, however, must not be seen as denigrating large items. Take for example No. 6. Here we have a seemingly large and cumbersome piece. Because of their sheer size and lack of practicality in today's world, breakfront wardrobes are not always easy to sell; quite often they are bought merely for the timber to be re-used for other smaller items. At this point, take note of No. 7; one can soon realize that with only a small amount of imagination and work, No. 6 can easily be converted into a breakfront bookcase, thus transforming an unwanted piece of furniture into a highly desirable and therefore saleable one.

6

7

1. *A Regency mahogany writing table.* 66 in. wide. Nov. '85, £8,200.
2. *A Regency mahogany writing table.* 54 in. wide. May '85, £3,400.
3. *A mahogany partners' pedestal desk.* 71 in. wide. Jun. '85, £6,500.
4. *One of a set of fourteen George IV mahogany dining chairs.* Feb. '86, £4,200.
5. *A pair of early Victorian mahogany bedside cabinets.* 16½ in. wide. Feb. '86, £900.
6. *An early Victorian mahogany breakfront wardrobe.* 102 in. wide. Apr. '86, £1,800.
7. *A Victorian mahogany breakfront bookcase.* 65 in. wide. Feb. '85, £3,600.

1

2

During the year from June 1985 to May 1986, twelve and a half thousand items of furniture have passed under the hammer at South Kensington and in the following pages we have selected and illustrated only a very small percentage of those items. Grouped into various categories, we discuss the merits or indeed lack of merit of each individual item in order to show how and why the prices for seemingly similar pieces can and do vary enormously. Before we look at the categories selected for this year's book, here is a brief update on the categories that were discussed in the *Popular Antiques Yearbook*, Volume 1.

1. **Dining Chairs**
   Two from a set of eight Regency mahogany dining chairs, including two open armchairs. May '86, £2,800.
   Chairs in sets of eight continue to be much sought after. On these, note the carving on the top rail and the simple turned tapering legs.

2. **Eighteenth-Century English Bureaux**
   A George III mahogany bureau. 41½ in. wide. May '86, £1,350.
   There has been no appreciable movement in price for bureaux over the last twelve months. Of its type, this one even though in need of restoration had the advantage of the reeded angles and original ogee bracket feet.

3. **George III Mahogany Tallboys**
   A George III mahogany tallboy. 45½ in. wide. Feb. '86, £1,900.
   As mentioned in *Popular Antiques Yearbook*, Vol. 1 (p. 27), the majority of George III mahogany tallboys fetch between £1,000 and £2,000. This one is an above average example in that it is not only well proportioned, but also has the ever popular decorative feature of blind fret carving to the frieze and uprights.

4. **Secretaire Bookcases**
   A Regency mahogany secretaire bookcase. 40 in. wide. June. '85, £2,600.
   As can be expected with a type of furniture that combines all the functions of display, writing and storage, the popularity of secretaire bookcases shows no signs of waning. Here we have a well-proportioned example with unusual glazing bars and original handles and feet.

3

4

5

6

7

8

5. **Davenports**
A Victorian walnut Davenport. 22 in. wide. May '86, £1,750.
An example to show how these burr-walnut Davenports with rising stationery compartments are regularly commanding four-figure prices.

6. **Boulle**
A mid-19th-century Boulle bureau plat. 45 in. wide. Feb. '86, £1,800.
Of the examples of Boulle furniture sold at South Kensington during the last year, this proved to be the most sought after, largely due to its excellent condition and graceful serpentine outline. When buying Boulle, bear in mind that any restoration needed can be difficult and expensive.

7. **George III Mahogany Serpentine Chests**
A George III mahogany serpentine chest. 38 in. wide. Aug. '85, £4,400.
A wonderful example; good shape and size with excellent attention to detail, namely the boxwood edging on the top and the ivory oval key escutcheons.

8. **Chiffoniers 1800–1850**
A Regency rosewood chiffonier. 45 in. wide. May '86, £2,500.
Although of a basic design, this is an above average example with well-figured rosewood, nicely beaded edge and beautifully detailed brass inlay.

9. **Pembroke Tables**
A late Georgian mahogany Pembroke table. 38 in. wide. Oct. '85, £850.
Oval examples are still second in popularity after the serpentine variety. No noticeable increase in demand for Pembroke tables was seen in 1985–6; the pedestal-supported examples are still comparatively inexpensive.

10. **Later Dutch Marquetry**
A Dutch marquetry cylinder bureau. 44 in. wide. Apr. '86, £2,300.
Although this example has very stylized decoration, when compared with examples illustrated in *Popular Antiques Yearbook*, Vol. 1, the price achieved was to have been expected.

11. **Card Tables**
A George III mahogany card table. 36 in. wide. July '85, £550.
A fairly plain example, the price was helped by the original trade label found underneath.

9

10

11

Extending Dining Tables

As you can see from these two pages, extending dining tables come in all shapes, sizes and designs. Apart from the obvious pointers that one should look for in buying any type of furniture – age, condition, originality, quality, etc. – there are many practical points to bear in mind when making your choice. Is it the right shape? Is it the right size? Will the legs get in the way of yours and your chairs'? Is it the right height? You do not buy an armchair without first sitting in it to make sure that it is comfortable, likewise you should not buy a dining table without making sure.

The first page concentrates on illustrating the variety of designs for extending dining tables, while the second looks in more detail at one particular type and shows some of the variations that one can find on that design.   *Hugh Edmeades*

Measurements on pp. 20–1 refer to length fully extended.

1. *Early Victorian, mahogany with two leaves,* 108 in. Jan. '86, £1,350. A good example of the most basic form of extending table. The table is opened to insert the leaves by means of a winding handle.

2. *Early Victorian, mahogany with two leaves,* 132 in. Nov. '85, £1,600. A more complicated version of No. 1 with the additional benefit of hinged flaps.

3. *Late Regency, mahogany,* 72 in. Jan. '86, £1,300. Drop-leaf examples such as this and No. 4 are principally popular because when not in use as a dining table, the flaps can be folded down to form a space-saving side table.

4. *18th-century Dutch, oak,* 80 in. Sept. '85, £3,500. An oval example of a drop-leaf table, but there are square, circular and rectangular examples as well.

5. *Victorian, mahogany,* 70 in. Mar. '85, £5,000. Simply known as 'Jupe' tables after the man who patented the ingenious method of extending a circular table while still keeping the circular shape, by means of revolving the top and inserting wedge-shaped leaves. Large versions of these tables have made as much as £40,000.

6. *George III style, mahogany,* 90 in. Nov. '85, £1,500. Although a modern reproduction, this is another method of extending circular tables, this time by clipping on the spare leaves to the outside.

7. *William IV, mahogany with four leaves,* 129 in. May '85, £3,800. As already seen in Nos. 5 and 6, here is another example of a centre pedestal-supported table capable of extension. The leaves are supported by 'runners' and by the four legs, which neatly fold away when the table is in the closed position.

8. *George III, mahogany,* 64 in. Oct '85, £3,500. Yet another ingenious method of extending single pedestal tables, here the leaf is spring-loaded and is concealed under the two side pieces when closed.

9. *George III, mahogany with one leaf,* 71 in. Mar. '85, £1,200. The most basic design, simply two tables put together. The only decorative feature is a satinwood crossbanded top, and this was added at a later date.

10. *George IV, mahogany with three leaves,* 124 in. Jan. '86, £2,800. While still basically two tables put together, the sliding action is more complicated and flexible, and of course gives a good maximum length.

11. *Regency, mahogany,* 112 in. Nov. '85, £2,200. This has the two end sections with a drop-leaf centre section; and so when not in use as a large dining table, you have three separate tables, with the use of the centre section on its own as a small dining table.

12. *Regency, mahogany,* 125 in. Jul. '85, £3,500. A similar table to No. 11, but not only is it that much longer, but also 12 inches wider; note the unusual 'spoked' castors.

13. *George III, mahogany,* 102 in. Aug. '85, £1,300. A provincial version of Nos. 11 and 12, of very poor quality.

14. *George III, mahogany,* 115 in. May '85, £2,600. Another three-part table seemingly very similar to No. 13, but of twice the quality, hence twice the price.

15. *Early Victorian, mahogany,* 125 in. Feb. '85, £3,200. Although only three parts are shown, this does have another identical centre section, and both have swivelling fold-over tops, and so for the price of one table, you have a pair of tea-tables and a pair of side tables.

16. *George IV, mahogany with three leaves,* 118 in. Jun. '85, £5,200. All in one section, and note the ingenious 'concertina' action making it as flexible as No. 10. Apart from this flexibility, the prime advantage of this table as compared for example with No. 15, is that in any position you only have half the number of legs to contend with.

9

10

11

12

13

14

15

16

Sideboards

The type of furniture that we know as sideboards today first became popular during the reign of George III, through the designs of such people as Robert Adam, Thomas Shearer and Thomas Sheraton, when the demand for pieces of dining-room furniture for storage and display purposes became ever increasing.

The origin of the sideboard dates back to the Middle Ages when 'dressers' were used to accommodate the various dining-room accessories. Hard on the heels of the dresser came the 'court cupboard' whose popularity lasted throughout the Tudor period and well into the 17th century. With the Restoration of the monarchy in 1660, the demand for dining-room furniture in which to store things began to wane. By the time Queen Anne succeeded to the throne in 1702, the emphasis was far more on display rather than storage, and this vogue continued throughout the first half of the century, as can be witnessed by the lack of cupboard and drawer furniture in the dining-rooms of this period. Instead of hiding away their possessions, people preferred to have them on view and so 'side tables' both grand and simple, and more often than not with a marble top, became the order of the day.

The second half of the eighteenth century saw many changes in style and taste, and a new 'type' of furniture was needed to accommodate these changes. The desire for storage space, not deemed necessary during the previous hundred years, became paramount once again, and various designs of sideboard, combining the usefulness of both side tables and cupboards, began to be produced. The requirement was for a piece of elegant furniture which could not only display but also house the 'accessories' pertinent to use in the dining-room. The ideal design soon became apparent. This was for a piece of furniture, standing on a combination of legs and fitted with enough drawer space for cutlery, table linen etc., and enough cupboard space or deep drawers to hold bottles. As one can see from the illustrations, this basic design not only fulfilled all the requirements, but also lent itself well to numerous variations. All these examples are made of mahogany and date from the period 1780–1810. However, one must be aware that such has been the popularity of the design, that not only did Edwardian cabinet-makers use it as a basis for their sideboards, but also modern craftsmen continue to produce these 'Georgian' style sideboards in great numbers.   *Hugh Edmeades*

Measurements on pp. 22–3 refer to width.

1. *Regency*, 79 in. Apr.'85, £3,400. A comparatively large example of graceful outline and with good attention to detail, as in the ivory diamond key escutcheons and the arcaded boxwood stringing.
2. *George III*, 48 in. Jul. '85, £2,900. From one extreme to another. Although this example is very standard in design, sideboards of only four feet are not common and are therefore much sought after.
3. *George III*, 76 in. Jun. '85, £3,000. Again a larger than average sideboard, this time of serpentine outline, with more decorative details than No. 1. Notice how the right-hand drawer is disguised as two short drawers to match the left side.
4. *George III*, 54 in. Dec. '84, £2,800. A more typical size, but well figured and with a generous satinwood crossbanded top. Although the stringing on the legs is similar to that on No. 2, the use of circular and oval bands on the drawers and doors is much more ambitious and satisfying.

1

2

3

4

5

6

7

5. *Regency*, 57 in. Apr. '85, £1,700. Slightly heavy in appearance, but an example of a sideboard on well-turned and reeded legs.

6. *Regency*, 57 in. Mar. '85, £1,400. Again, although slightly heavy in appearance, the ebony stringing and brass lion mask and ring handles are good features.

7. *Regency*, 54 in. Jul. '85, £1,350. Note the more ambitious use of the ebony decoration compared to Nos. 5 and 6. Here the maker has done away with the two central legs, but has added a brass curtain rail.

8. *George III*, 60 in. Nov. '84, £1,000. A relatively low price, but this was accounted for by the need for extensive restoration.

9. *Regency*, 54 in. Sept. '85, £900.

10. *Regency*, 46 in. Jan. '85, £900. Both this and No. 9 are two examples illustrating the most basic of designs with a minimum of decorative detail.

8

9

10

Oak — A Stronger Market

Having been fairly sluggish since the late '70s, the market in oak furniture has picked up well over the last two years. Oak can be read here as a generic term for early furniture and traditional country pieces made with varying degrees of attention to the fashions of the day. Pre-18th-century oak has enjoyed a vogue since the early 19th century, its associations well suiting the romanticism typified by Walter Scott's novels.

The relatively crude constructional methods of the joiner, the availability of old panelling and other architectural fittings such as staircase balusters, and the scarcity of precise historical records of design have combined to make oak a peculiarly suitable target for the fakers. Today, the larger proportion of pieces on the market have either been embellished, adapted or completely made up by these ingenious entrepreneurs. As the wood used may have undergone perhaps 150 years of genuine ageing, spurious pieces can be extremely difficult to detect. Indeed many books on the subject, particularly those from earlier in this century, are scattered with illustrations of undetected fakes. It is therefore a field through which the purist must tread with care.

Some of the commonest fakes are coffers made up from old panelling, and joint stools using staircase balusters for legs. Later carving on genuine pieces, often done as a hobby by amateur Victorian carvers, is another problem. It can most commonly be found applied to coffer fronts, but the food cupboard (No. 1) had also received this unwelcome attention. Without the addition of indiscriminate carving and a spurious date, it would have been worth about the same as No. 2. As it was, it was reduced to a price comparable with that of No. 4, a straight Victorian creation of Jacobean inspiration, made without intent to decieve, such as was produced in large quantities from the mid-19th century.

However, the stools in No. 15 on p. 26 escaped 'improvement'. To find a set of six is a rarity and with their fine rich patina and colour, they commanded a hefty premium. The long stool (No. 5) came out of a Welsh stable, and judging by its grey complexion and lack of patina had been there some time. It was, however, completely original and had a good provenance. Because of the aforementioned problems, good provenance is a particular bonus with oak, but it is important to bear in mind that many houses may in fact have been refurnished with oak a hundred or so years ago, much of it supplied as genuinely old by less than scrupulous dealers.

1. *Carved oak press cupboard, 17th century, with some later carving.* Oct. '85, £500.
   Press cupboards are often miscalled 'court' cupboards, but the true court, which was the ancestor of the press, had no doors (see No. 4). The carved motifs on pieces such as this can often provide a clue to the locality in which they were made. (See V. Chinnery: *Oak, the British Tradition,* Antique Collectors' Club, 1979.)

2. *Oak press cupboard, late 17th century.* Oct. '85, £2,000.
   A price which demonstrates the importance of original condition, although most pieces of this age show signs of repair.

3. *Oak and fruitwood dresser.* Christie's King Street, May '85, £4,536.

4. *Victorian court cupboard.* Nov. '85, £550.
   The very first court cupboards were open at the back as well, and this is a copy of a transitional design.

Dining chairs have, as always, proved in demand and a particularly popular model is the Derbyshire chair. The harlequin set of five chairs (similar but not matching), dating from the 17th century, are strong, very usable and of good bold design (No. 6). The Carolean chairs (No. 7) are altogether more delicate, and are likely to be relegated to the side of the room by us aficionados of the Parker Knoll. They provide fine decoration, redolent of the period, all the same. This pair was in good clean condition—being most commonly made of walnut they can be susceptible to worm—and examples in poorer condition can still be bought for much less.

The Windsor chair continues in great demand, the classic design of the early 19th-century pair in yew and elm (No. 9) having a considerable edge over their heavier Victorian counterparts (No. 10).

Neither of the dining tables illustrated is of great age, but they are clever copies, with well-simulated wear and a close attempt at genuine colour and patination. Gatelegs of good size (No. 11) are in much demand and even if not genuine will fetch a high price. In the draw-leaf refectory table (No. 12) we can see how the stretcher is undulated as if by generations of feet, although the squared corners have been left rather inconsistently true for so much wear. The carving also is rather too sharp, the finish too glossy and shallow, and the colour lacking that complexity that only several hundred

5. *Oak long stool, 17th century.* Feb. '86, £1,050.

6. *Set of five Derbyshire chairs, early 17th century.* Christie's King Street, Jan. '86, £2,376.

7. *Pair of Carolean chairs.* May '85, £1,188.

8. *Chest of drawers, George III.* Dec. '85, £600.

9. *Pair of yew and elm Windsor chairs, early 19th century.* Jun. '85, £2,600.

10. *Pair of Victorian Windsor chairs.* Jul. '85, £1,000.

Oak continued

11

12

13

14

years can lend it, but an impressive model all the same.

The addition of some fruitwood with its wonderful lustrous colour will also always add greatly to a price, No. 12 being a good example.

The price for the handsome Georgian dresser (No. 13) is around the average at the moment for such a piece with a plate rack. The less elaborate dresser base (No. 16) provides a useful piece of dining-room furniture more in line with our idea of a sideboard.

Oak used in a less vernacular tradition would seem at the moment to be the most undervalued section of the market. No. 14 will, when the later bracket feet have been replaced with buns, be a beautifully proportioned Queen Anne chest. No. 8 is an excellent George III example, with mahogany crossbanding, fluted quarter-column angles and ogee bracket feet. Their equivalents in walnut and mahogany respectively could be expected to make several times the price. *James Graham-Stewart*

11. *Gateleg dining table.* Aug. '85, £2,200.

12. *Draw-leaf refectory table.* Apr. '85, £2,200.

13. *Oak dresser, 18th century.* May '85, £2,800.

14. *Chest of drawers, Queen Anne.* Feb. '86, £650.

15. *A set of six joint stools, early 17th century.* Christie's King Street, Nov. '85, £25,920.

16. *Oak dresser base, 18th century.* Mar. '85, £1,700.

15

16

'Louis Style' Furniture

Pieces made in the style of the great period of French furniture of the reigns of Louis XV (1715–74) and Louis XVI (1774–93) have been in much demand since the mid-19th century. Both 19th-century and relatively modern copies can achieve high prices at auction. Nos. 1 and 2, for example, were both made within the last fifty years. Both were nicely, if not exquisitely made, with a good combination of marble tops, marquetry and ormolu mounts within a curvaceous form to create a harmonious whole — no mean feat with such rich and diverse ingredients. They have the added advantage of being in pairs and of small size.

Nos. 3 and 4 fetched the same price. They have little else in common. No. 3 is showy and crude, a good example of the Louis XV style badly misinterpreted by a modern maker, in whose hands the various decorative elements appear to have got out of control, each asserting itself at the expense of any unity and harmony the piece might have achieved as a whole. It is bold and impressive all the same, and such pieces do find a ready market. No. 4 is much more restrained, with good mounts and veneers. A vitrine cabinet of similarly successful design and execution might be expected to achieve a much higher price.

The bureau plat (No. 6) is true to the magnificence of its precursors, with confident curves and boldly chased mounts. No. 5 shows the caution of a maker not so confident in the language of the style, and the result is weak and a little awkward.   *James Graham-Stewart*

1. *One of a pair of kingwood marquetry and ormolu mounted petit commodes, Louis XV style, 20th century. 29 in. wide. Dec. '85, £4,500.*

2. *One of a pair of Louis XV style kingwood tables en chiffoniere, 20th century. 15 in. wide. Nov. '85, £3,400.*

3. *A Louis XVI style vitrine table, late 19th century. 27 in. wide. Nov. '85, £2,400.*

4. *A kingwood and Vernis Martin vitrine cabinet of Louis XV inspiration, 20th century. 54 in. wide. Jul. '85, £2,400.*

5. *A Louis XV style kingwood bureau plat, 20th century. 44½ in. wide. Nov. '85, £1,500.*

6. *A Louis XV style bureau plat, mid-19th century. 63 in. wide. May '85, £5,500.*

Edwardian Painted Furniture

It is not difficult to understand the continuing popularity of furniture decorated with light rococo painting in the manner of Angelica Kauffmann, Cipriani and Bartolozzi. First popularized in the last quarter of the 18th century, it re-emerged as an important style at the turn of the 19th and 20th centuries. In many ways, the circumstances of its revival are similar to those of its conception – just as Adam's superficial decorative ornament in light relief moved away from the heavy carving typical of the mid-18th century, so did Edwardian cabinet-makers react against the bold form and decoration prevalent in later Victorian furniture.

The painting on Edwardian furniture usually consists of husks, flower swags and sprays, urns and masks – all painted in bright, naturalistic colours. However, the later pieces do have a tendency to be overdecorated (No. 1), perhaps in response to the closer, more exaggerated figuring of the East Indian satinwood favoured by the Edwardians, as opposed to the bolder West Indian wood used by the Georgians.

The suitability of this type of high quality, delicately proportioned, light furniture to the modern home guarantees a strong market, and consequently a high price at auction. The importance of the painted decoration is reflected in the prices of Nos. 1 and 2. No. 2 is of serpentine form and in normal circumstances would demand a higher price than the more simple bowfront, but No. 1 sold for some £600 more. It is also interesting to note how the painted Edwardian example of No. 1 compares in price with its unembellished Georgian counterpart, No. 3 – the desirability of age and rarity are matched by the painted decoration.

Apart from the painting, the price of this type of Edwardian furniture appears to be dependent on type of wood. The rich tones of mahogany and satinwood both accept with some ease the light rococo decoration and are therefore used most commonly. The strong pattern of rosewood is not used so successfully and is therefore rarer, and yet less desirable. Nos. 4 and 5 show two pairs of similar display cabinets. No. 4 has the more complex form and is slightly better balanced. However, the satinwood pair (No. 5) realized some £1,000 more. Further evidence of the greater value of satinwood as opposed to mahogany can be found in Nos. 6 and 7. Once again, the mahogany example has a more complicated form, with drawers below the secretaire drawer rather than the cupboard doors of the satinwood example. The price difference is still £800 in satinwood's favour.

Painted satinwood furniture has continued to be produced up to the present, the quality never matching that of the Edwardians. No. 8 is a later piece, any classical elegance lost by the ungainly stand, and it is not of such high quality of construction. It contrasts sharply with No. 9, which represents the quintessence of Edwardian painted furniture. Here the craftsman delights in his ability to complicate form, and yet does so with restraint. Likewise, the painted decoration is subtle, not over elaborate, creating the lightness, delicacy and grace that is the strength of this furniture, ensuring its popularity and making it an attractive investment.

Edward Dolman

1

2

3

Measurements refer to width.

1. *An Edwardian satinwood bowfront chest.* 43 in. Apr. '86, £2,600.

2. *An unpainted Edwardian satinwood serpentine chest.* 42 in. Feb. '86, £2,000.

3. *A George III bowfront satinwood chest.* 46 in. Aug. '85. £2,600.

4. *A pair of Edwardian mahogany and satinwood banded display cabinets.* 29 in. Feb. '86, £1,800.

5. *A pair of Edwardian satinwood display cabinets.* 29 in. Nov. '85, £2,800.

6. *An Edwardian mahogany secretaire bookcase.* 35 in. Nov. '85, £2,800.

7. *An Edwardian satinwood secretaire bookcase.* 44 in. Aug. '85, £3,500.

8. *A satinwood bureau-on-stand, post-Edwardian.* 36 in. Jan. '86, £1,400.

9. *An Edwardian satinwood display cabinet.* 41 in. Jan. '86, £2,400.

Georgian Tripod Tables

The beginning of George II's reign saw the introduction of the tripod table. It first appeared as a tea or small supper table, the earliest examples having dished compartments in the top to support plates, cups and saucers (No. 1). Tea drinking at this time had become a popular pastime in 'smart' society. The expense and importance of tea resulted in the earliest tripods being of the highest quality, often decorated with brass inlay (No. 1), and it is this inlay that allows us to attribute the manufacture of these tables to the workshops of John Channon, possibly influenced by the work of Abraham Roentgen (1711–1793), father of the better known German maker, David Roentgen (1743–1807).

When assessing the value of a Georgian tripod table, the two most important considerations are its level of ornament and the originality of its condition. Of course, the patina and colour of the wood are also important; a good quality Georgian tripod table made in a wood other than mahogany is rare, and this can increase value (No. 2). However, with regard to ornament, in most cases the higher quality the table, the greater the level of decoration.

1

2

3

The obvious practicality of this type of table soon resulted in the expensive dished tea tops being replaced by cheaper, plain tops geared to more general uses. The popular 'pie-crust' moulding (Nos. 3 and 6) enhances the tables' value, as does a top that has been turned to produce a rim (Nos. 2 and 4). However, beware of the latter – a plain top can always be turned later to give the impression of quality. A recently turned top can be spotted simply by measuring along the grain and across it. If the two measurements are the same, there has been no shrinkage in the wood and it is probably a late modification. The top can also appear rather thin with signs of the fixing bolts to the support appearing on the surface. A 'bird-cage' device enabling the top to tilt is also a sign of quality and can increase the value of the table (Nos. 3, 4, 5 and 7). The crispness of carving on the base also denotes a higher level of craftsmanship (No. 8).

1. *A mid-Georgian mahogany table in the manner of John Channon, inlaid with brass lines.* 23 in. Edward James Collection, West Dean Park, June '86, £11,000.

2. *A mid-Georgian burr yew table.* 23 in. Christie's King Street, Oct. '85, £3,132.

3. *A Georgian mahogany table.* 32½ in. Feb. '86, £1,350.

4. *A mid-Georgian mahogany table.* 33 in. Feb. '86, £900.

4

The nature of the tripod table as a portable, practical piece of furniture means that damage of some sort is almost unavoidable. It is very rare indeed to come across a table without any restorations or repairs. Most commonly the top and bottom are 'married' together – the original top or bottom having been replaced from another table, often of the same period. Always look on the underside of the top for any signs of fixings to a previous support, and try and gauge the overall balance of the table. A top must sit easily on its support, appearing neither too large nor too small, too heavy or too light. No. 8 has a rather ungainly feel and is quite possibly a marriage. Legs are often replaced and should be carefully examined for consistency of age and colour. The fixing point between top and support is also often damaged and replaced.

All the above factors must be taken into account when placing a value on a tripod table. Generally speaking, the market for these tables is strong and consistent. A high quality table in its original form can therefore be a sound and enjoyable investment.

Edward Dolman

5. *A mid-Georgian mahogany table.* 30 in. Feb. '86, £700.
6. *A mid-Georgian mahogany table.* 29 in. Mar. '86, £600.
7. *A George III mahogany table.* 30½ in. May '86, £950.
8. *A George III mahogany table.* 29 in. Mar. '86, £700.
9. *A mid-Georgian mahogany table.* 31 in. Jan. '85. £350.

Wine Coolers and Cellarettes

The two terms, wine cooler and cellarette, are often incorrectly used. A cellarette is a piece of furniture that can hold bottles, and only when it is lined with a material such as lead or zinc can it be called a wine cooler.

Although, as we have seen, sideboards were often fitted with a 'cellarette' drawer, the number of bottles a sideboard could house was limited, and so during the 18th century we see the emergence of a new price of furniture, specifically designed for bottles.

During the late Georgian period, many wine coolers/cellarettes were designed more for function than for beauty (Nos. 1–2), being simple oval mahogany tubs bound in brass and on plain stands. More attractive were those that were covered (Nos. 4–6), often with a domed lid. The most successful and decorative examples were a combination of these two types (Nos. 7–11). Here we find hexagonal or octagonal boxes bound in brass with hinged lids, sitting on detachable or attached stands. By the start of the nineteenth century, the archaeological interest of the period could be seen in the sarcophagus-shaped designs used for wine coolers/cellarettes (Nos. 12–14.)

Hugh Edmeades

Measurements on pp. 32–3 refer to width.

1. *A George III mahogany brass-bound wine cooler,* 25 in. Christie's King Street, May '85, £2,268. Compared to Nos. 2 and 3, note how much deeper this is.

2. *A George III mahogany brass-bound wine cooler,* 24 in. Jan '86, £1,250. Very much the poor relation of No. 1 in every aspect,

with similar 'C' scrolled brackets, but lacking the quality.

3. *A George III mahogany brass-bound wine cooler,* 27 in. Jan. '85, £900. Sold a year before No. 2, but the price difference was due to the fact that the stand was a later replacement. See how the handles appear to be too heavy for the piece.

4. *A George III mahogany cellarette,* 16 in. Nov. '85, £1,400. A good example of the lidded cellarette, only 16 in. wide but nicely crossbanded – and totally original.

5. *A George III mahogany cellarette,* 22 in. Christie's King Street, Jan. '85, £1,296. A larger example than No. 4, but again totally original.

6. *A Regency mahogany cellarette,* 20 in. Christie's King Street, Jan. '85, £1,296. Although of a later date than No. 5, it fetched the same price, partly due to the Irish trade label found inside.

1

2

3

4

5

6

7. *A George III mahogany brass-bound wine cooler,* 20 in. May '85, £2,200. A beautifully figured piece of mahogany. This one still has its originally tap underneath to drain away the water. The turned reeded legs are an unusual feature, as most of them were simply square.

8. *A George III mahogany brass-bound wine cooler,* 19 in. Christie's King Street, Jan. '85, £2,052. Another octagonal example, this time with a segmented lid centring a satinwood panel. Unfortunately the stand is not contemporary, hence the lower price than No. 7.

9. *A George III mahogany brass-bound wine cooler,* 19 in. Christie's King Street, Oct. '85, £1,512. Compared with No. 8 this piece is badly proportioned, and even though the stand is original, it is relatively dull.

10. *A Regency mahogany brass-bound wine cooler,* 18 in. Mar. '85, £1,300. Just for a change, an example of an hexagonal wine cooler.

11. *A George III mahogany brass-bound wine cooler,* 21 in. Oct. '83, £900. I have included this one to show how prices for these wine coolers have increased over the last two years. The stand is again unimpressive but the piece is of the same quality as No. 9.

12. *A Regency mahogany cellarette,* 32 in. Jul. '85, £1,300. An example of the sarcophagus shape that was used throughout the first half of the 19th century.

13. *A George IV mahogany cellarette,* 25 in. Christie's King Street, Jan. '85, £540. Later and less interesting than No. 12, and of course that much smaller.

14. *An early Victorian mahogany cellarette,* 30 in. May '85, £400. A very dull and plain example, its one saving feature being the shape of the lid.

7

8

9

10

11

13

14

Canterburies

The term 'Canterbury' appears for the first time in Thomas Sheraton's *The Cabinet Dictionary* of 1803, where it is used to describe various small galleried supper-tables to hold cutlery and plates by the side of the dining table; it can also be called a forerunner of the modern trolley. The name derives from the fact that the then Archbishop of Canterbury was supposed to have been the first person to order such a table. However, what is now universally termed a Canterbury is a small low piece of furniture with slatted divisions used originally to hold sheet music, but now more commonly to hold magazines.

The earliest examples dating from the Regency period are relatively standard in design (Nos. 1–3). Usually made of either mahogany or rosewood, they are fitted with a number of slatted divisions above a drawer, and it was not until the Victorian period (Nos. 5–6), that designs became more adventurous, allowing the craftsman to show off his many skills in different ways. It was also during this period that a shelf or shelves began to be added above the divisions, thus combining the functions of the Canterbury and the whatnot into a single piece of furniture (see No. 7).   *Hugh Edmeades*

Measurements refer to width.

1. *Regency, mahogany*, 20 in. Christie's King Street, Oct. '85, £2,052. A superb quality example, note the ring turning on the legs by the drawer.

2. *Regency, rosewood*, 19.5 in. Christie's King Street, Jan '85, £1,296. Although this one has four divisions and the advantage of a carrying handle, it lacks the quality of No. 1.

3. *George III, mahogany*, 18 in. Aug. '85, £800. Slightly older than the previous two, but an example of a Canterbury at its most basic.

4. *Regency, rosewood*, 17 in. Mar. '85, £420. Here instead of a drawer we have a shelf. The slats and the turned spindles make it too fussy, but even so, not expensive at £420.

5. *Victorian, walnut*, 22 in. Jan. '85, £650. Unusual that it is totally enclosed; a good piece of figured walnut with a simple inlaid front and crossbanded domed top.

6. *Victorian, walnut*, 19 in. Feb. '85, £600. A good example of a fret-carved Canterbury.

7. *A Victorian walnut Canterbury/whatnot*, 23 in. Mar. '85, £800. Here we see how a Canterbury and whatnot can be combined, a useful decorative piece of furniture with good fret-carved panels and gallery.

1

2

3

4

5

6

7

Whatnots

As already mentioned (p. 22), the desire of the late 18th century for displaying possessions created a need for new types of furniture. One such type that evolved during this period was the whatnot, an awkward and unspecific name for a piece of furniture that could be used to display a variety of objects.

The earliest examples, in the same way as Canterburies, were very standard in design, usually consisting of four rectangular shelves on turned supports with one of the shelves fitted with a drawer, and so with these early examples it is the quality of craftsmanship that is the deciding factor when it comes to price.

As the 19th century progressed, the cabinet-makers became more ambitious with their designs. First of all, the shelves began to be more graduated and shaped. Secondly, because of the easier access to materials, mahogany soon lost its predominance as the wood for whatnots, and by the middle of Queen Victoria's reign whatnots were being made in all sorts of woods. Hence putting a price on a Victorian whatnot is less easy, because there are more factors to consider than with the earlier standard examples. *Hugh Edmeades*

Measurements refer to width.

1. *George III, mahogany,* 18 in. Jan. '85, £550. A very plain standard example.

2. *George III, mahogany,* 20 in. Mar. '85, £950. A superior example dating from the same time as No. 1. The top is hinged to form a bookrest. Nicely turned supports, but it would have made more had the drawer been on the bottom shelf.

3. *George III, rosewood,* 20 in. Sept. '85, £750. Very similar in appearance to No. 1, but more expensive owing to the rosewood and the overall quality.

4. *Early Victorian, mahogany,* 16 in. Nov. '85, £600. Slightly later in date than Nos. 1–3, but of good quality and that much more interesting than No. 1.

5. *Early Victorian, mahogany,* 21 in. Nov. '85, £600. Although heavier in appearance than No. 4, this example made the same money, owing to its larger size and more detailed turning.

6. *Late Regency, mahogany,* 18 in. Dec. '84, £300. Once a good whatnot, but with the rear half now enclosed by doors, giving it an awkward and clumsy appearance.

7. *Victorian, thuyawood,* 28 in. May '85, £1,150. A beautiful piece of furniture of the highest quality. Note all the details, the bowed shelves, the brass gallery and finials and the gently tapered legs.

8. *Victorian, satinwood,* 28 in. Mar. '86, £400. An example of a corner whatnot of serpentine outline. An above average example, but the quality of the twist-turned uprights and fret-carved cresting could have been of a higher standard.

Furniture Miscellany

Furniture cannot always be neatly labelled and pigeonholed. It is as varied as mankind, and there are endless oddities, eccentricities and flights of fantasy. While the usual essentials of quality and craftsmanship obtain no less for one-off pieces, occasionally an element of pure fun – or even farce – can produce weird and wonderful prices. Here is a selection of individual items which are worth illustrating for themselves.

Hugh Edmeades

1. *A Venetian giltwood and composition day bed, 19th century.* 81 in. long. Nov. '85, £1,400. Although quite obviously in need of extensive restoration, an extremely comfortable day bed. Note the unusual entwined dolphin arm terminals.

2. *A Regency mahogany reading chair.* May '85, £1,500. Sometimes erroneously known as cock-fighting chairs. This one needed some restoration and is too heavy in appearance to be called a good example. Note the signs of transition from classical design to Victorian gothic.

3. *A Regency rosewood music chair.* June '85, £550. A very pretty example in full working order with a distinctive lyre-shaped splat.

4. *An Anglo-Indian padouk planter's chair, 19th century.* Oct. '85, £1,000. A very superior example, presumably commissioned by a very superior client.

5. *An Indian camel centre table.* 29 in. Dec. '85, £650. There are plenty of 'elephant' tables about, but how often do you see one of these?

6. *A Korean elm and pine chest, late 19th century.* 39 in. wide. Apr. '85, £550. An above average example of a type often seen in the salerooms. Older Chinese furniture can be very expensive indeed.

7. *A Damascan parquetry games table.* 36 in. wide. Dec. '85, £1,200. Not to everyone's taste, but handy if you play cards, draughts and backgammon.

8. *One of a set of four Damascan armchairs.* Jan. '85, £2,200. Although a variety of Damascan games tables appears each year, armchairs are less common, and a set of four is very rare.

1

2

3

5

4

6

7

8

9. *A Regency iron and wrought iron painted washstand.* 35 in. wide. Nov. '85, £1,900. An unusual and highly decorative piece. Very few Regency washstands made of wood could command such a price.

10. *A George III mahogany bidet.* 23 in. wide. Apr. '85, £550. A far more practical shape than the later rectangular examples, with the added luxury of a tap.

11. *a & b A satinwood kneehole dressing table labelled Maple and Company, c. 1935.* 33 in. wide. Apr. '85, £1,700. At first glance this appears to be a straightforward dressing table, but when opened it reveals an Aladdin's Cave of fittings.

12. *A late Victorian portfolio stand.* 45 in. wide. Jan. '86, £700. Perhaps not as sightly as some open folio stands, but a clean example of the enclosed variety.

13. *An overstrung boudoir 7 octave grand piano by Pleyel, No. 168269.* Apr. '85, £5,500. Not only a musical instrument, but a highly decorative piece of furniture.

14. *An Edwardian satinwood revolving bookcase.* 56 in. Jul. '85, £1,800. An example of Edwardian furniture at its best, delicately painted with 'Adamesque' motifs, but perhaps not the most practical of bookcases. The basic design was first patented in the Regency period.

15. *One of a set of four oak double-sided library bookcases, each 113 in. high, 102 in. wide and 62 in. deep.* Sept. '85, £6,500. These won the prize for the heaviest lot of 1985. This one is numbered 58 and 59, and if you know the whereabouts of the missing numbers, the furniture porters prefer that you keep quiet!

9

10

11

12

13

14

15

2. *Western Ceramics and Glass*

Introduction
by Paul Barthaud

The following pages are intended both to stand in their own right, and to be an extension to some of the areas covered by the previous volume of *The Popular Antiques Yearbook*. Before summarizing, I would like to make some observations on the markets examined last year. The percentage increases quoted here are based on recent prices obtained for items similar to those in Volume 1.

The market for 18th-century English blue and white porcelain, using the simple comparison process mentioned above, shows an increase of 79.7% – so much for simple comparisons! I would not put forward this figure as being a correct reflection of the whole market, although there was a varied selection of items illustrated in the last edition. Certainly there has been an increase in prices with the 'better' examples again showing the highest increases, but a more realistic price increase percentage is probably in the region of 25%.

Due to a lack of English delft coming on to the market this year, it is very difficult to suggest a percentage increase. For instance, there have not been any really good early royalty chargers. Standard large dishes have probably shown increases of 10%, but there has been notable movement in the price of albarelli (drug jars), with even poor examples realizing in the region of £200 – an increase of about 20%.

Staffordshire figures have again proved to be very popular, with some prices doubling over last year's amount and an average increase of 50%. There have been some fears that the increasing strength of the pound sterling against the dollar, discouraging American buyers, could depress the market. These fears have proved groundless.

There is still no specialist market in the wares of the French porcelain factory popularly referred to as 'Samson'. There has been an increase in prices, but as part of the general demand for 'decorative' porcelain (see pp. 40, 41).

1

2

1. *A Staffordshire group of bull-baiting.* Mar. '86, £80.
   This is a 20th-century model of a once popular rural sport. 'Copy', 'fake' and other emotive terms are applied to this type of later pottery, but the modelling of the animals is good and I feel that such pieces should stand on their own merit, as long as they are honestly described.

The article on Royal Doulton figures in Volume 1 of the *Yearbook* included a comment that there might be record prices to come. This has proved to be correct, with several examples similar to those illustrated having doubled in price. However, the current feeling and performance at auctions would suggest that, like the character jugs on pp. 44, 45, this market is due for a revaluation – downwards.

Wemyss has been fairly static in price for the standard shapes and designs. However, the rarer examples have shown increases of 50% or more. A book to be published in the near future should generate more interest in this field.

English drinking glasses and decanters have shown a strong upsurge in interest, and a corresponding rise in prices (32% and 25.6% respectively over last year's examples). Looking back at the two articles in Volume 1, it is rather apt that the last word is 'rewarding', although this was not intended as a purely commercial observation.

The prices for the decorative glass novelties referred to as 'Friggers', have been static even though there are fewer pieces being offered for sale.

Of the large amount of Bohemian glass sold, we last year illustrated only very few items. This field shows an increase of 9.3%. Because we feel that this is an important market, we have devoted a much larger section to it in this year's edition.

To summarize, the general trend in this area of ceramics and glass is for the best examples to show the largest percentage increase in value.

This year, we have chosen some broad headings in 'Decorative Porcelain' and 'Scottish Pottery', as well as very specific markets such as Royal Worcester and Royal Doulton character jugs. Bohemian glass and Dutch delft are generic titles for groups of factories. All of these are established markets. The market for Staffordshire animals has emerged in strength more recently, and could be argued to be a fashion rather than a market, but time will tell.

Taking a broad look at these markets, I am pleased to see that two factors which could have adversely affected prices have had no major effect. These are the emergence of certain groups of fakes, and the strength of the pound against other currencies. Fakes on the market include

Wedgwood black basalt, Clarice Cliff, pot lids, Royal Worcester, Staffordshire figures, Meissen . . . as the list lengthens, they seem to deserve a book in their own right! The strength of the pound has traditionally had a more direct effect, causing prices to level off or fall as overseas buyers hang back, awaiting a swing in values to their advantage. This is particularly true of American buyers, who are a major force in this area of the 'fine arts'. But neither of these two factors has undermined confidence, and there is no reason why this market should not continue on an overall upward course – but with some fluctuations within certain subjects.

2. *A Staffordshire group of bull-baiting, by Obadiah Sherratt, c.1825.*
   The real thing. As a damaged and restored example this could be worth £2,000 to £2,500. A perfect group might make up to £4,000. From this you can see that No. 1 is something of a variation on the theme rather than a faithful copy.

3. *A Royal Worcester vase painted by Baldwyn.* 18 in. Apr. '86, £1,700.
   The estimate on this lot was £2,000–£3,000. This was based on the strong market for smaller examples, and the commercial nature of the subject. Yes, it was an intentionally high estimate, and on the day, the 'market' was not strong enough to push the price further. This sale could well have signalled a weakening at the top of the prices for Royal Worcester.

4. *A Royal Doulton figure of Uriah Heep (HN554).* Mar. '86, £120.

5. *A Royal Doulton figure of Cicely (HN1516).* Oct. '85, £360.
   In 1984 this figure was sold for £120. If it were to be offered for sale now (mid-1986), it would probably be bid to about £400.

6. *A Royal Doulton figure of the Sunshine Girl (HN1344).* Oct. '85, £680.
   This type of 1930s figure was the fastest market mover among Royal Doulton figures. The price is now static, and a similar figure offered now would probably realize less.

Later Decorative Continental Porcelains

1   2   3

This is a very broad area which cannot be covered in detail in a brief article. However, these decorative wares also account for a very substantial section of the market, and a few guidelines may be helpful.

The bulk of them were produced in Germany and France in the latter part of the 19th century. German production was centred in the small Thüringian factories of Volkstedt, Sitzendorf, Potschapel and many others – termed 'Dresden' as a group. The French porcelains were produced in factories around Paris, and were in the Sèvres style. These are termed 'Sèvres' or Sèvres pattern.

German pieces tend to be figural in subject, painted with lovers in gardens or figures supporting candle sconces. The French porcelains tend to be characterized by various shades of blue as the ground colours. 'Jewelling' was used on pieces of better quality, and was produced by using white or pink enamel.

Quality of decoration can vary enormously, and you should look to the detail, or lack of it, of the hands and costumes. The gilding and the ground colour are also important. The gilding must not be rubbed, and there is a general preference for dark blue as a ground colour.

Factory marks are of less importance in this market than other areas of ceramics. Examples from the German factory of Meissen do command higher prices, and can increase the price by 50% or more. Marks on the 19th-century French porcelains are mainly variations on the Sèvres mark of interlaced L's. The letter in the centre of these L's, which should be the date code for the year of manufacture, usually shows a false early 18th-century date (No. 7). Prices are also directly influenced by size, with the higher prices being obtained by, say, a pair of Sèvres-pattern vases in excess of 36 inches high, with jewelling.

In common with all ceramics, prices are affected by damage. However, the presence of large amounts of colourful decoration makes repairs relatively easy, and successful. Minor cracks will devalue a piece by perhaps 10%.

Like many popular markets there are modern copies, particularly of the French porcelains. I have seen one particular subject, a shepherd boy and girl seated with a lamb, on dark blue-ground vases and boxes. They are of undoubted 20th-century manufacture, and are of overall good quality, but examining the figures carefully you can discern a printed outline, and this is a good guide to spotting a modern piece. Altered and erased marks are also known, with Limoges being a favourite factory for this sort of attention. These can be discerned by poor-quality gilt metal mounts, a lack of overall decoration and a lightness in weight.

The low to middle price range, £100 to £700, attracts a very mixed bag of buyers, whereas the top end of the market, £1,000 plus, has seen a trend over the last few years with many Middle Eastern buyers withdrawing and their place being filled by buyers from Japan. This has particularly affected the price of plaques, with good Berlin examples realizing over £2,000 – but beware of faked KPM (Berlin) marks (No. 3), and look to the detail of the painting for confirmation of an attribution. Berlin or Meissen examples will be very fine with depth to the overall composition, and clear lines to the face and hands.   *Paul Barthaud*

1. *A German porcelain plaque painted with a young girl in white diaphanous robes holding an oil lamp*, 13 in. May '86, £950. Not a commercial subject but good-quality painting.

2. *A German porcelain plaque painted with a young girl holding a basket of fruit.* 13 in. May '86, £450. This is a better subject but does not have quality to the painting. The brush strokes are broad, and the piece gave an overall messy appearance which is not obvious from the illustration.

3. *The Berlin factory mark found on the reverse of No. 2.* This piece was not a Berlin example, and exemplifies the caution you should use with Continental porcelain. A Berlin example would be of finer quality than either No. 1 or No. 2.

4. *A Sèvres-pattern blue-ground box and cover, 20th century.* 9 in. wide. May '86, £150.

5. *The Sèvres mark on No. 4.*

6. *A Sèvres dark-blue-ground vase.* 14 in. May '86, £400. A typical late-19th-century example, with a softer tone of decoration, and much finer gilding.

7. *The mark on the base of No. 6 with an 18th-century date letter.*

4   5

7

9

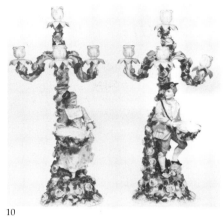

11

10

8. *A pair of Paris vases, each painted with two panels of figures in river landscapes. 14½ in. Apr. '86, £250. Although in the Empire style these date to c.1870. The gilding is rubbed, which is often the case with this class of French porcelain.*

9. *A Sèvres-pattern centrepiece with gilt-metal mounts and the painted panels signed, on a dark blue ground. 21 in. Jul. '85, £900. The mounts were not good-quality, and single bowls are not normally popular. This, therefore, was an unexpectedly good price.*

10. *A pair of Sitzendorf candle-holders. 21 in. Apr. '86 £650. The top sections lift off; typically there was damage to the sconces and flowers.*

11. *The blue AR mark on the bases of No. 13. This mark is sometimes confused with the 18th-century Meissen original. In shape the vases are more rounded than the originals, the designs are unlike any you would find on early 18th-century porcelain, and the ceramic body is totally different. These later pieces are sometimes attributed to the decorator and manufacturer Helena Wolfsohn.*

12. *A massive Sèvres-pattern gilt-bronze mounted oviform vase and cover painted with a medieval battle scene. 60 in. overall, on carved wood plinth. Christie's King Street, Jan. '86, £4,928.*

13

14

13. *One of a pair of Dresden vases and covers painted with figures in gardens and flowers on pink grounds. 14 in. Apr. '86, £520.*

14. *A late Meissen group of nymphs netting Tritons. 11½ in. May '86, £650. Minor damages to the fingers and decoration.*

15. *Left – A Sèvres-pattern turquoise-ground gilt-metal-mounted vase, in the style of the Sèvres service made for Catherine the Great. 10¼ in. Christie's King Street, Jan. '86, £263. Centre – A Sèvres-pattern turquoise-ground trembleuse cup, cover and saucer, Christie's King Street, Jan. '86, £767. This was a good price for which I have no explanation other than the fact that two people wanted it. Right – A Sèvres-pattern gilt-bronze-mounted turquoise-ground vase. 10¼ in. Christie's King Street, Jan. '86, £329. The cover was not original and the vase had been repaired.*

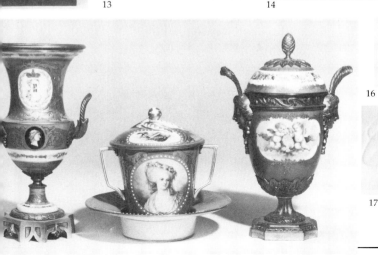
16

17

16. *The crossed swords mark on the base of No. 14. The bar below the swords shows that this piece was sold originally as a second.*

17. *The mould numbers also on the base of No. 14. The Meissen mark causes great problems of attribution for many people. On figures you should look for these numbers as well as the mark, and their absence should be viewed with suspicion.*

Dutch Delft

Delft is a term for tin-glazed earthenware originating from the Netherlands and England. In the Netherlands there were potteries in Rotterdam, Haarlem and the Hague in the early 17th century, and Delft from 1658 – but it was this latter town, Delft, which came to dominate production. The potteries sprang up from breweries, which had been vacated by a decline in brewing after a fire, and adopted such tavern names as the 'Three Bells', or 'Claw'. These names were also incorporated as factory marks. However there are many 19th- and 20th-century copies of these marks, and they should not be used as a sure guide to dating.

The majority of the production was dishes, plates and other simple shapes, but large and elaborate pieces were produced such as the multi-tiered tulip vases of the type on display at Ham House. Figures and animals were also produced, of which the most common are cows. These can be in blue and white or polychrome, and again, caution must be used to avoid later copies or fakes. You will find that later pieces tend to be a lighter, 'watery' blue and to have elaborate marks painted on the bases. Any piece actually inscribed 'Delft' will be of later manufacture, and will tend to be lead-glazed. These later pieces are often in the earlier styles, and regularly arrive into our reception area via clients who have purchased them in street markets in the hope that they have a bargain. In general terms you will find that 18th-century examples will have a pitted look to the underside of the bases and a pink appearance to the foot rim.

Dutch Delft is an international market, with prices starting from about £30 for plates of the plainer patterns, up to many thousands of pounds for large and important dated examples and figures.

In commercial terms the more desirable patterns are the elaborate chinoiserie subjects and interesting battle or figure scenes. For example a 14-inch dish painted in blue with flowers will be in the region of £100, while a similar dish with Oriental figures will realize in excess of £200.

Damage, or the absence of it, will affect the price. Minor chips are acceptable to buyers, and will not greatly cheapen an item. However, it is not easy

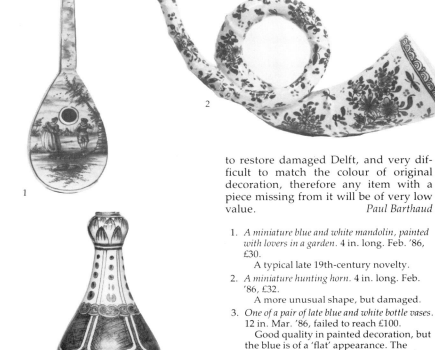

1

2

to restore damaged Delft, and very difficult to match the colour of original decoration, therefore any item with a piece missing from it will be of very low value.
Paul Barthaud

1. *A miniature blue and white mandolin, painted with lovers in a garden.* 4 in. long. Feb. '86, £30.
   A typical late 19th-century novelty.
2. *A miniature hunting horn.* 4 in. long. Feb. '86, £32.
   A more unusual shape, but damaged.
3. *One of a pair of late blue and white bottle vases.* 12 in. Mar. '86, failed to reach £100.
   Good quality in painted decoration, but the blue is of a 'flat' appearance. The design is in the style of the Chinese porcelain of the Wanli period (1573–1619). The low value reflects the lack of interest in 20th-century pieces.
4. *One of a pair of polychrome wall plaques, dated 1766.* 13 ½ in. Christie's East, New York, Jan. '86, $3,740 (£2,674). Has minor chips.
   Tiles and plaques are a specialist subject in their own right.

4

5

5. *A polychrome tile picture painted with a French poodle, enriched in manganese.* 14¼ by 10 in., minor chips, wood frame. 3 × top estimate, Christie's New York, Jan. '86, $1,980 (£1,416).

6. *A polychrome figure of a Chinese sage.* 6⅝ in. Christie's Amsterdam, Sept. '85, DF.10,440 (£2,377).
   Early 18th-century figures are rare.

7. *A pair of manganese tile pictures.* 20 × 15½ in., minor damages. Christie's East, New York, Jan. '86, $1,980 (£1,416).

8. *A blue and white tobacco jar for 'Violet' tobacco, metal cover.* 9⅞ in. Christie's Amsterdam, Sept. '85, DF.1,392 (£317).
   Tobacco jars were a popular subject in Delft.

9. *A blue and white tobacco jar for 'Spaanse' tobacco, metal cover.* 9¼ in. Christie's Amsterdam, Sept. '85, DF.1,392 (£317).

10. *One of six polychrome plates painted with elaborate patterns of panels of single flowers.* 9⅛ in. diam. Christie's Amsterdam, Sept. '85, DF.3,480 (£792).

11. *One of four polychrome plates painted with baskets of flowers.* 9⅛ in. diam. Christie's Amsterdam, Sept. '85, DF.1,624 (£370).

12. *A blue and white dish painted with the Peacock pattern.* 13 in. diam. Apr. '86, £280.
   A typical and common example of the products of the 1760s and later. Many people see this design as a bowl of flowers

6   7

rather than a peacock. Minor rim chips are acceptable on these large dishes, and do not greatly reduce the value.

13. *A garniture (set) of five, blue and white vases.* 11¼ – 15 in., finials damaged. Christie's Amsterdam, Sept. '85, DF.5,220 (£1,188) (estimate DF.800–1,200). The estimate appears to have been rather low. This type of vase is not uncommon, but a complete garniture is rare and desirable.

14. *A jug of the Roistering Dutchman,* c.1740. 13 in. Sold at Weston Park, Shropshire, on the premises. May '86, £550.
   This figure was in a very sad state with most of the enamels missing, leg and hand restored. The interest shown in this lot was surprisingly strong, and was eventually sold near the top of the £400–£600 estimate to a 'telephone bidder'.

9

10   11   12

14

Royal Doulton Character Jugs

The following abbreviations are used for sizes:

L   – large   (5¼ – 7½ in.)
S   – small   (3¼ – 4 in.)
T   – tiny   (1¼ in.)
sp – special   (4½ in.)
M – miniature   (2¼ – 2½ in.)

These light semi-earthenware jugs were launched in 1934 with John Barleycorn (No. 4) designed by Noke, which was based on the earlier stoneware whisky jugs with moulded smiling faces. This was quickly followed by a mixture of 'Olde English' and Dickensian subjects – Old Charley, Dick Turpin (No. 8), Simon the Cellarer, Sairey Gamp (No. 3) and Parson Brown (No. 12). The initial popularity has proved to be enduring, with new models supplying the modern demand. Some of these are early models remodelled. Dick Turpin was in production from 1935 to 1960 and has sold for £95, but the second version which was in production through to 1981 will only realize half that amount.

The present market has developed over the last three years as part of a wide demand for later Royal Doulton production wares. As with figures, the current market value will depend not only on the subject, but also on the length of time that the jug was in production. An additional factor when deciding on potential price is size – certain subjects were produced in different sizes in smaller amounts.

A good example of the difference that length of production can make was the Punch and Judy Man, produced from 1964 to 1969, which has realized £360, while Old Charley, which ran from 1938 to 1983, has realized only £42. Some examples were in production for even shorter periods, and these can sell for more than £1,000. The 'Hatless' Drake, for example, has sold for £2,900 (No. 5).

The size has less influence on the price of the majority of subjects, with large Toby Philpots realizing £65, small £40, and miniature £30 (No. 7). Exceptions to this are the six special Dickens character jugs. One type of rarity which is well worth looking out for is jugs in the white. These are said to be 'seconds' (slightly faulty), and were sold to employees. We have not sold a white character jug, but a four figure sum might be expected.

In keeping with other 20th-century ceramics, condition is of vital importance, even a small crack or repair depreciates the value by 50% or more.

The market has been very strong, but auction prices would suggest that there is currently a re-appreciation of values. The rarer examples are selling around their early 1985 prices or a shade under, and more common types are proving difficult to sell. This may well prove to be a lull before an upsurge, which often happens to new markets, but time and the buying public will be the only arbiters.

Recommended reading: Kevin Pearson, *The Character Jug Collector's Handbook.*   *Graham D'Anger*

1. *Toothless Granny (L).* Nov. '85, £550.
   This represents an increase of £30 over 18 months.

2. *Granny (L).* Nov. '86, £35.
   This jug was in production from 1935 to 1983. I have encountered this standard jug with the tooth ground out to try and pass it off as the more rare version.

3. *Sairey Gamp.* Nov. '85, £10 (S), £25 (L).
   This is a typical price difference for the varying sizes of the common jugs.

4. *John Barleycorn.* Oct. '85, £70 (L), £40 (S).
   This is a later version of the first Doulton character jug, and may well have been inspired by the stonewares produced by the Martin brothers.

5. *'Hatless' Drake (L),* Nov. '85, £2,900.
   This high price attracted several more examples on to the market, and an average price is currently £2,000.

6. *Drake (L).* May '85, £80.
   This is the standard version.

7. *Toby Philpots.* Oct. '85, £30 (M); Sept. '85, £40 (S); Mar. '85, £65 (L).
   (L) & (S) were in production from 1937 to 1967, (M) from 1939 to 1969. All versions are common.

8. *Dick Turpin.* Mar. '85, £95 (L); June '85, £45 (S); June '85, £25 (M). This model is the first of two versions.

9. *Mephistopheles (L).* June '85, £1,200 (two sides shown).
   This model was in production from 1937 to 1948 and is the first double-sided jug made.

10. *Farmer John (L).* Oct. '85, £70.
    In production from 1938 to 1960, modelled in similar style to John Barleycorn.

11. *Paddy (L).* Oct. '85, £80.
    In production from 1937 to 1960, and has doubled in price during 1985–6.

12. *Parson Brown.* Jun. '85, £60 (L); Oct. '85, £40 (S).
    Both were in production from 1935 to 1960.

Royal Worcester

This term is used to distinguish between later and earlier Worcester wares. The Worcester factory adopted the title 'Worcester Royal Porcelain Company' in their Articles of Association in 1862. The earlier factory is remembered in the shape of the marks on its wares: the number 51, referring to the founding of the original factory in 1751, features in the centre of the standard mark.

The late Victorian period saw many new ceramic ideas and techniques, and the Worcester factory was an integral part of these changes. The use of the light Parian (a semi-porcelain) body for decorative wares, as well as figures, provided a very good surface for the often elaborate painted designs and detailed gilding.

The factory produced a wide range of shapes — particularly vases. These provided simple broad surfaces for the artists to embellish with animal and fruit patterns. It is these signed artist examples which form the main commercial backbone of the market.

John Stinton with his scenes of Highland cattle is the best known and most prolific of the artists, and he signed himself as J. or John Stinton. His brother, James Stinton, was also a painter at the factory, and the signature Jas. Stinton will be found on wares depicting exotic birds perched on branches. Harry Davis and Ernest Barker are less common, and their preferred subjects were sheep in landscapes or among mountains. Charles Baldwyn, signing himself C. H.

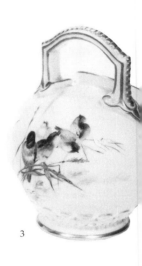

C. Baldwyn, painted swans in flight. On plates and dishes the list lengthens considerably with Ayrton, Townsend and Ricketts, but the market has promoted Richard Sebright to the first position as the most commercially desirable of this group of painters. William Powell, with his fine bird paintings, is found on plates and vases. These are distinctive, often with storks in desert-like settings below bright blue skies.

The fashion and esteem for the above have changed over the years. Currently the 'most saleable' in commercial terms would be Baldwyn, Powell, larger pieces by John Stinton, and services or pairs of plates by Sebright. This is of course a generalization, and there are other rarer artists, such as Thomas Bott, whose work commands high prices at auction.

One other name to look out for is George Owen. He specialized in very fine pierced wares, which are referred to as 'reticulated'. These delicate pieces, usually vases, are lightly decorated with gilding, and signed pieces are highly prized. The signature is scratched into the ceramic body, normally on the base. A signed vase of, say, four inches high will fetch in the region of £500 while an unsigned example of similar size may sell for under £50.

1. *A baluster ewer applied with a flowering branch on a pale yellow ground, 1880 (and two others). 13 in. Nov. '85, £120.*

2. *A baluster vase painted with raspberries c.1900 (and one other). 4 in. Nov. '85, £140.*

3. *A spoon-warmer painted with birds perched on grasses, 1883 (and three other Worcester pieces). 4½ in. Nov. '85, £220.*

4. *A plaque painted with swans in flight on a blue ground by Baldwyn, cracked across base, c.1900. 15¾ in. diam. Mar. '86, £400.*
   This was in line with our estimate.

5. *A two-handled slender baluster vase and cover painted by H. Davis with two polar bears on an iceberg, c.1903. 17 in. Jul. '85, £2,800.*

6. *Part of a dessert service painted by Shuck with fruit within richly gilt dark blue and pink borders, comprising two square dishes, two circular plates, two oval dishes and twelve dessert plates, c.1917. Jul. '85, £2,500.*

7. *A two-handled cup depicting Worcester Rowing Club by Powell, the reverse with a coat of arms, dated 4 May 1905. 4½ in. Aug. '85, £200.*
   An unusual design on a Hadley's model.

The age of a piece is not a major factor affecting price but pre-1920 should be preferred and any piece with the standard factory mark in black (modern wares) should be avoided. The dating of Royal Worcester is quite simple, using a date code system centred around the mark. The letter A designated the year 1867, and each subsequent year progressed through the alphabet (omitting some letters) until 1891, when the shape of the crown device was changed and the word England added. 1892 is shown as one dot to the left of the crown, and so on until 1915 (24 dots). 1916 is a small star-like symbol below the main mark, 1917 is a dot to the left of the star, and so on to 1927. Below the date code will be a number which is the registered shape number from the factory design book. (A full list of marks can be found in several specialist books on factory marks.)

A piece without a date code and shape number should be treated with suspicion as a deliberate forgery. There are fakes with these omissions, particularly plaques decorated with Highland cattle, coming on to the market in small numbers, but these are unlikely to have any long term effect on prices.

The market for Royal Worcester has been strong for many years, with collectors in the Midlands and overseas in Australia and America. Some interest has been noted from Japanese buyers, but this has yet to develop. The strength of the pound against the Australian dollar gave rise to worries about a fall in the market towards the end of 1985, but this has not materialized. The market seems as strong at all levels as it has always been.

6

7

The new collector of limited means may like to look to cups and saucers as a starting point, or perhaps thimbles? Figures are another option, with prices from about £30. These are of good quality and are under-priced in comparison to all other wares. The two areas of this market which should be avoided are Dorothy Doughty birds, and limited editions. The former includes a series of American bird subjects which have been pushed up to very high prices in America. £1,000 plus was not unusual. Unfortunately these models are so fragile, with very delicate flowers and grasses, that they are very easily damaged and have become unfashionable. A slightly damaged example would probably realize under £400 at the present time at auction. Limited editions rely on investors buying with a view to a profit, but this has not materialized to date.

(The standard reference book is: *Royal Worcester Porcelain*, by Henry Sandon.)   *Paul Barthaud*

8. *One of a pair of two-handled oviform vases with tall necks, painted with flowering vines outlined in gilt on ivory grounds, 1890.* 12 in. Sept. '85, £300.

9. *A ewer with serpent handle, painted with flowering vines on an ivory ground, 1895.* 11½ in. Sept. '85, £120.

10. *An urn-shaped vase painted with fruit on a dark blue ground by Sebright, finial repaired, c.1914.* 9½ in. Nov. '85, £280.

11. *A two-handled globular vase and cover with pierced neck, painted with sheep in a highland landscape by H. Davis, c.1920.* 10 in. Jul. '85, £2,800.

12. *A three-handled goblet, painted with brightly coloured birds by Shuck, 1904.* 10½ in. Jul. 85, £320.

12

9

10

11

Staffordshire Animals

The popularity of Staffordshire figures has been apparent over the past two seasons, and the current trend centres on animal subjects. The early Pratt or Wood type figures are not easy to date. Most were produced in the latter half of the eighteenth century, and these earlier figures are generally squirrels, sheep, deer, cows and homely animals (No. 1).

The Victorian age saw a continuing interest and excitement in travelling fairs and menageries. At these shows beasts from all over the world were exhibited in England, sometimes for the first time. These animals caused a great stir in the potteries and so started an animal revolution. Brightly coloured figures were produced of lions, leopards, camels, giraffes, birds and the ever popular elephant (No. 5). Rabbits, cats, birds and dogs, however, were not forgotten, and production continued (No. 3). Isaac van Amburgh, the celebrated American Lion Tamer, toured England in the mid-19th century, and one of his feats involved training a lion to lie down – or in this case, sit – with a lamb recumbent at its feet (No. 2). Zebras were produced in pairs, the demand being enough for the potters to use moulds originally intended for the production of horses (No. 6). Cat figures are generally considered to be rare and are most sought after (No. 7). Tureens with covers modelled as hens, doves and ducks have recently attracted enthusiastic bidding (No. 9). Production continued to be strong throughout the 19th century, and even events such as the Crimean War (1854–6), when human figures also sold well, failed to reduce the demand for animals.

At the end of the century cruder versions, often reusing earlier moulds, were still produced (No. 10). The vast numbers of animals produced in the Victorian era present a wide choice to collectors, and some models are found reasonably inexpensively (Nos. 8–11). However, unusual models can cause prices to soar (Nos. 8).

Beware of late reproductions – produced in Staffordshire and on the Continent (Nos. 14–15). The Staffordshire reproductions are invariably too light in weight, the colours poor and faded. The bodies are often covered in mock crazing to simulate age, the pottery paste is too smooth to the touch, and the gilding often too bright. The Continental pieces are porcelain, and usually once handled easy to detect. The bodies are too shiny, glasslike and hard. However, Continental reproductions are always well modelled and the colours bold, making them very alluring to the inexperienced eye.   *Mark Hales*

1. *A rare model of a Horse c.1790*, April '86, £800.
2. *'Van Amburgh Circus Act', lion and lamb group*, c. 1848. Feb. '86, £280.
3. *One of a rare pair of Rabbits with gilt markings*, c. 1855. Apr. '86, £1,200.
4. & 5. *'Beasts from all over the world': a rare model of a heron and a circus elephant*, c.1850. Apr. '86, £220, £150.

1

2

4

5

3

6. *A pair of zebras. These are correctly moulded without flowing manes, c. 1855.* Apr. '86, £220. A mane would indicate a revised horse mould.

7. *A cat c. 1855 (head restored).* Feb. '86, £85. Cat figures are much in demand.

8. *A pair of dogs, c. 1850,* Apr. '86, £150. Dogs are frequently found, and generally quite inexpensive, but extras, such as the baskets (No. 11) can boost prices.

9. *A duck tureen, c. 1845.* Apr. '86, £120. Examples such as these recently have become popular.

10. *A pair of Camels, c. 1890.* Feb. '86, £350 These were probably produced using earlier moulds.

11. *A pair of dogs, c. 1850,* Apr. '86, £350.

12. *One of a pair of Dalmatians, c. 1845,* Apr. '86, £320.

13. *One of a pair of Dalmatians, c. 1895,* Apr. '86, £45.

14. *A swan inkwell, Continental, c. 1920,* Apr. '86, £20.

15. *A swan inkwell, Staffordshire, c. 1860,* Apr. '86, £50.

6

7

8

9

10

11

13

14   15

Scottish Pottery

1

2

The only tin-glaze factory in Scotland, as far as we know, was Delftfield. It was founded around 1748 near what is now James Watt Street in Glasgow. The factory exported large quantities of its wares, so very little comes on to the UK market. It is also difficult to identify from other delftware as it is rarely marked. The catalogue produced by Glasgow's Kelvingrove Museum for their important Delftfield Exhibition in 1986 is one of the few reference works available on the factory and is a valuable guide to types of decoration used.

No. 2 was commissioned by the Roberton Hunt of Lanarkshire in 1771. The bowl had sustained considerable damage during its 200-year existence, but none the less sold to the People's Palace Museum, Glasgow. In the same sale an undocumented centrepiece *c*.1765, also restored, still sold well (No. 1).

The 19th century saw Glasgow with a plethora of potteries. One of the most successful was the 'Glasgow Pottery' or Bell's Pottery as it became known, after the two brothers who founded it.

Bell's jugs, plates, bowls and services can all be bought easily in the saleroom. A 32-piece blue and white part dinner service printed with the 'Triumphal Car' pattern sold for £100 in January '86, a blue and white octagonal ewer for £42 and a commemorative jug of 'Burns Centenary' for £38. Bell's products, therefore, are well within the range of the modest collector, although, obviously, hand-painted pieces incur a premium.

The Possil Pottery was another successful Glasgow factory, particularly their 'Nautilus' porcelain range. A full tea service would fetch around £150–£250 at auction, a jardiniere £100 upwards – although a two-handled example moulded with cherubs holding garlands raised £160 in January '86.

At Pollokshaws in Glasgow the Victoria Pottery produced Staffordshire type figures but also large numbers of transfer-printed mugs. A typical 'Yarmouth' pottery mug printed with a salmon lying on a bank would fetch £15–£20 (see No. 3).

In recent years Scottish ceramics have shown a steady growth in popularity. Wemyss Ware in particular boasts an enthusiastic following whether it's for pigs and other pieces (see *Popular Antiques Yearbook*, Volume 1) painted in the distinctive livery of pink cabbage roses and oily green foliage or for the more unusual pieces such as a bedroom set painted with dragonflies (No. 4).

Other East Coast pottery centres included Portobello, Prestonpans and Westpans. William Littler, an Englishman, founded one of the first potteries recorded at Westpans. Early Westpans pieces rarely come on to the market but when they do they have a greedy audience. A pair of sauceboats offered in London in February '86, took £1,026.

Nos. 6 and 7 illustrate wares produced by the Gordons factory at Prestonpans, established in the early 18th century. Large quantities of jugs were made with embossed figures on the side, and No. 6 did well – the new owner no doubt appreciating the two legends on the jug 'I'm happy now o'er happy' and an effusive 'Let gang your grips'.

1. *A Delftfield blue and white centrepiece, c.1770, restored.* Aug. '84, £1,050.

2. *A Delftfield documented blue and white punch bowl, damaged.* Aug. '84, £5,200.

3. *A Pollokshaws mug by D. Lockhart & Co.* 3½ in. These make about £10 to £15 each.

3

4

5

6

7

A successful line with the Portobello factory seems to have been carpet bowls. This was a popular pastime for the upper classes in the 19th century, and the bowls now crop up regularly at auction. They usually sport striped, sponged or mottled decoration in primary colours and fetch in the region of £20 each (see No. 5).

The work of Jessie Marion King (1875–1949) is regularly featured at auction, both her delightful illustrations and her studio pottery. The latter is becoming increasingly sought after by collectors with prices ranging from around £40 for an egg cup to the low hundreds for vases and mugs (No. 9). Other studio potters worth watching for in the saleroom are Elizabeth Mary Watt, Ann Macbeth and Helen Watson.

Standard reference books on Scottish pottery are, unfortunately, in short supply. The only general books covering the subjects are J. Arnold Feming's *Scottish Pottery* published in 1923 and reprinted

in 1973; and more recently Patrick McVeigh's *East Coast Potteries 1750–1840*. A book on Wemyss Ware by Peter David and Robert Rankine is due out soon and there are numerous booklets, pamphlets and newsletters which have been produced by the Scottish Pottery Society since its inception in 1972.

Paul A. Howard and Jackie Lacey
All items mentioned or illustrated here were sold by Christie's Scotland.

4. *A Wemyss ewer and basin.* Diam. of basin 15¼ in. Jan. '86, £500. An almost identical ewer and basin made £480 at the same sale while a soap dish and two toothbrush mugs in the same pattern made £190.

5. *A group of Portobello carpet bowls.* Jan. '86, £20 each.

6. *A Prestonpans jug, damaged.* 6 in. Jan. '86 £160. This was a good price considering the damage, largely accounted for by the appeal of the mottoes.

7. *A Prestonpans jug by R & G. Gordon,* c.1820. 6 in. Mar. '85, £380.

8. *A Bo'ness pottery parrot.* 12¾ in. May '86, £100.

9. *A studio pottery mug by Jessie Marion King.* 4½ in. Jan. '86, £160. A ribbed oviform vase fetched £320 in the same sale. Jessie Marion King's work is identified by her initials, JMK, a rabbit and a gate.

10. *Attributed to Portobello, a salt box or 'saut bucket', inscribed with the owner's name and dated 1850, damaged.* Aug. '84, £150.

8

9

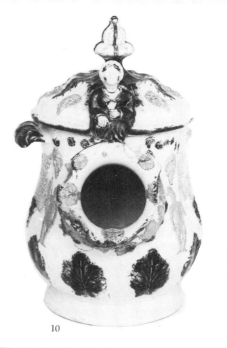

10

Bohemian and Coloured Glass of the 19th Century

The 19th century produced a wonderful variety of glassware, from clear, plain glass, relieved from austerity with diamond-cutting, fluting and faceting, to the smooth beauty of opaline glass or the richly ornate Bohemian style with its elaborate shapes and styles, enamelled and gilt, cut and cased – often all combined on a single item.

The manufacture of coloured glass in the 19th century produced many fine examples, blending colours with gilding and engraving to good effect; but by the same token, there was no restriction to the creative imagination, as though the glass makers were competing to see who could smother a piece with most decoration – often with very garish results (No. 16, overleaf).

1

The Bohemian, or 'Biedermeier', glass dominated the market throughout Europe. Britain abandoned her lead-crystal with its emphasis purely on the proportion and brilliance of the glass itself in favour of the growing trend for a more vibrant style. In contrast with the strict patents of the Venetian glasshouses of the 16th century and those in England in the 18th century, which guarded their formulae and techniques with a passion bordering on fanaticism, many of the Bohemian artists travelled throughout Europe teaching their skills. Some settled in England to the benefit of the factories at Stourbridge, such as Richardson and Bacchus & Sons. It is interesting to note the change in style between the early 19th-century English coloured glass, adhering to the popular 'Bristol' blue and green and maintaining the traditional proportions (No. 1), and the cranberry overlay decanter, probably from the Webb factory and dating from the third quarter of the 19th century (No. 2). The popularity and demand for Victorian cranberry glass has been consistently strong for the past two or three years, as the difference in prices shows. Another example of the present enthusiasm for good quality glass is illustrated in Nos. 3 and 4, the Moser wine glass and the English 'Bristol' green wine glass. Both are fine examples of their type, yet the difference in price is remarkable. The trend now, in the middle range of antique glass, seems to lean towards the elaborate and decorative.

The most popular Biedermeier glass, notably Lithyalin, a polished, opaque glass marbled in red, blue and green (the most renowned artist being Friedrich Egermann) was widely copied by other European countries and reached its height in the 1830s and 1840s.

2

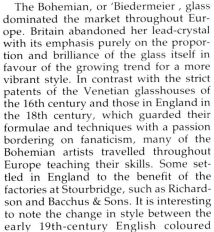

3   4

1. *Two flagons of deep blue and green glass, late 18th century/early 19th century. Oct. '85, £100.*

2. *English 'doughnut' shaped decanter and stopper, possibly Webb, mid-19th century. Oct. '85, £320.*

3. *A Moser wine glass applied and gilt with insects, acorns and oak leaves. Oct. '85, £180.*

4. *An English green fluted wine glass, early 19th century. Oct. '85, £38.*

The greatest Bohemian influence on the production of coloured glass elsewhere was in cased or overlay glass, and opaline glass. By the mid-19th century England was competing strongly with Bohemia in the production of all manner of overlay wares, from beakers and vases to scent bottles and decanters, producing some very fine examples, as No. 11.

English glasshouses not only successfully imitated the Bohemians in coloured overlay with decanters, wine glasses, finger bowls and vases, cut with window shaped panels, flowers and foliage to reveal the colourless glass under the outer layer, but were innovative in their own style, taking ideas from other European glasshouses and adapting them to produce very distinctive Victorian decorative glass, notably the introduction of cranberry glass (No. 8). Cranberry centrepieces, decanters, jugs, sugar bowls, sugar sifters, plates, bowls and drinking glasses—every imaginable piece of functional table glass—were enthusiastically made in cranberry, blue, green, amber and amethyst glass.

While English glasshouses were busy exploiting the demand for cased glass, those in France had developed and mastered the technique of opal glass. 'Opal', 'opaline' and 'opalescent' glass are, as the names suggest, comparable to the opal gemstone, with differing degrees of translucency. Early opaline glass was often made in opaque milky-white, but

5

6

7

also in dark blue, amethyst and black (No. 5). The finest examples of French opaline glass date from 1840 to 1870, notable factories being Baccarat and St Louis. *(continued overleaf)*.

5. *A pair of French blue opaline baluster-shaped vases, finely painted and gilt with exotic birds and flowering foliage, mid-19th century.* Oct. '85, £300.

6. *A pair of Continental brightly painted and gilt vases, late 19th century.* Oct. '85, £320.

7. *A set of Austrian champagne glasses by Fritz Heckert, beautifully gilt and painted in bright colours with garlands of flowerheads, c.1900.* Oct. '85, £260.

8. *An English pink opalescent épergne, with flowerholders and barley-twist canes.* Oct. '85, £420.

9. *A late pair of English ruby-stained decanters and stoppers with silver rims.* Oct. '85, £160. The engraving and diamond-cutting are very poor, but it is interesting that they managed to realize this price – I can only assume that it is because they are 'decorative' items.

9

Bohemian and Coloured Glass cont.

No. 5 is typical of the way in which this type of glass was modified from Bohemian examples. Here the emphasis, as in No. 17, depends mainly on the intrinsic beauty of the opaline itself, and not on the enamelling and gilding. The graceful, flowing shape of these vases with the slender flaring neck and smooth oviform body is complemented by the entwined bands of flowering foliage, rather than competing with them. The effect is 'finished' and complete. In this respect, it rivals the finest Bohemian flashed, cased and opaline glass, such as the bowl and cover in No. 15. The ochre and cream bands of fruiting vine, enriched with gilt, rest naturally on the deep ruby-flash ground, and this is a superb example of ornate Bohemian craftsmanship.

Engraving on flashed glass was a speciality of Bohemian factories and reached a peak of excellence in the mid-19th century. No. 10 illustrates one of the most commonly found subjects, stags and deer grazing in a continuous woodland scene, and although by no means a rarity, good examples continually command strong prices at auction. Spa scenes are another popular form of engraving, such as No. 14.

The quality of many later pieces of coloured glass throughout Europe and Britain deteriorated towards the latter end of the 19th century (No. 6). The engraving all too often lacked the detail and the imaginative use of classical, mythical or historic subjects of the earlier pieces. Cased glass was often replaced with the cheaper and quicker method of staining in colours ('flashed'), the overall impression being mass-produced (No. 9). Obviously the prices reflect this. A market that for many years was the exclusive preserve of the rich had become accessible to all, but as it did so, much of the original beauty and quality died.

Bohemian and coloured glass from the 19th century is not rare and a potential collector should not be faced with too many difficulties in finding early items of superb quality (Nos. 13 and 18). The main obstacle, as with many specialist antique markets, is the sheer cost of acquiring such good items. The demand for Bohemian and coloured glass is very strong, and prices, especially at auction, can range from about £100 up to several thousands – but it is more than possible to build a very pleasing collection at under £200 an item.   *Helene Venning*

10. *A Bohemian ruby-flash goblet, engraved with stags and deer grazing and running in woodland, c.1840. Mar. '86, £320.*

11. *A part set of five Webb green-overlay wine glasses, finely cut with garlands of flowering foliage and ovals, on slender inverted baluster stems. Oct. '85, £150.*

12. *A pair of French pale-green opaline vase lustres gilt with scrolling foliage, c.1865. Oct. '85, £220.*

13. *A Bohemian white-overlay, ruby-flash, tulip-shaped vase, c.1850, cut, painted and gilt with panels of diamonds, flowering foliage and scrolls. Mar. '86, £200.*

10

11

12

13

14

15

14

14. *A pair of Bohemian ruby-flash jugs, engraved with views of named buildings, outlined in gilt, c.1855. 13 in. Jul. '85, £550.*

15. *A Bohemian ruby-flash bowl and cover, modelled in the form of a fruit, enamelled in ochre and cream, picked out in gilt, with trailing vines, c.1845. 6½ in. Jul. '85, £280.*

16. *A pair of late Bohemian pink-flash vases, densely gilt and coloured with stylized flowerheads and foliage, applied with coloured beading, c.1880. Jan. '86, £700.*

17. *A rather more tastefully decorated French opaline baluster vase, painted with flowering foliage, with powder blue borders outlined in gilt. Jan. '86, £180.*

18. *A pair of Bohemian fluted white-overlay ruby-flash goblets. 10 in. May '86, £780. The cutting and gilt decoration is of good quality, but the interesting feature on these goblets is the red and white twist stems. This is not an extremely rare feature but certainly uncommon enough to raise the price.*

16   17   16

18

3. *Oriental Ceramics and Works of Art*

Introduction
by Nicholas Pitcher

Changes in the market for Oriental ceramics and works of art have been very gradual over the past year, and therefore not always easy to perceive at the time. A study of prices realized this year compared with last, however, has revealed certain movements. I could summarize the general atmosphere this season by saying that if an object is an extremely good example of its type, or unusual in any way and, above all, perfect, it would realize a good price, and probably improve on last year's. Should this hypothetical object be a bad example, damaged or run of the mill, it would in all likelihood make less than a year ago.

Some of the best prices seen this year in the low to middle segment of the market have been for top quality Satsuma ware (Nos. 1, 2), particularly by the likes of Yabu Meizan and Kinkozan. Low grade or damaged wares, however, have dropped slightly in price, as have most of Satsuma's routine relations such as Kyoto and Kyo-yaki pottery. Other 19th-century Japanese wares have remained fairly constant in price, although some early Arita and Imari is still, in my opinion, undervalued (see pp.62–3). While on the subject of Japanese works of art, cloisonné enamel, to which the same theory applies, is worth mentioning. The best items, completely unblemished, have sold extremely well (No. 3), whereas their more commonplace or damaged counterparts are in very little demand. Incidentally, look out for silver tablets on the bases of fine examples, usually bearing the signature of Namikawa, which can quadruple the price.

Chinese export porcelain is extensively covered on pages 58–9, so it is not necessary to eleborate further than to say it is still very much in demand, as are export paintings (No. 5). I cannot broach the subject, however, without a mention of surely the highlight of the year in this field – the

1

sale of the 'Nanking Cargo' in Amsterdam in April. Some 150,000 pieces of Chinese porcelain were salvaged for this sale from the wreck of a Dutch ship which sank in around 1750. The tremendous publicity, and the romanticism of the sale, captured the imaginations and hearts of people all over the world, with most pieces making five or ten times more than equivalent articles would without this rich provenance.

One other aspect of Chinese export porcelain is worth touching on here, and that is 'clobbered' or later decorated wares, particularly those painted in Holland. This used to detract enormously from the value of a piece, but now it appears not to matter so much.

Sadly, not all Chinese ceramics have been as popular this year as export porcelain. Qing dynasty (1644–1912) 'mark and period' wares have taken a plunge since the virtual collapse of the Singapore market and the uncertainty in Hong Kong, the more ordinary examples making perhaps half what they would have done three years ago (No. 4).

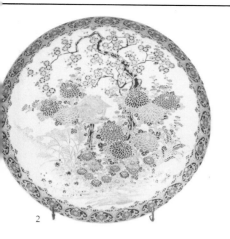

2

3

4

In addition to these, but for different reasons, I am sorry to say that lesser examples of Ming dynasty porcelain (1368–1644) have fallen in value. In my article 'Ming – Priceless or a Bargain?' in *The Popular Antiques Yearbook*, Vol. I, I stated that perhaps these wares were underrated – since when copious amounts have appeared on the market and prices have fallen even further. The same applies, for the same reason, to early Chinese pottery, which has arrived in the West in vast quantities (No. 6). I must qualify this, however, by reiterating, as I said last year, that the very best specimens of early pottery and later 'mark and period' pieces have still deservedly maintained their high levels.

Finally, I have illustrated the two bowls (No. 7) to show that academic interest and age alone are not enough to ensure an elevated price at present. Personally, I was fascinated by these bowls and would love to have had them in a collection. I am clearly in a minority there!

5

1. *A miniature Yabu Meizan box and cover, Meiji period.* 1½ in. diameter. May '86, £520.

2. *A Satsuma circular dish, Meiji period.* 14 in. May '86, £750.

3. *A small Japanese cloisonné koro and cover, Meiji period.* 4¼ in. wide. Feb. '86, £480.

4. *A famille rose yellow-ground bowl with blue and white interior, Daoguang seal mark and period.* 6 in. diameter. Sept. '86, £600.
   Three or four years ago, bowls like this were regularly making £800–£1,200.

5. *A large Chinese export painting in colours on paper, early 19th century.* 24 × 47 in. Sept. '85, £2,500.

6. *A Chinese celadon-glazed pottery footed jar, c.10th century.* 9 in. May '86, £170 (unsold).
   Up to five years ago, this jar could have realized between £500 and £1,000.

7. *A Chinese late Ming blue and white bowl, c.1635 (cracked).* 8½ in. diameter; *and a Japanese Arita copy, c.1690.* 9 in. diameter. Sold together, May '86, £200.

6

7

Chinese Export Porcelain

Once again, this year has seen large sums paid for rare or unusual examples of Chinese export porcelain from the Kangxi (1662–1722) and Qianlong (1736–95) periods. Large dishes, tureens and bowls are among the most desirable (Nos. 1 and 2), even if damaged (No. 3). Similarly, vases of all kinds have done well, even if mounted as lamps or candleholders, which combination adds interior decorators to the list of buyers (No. 4). Armorial porcelain is and always has been popular (Nos. 5 and 6), though its condition and the identification and importance or otherwise of the arms displayed are certainly relevant. Standard teaware is common, and individual pieces realize comparatively little. An unusually large or perfect service, however, will attract stronger bidding (No. 7). Much rarer are candlesticks, which are desirable in any shape or form, again even when damaged (Nos. 8 and 12). Chinese Imari, having been a poor seller in the last few years, has picked up (No. 9), while equivalent pieces of blue and white are still doing reasonably well, but only if perfect (No. 10). It remains to be seen what effect the sale of the 'Nanking Cargo' will have on the market for more ordinary Qianlong blue and white porcelain. Meanwhile Kangxi period blue and white has not moved noticeably since last year, good colour and shape being the important factors. Finally, figure and animal subjects have retained their high price levels (No. 11).   *Nicholas Pitcher*

1

2

3

1. *An unusually shaped famille rose soup-tureen and cover, Qianlong.* 13½ in. wide. Christie's King Street, Mar. '86, £4,320.

2. *A rare famille rose punch-bowl decorated with a European hunting scene, Qianlong.* 16 in. diameter. Christie's King Street, Mar. '86, £3,672.

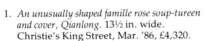

4

5

6

3. *A famille rose bowl decorated with immortals, Qianlong.* 14 in. diameter. May '86, £260. A smaller, much more common bowl than No. 2, and badly cracked. The price shows that export bowls of all types are popular.

4. *One of a pair of famille rose vases, Qianlong, gilt-metal mounted with candleholders.* Overall height 17 in. Dec. '85, £1,600.

5. *A small famille rose armorial salt painted with the arms of Molleson,* c.1755. 3¼ in. wide. Mar. '86, £550.

7

8

6. *A famille rose armorial soup-tureen and cover, Qianlong (badly cracked).* 13 in. wide. Sept. '85, £900.

   As a tureen and an example of armorial porcelain this piece is doubly desirable even though damaged.

7. *Three pieces from a famille rose tea-service, Qianlong, comprising a teapot, cover and stand, milk-jug and cover, tea-caddy and cover, slop bowl and cover, spoon-tray, six tea bowls and saucers.* Mar. '86, £2,000.

   An unusually complete tea service with very little damage. The price is much more than the total value of the individual pieces.

8. *A pair of rare famille rose candlesticks modelled with hounds, Qianlong (one repaired).* 7 in. Sept. '85, £2,700.

9. *A Chinese Imari circular dish, Kangxi.* 14 in. Dec. '85, £350.

10. *A blue and white circular dish, Kangxi.* 12½ in. May '86, £150.

9

10

11. *A composite set of ten famille rose immortals, Qianlong.* 9 in. (approx.) Jan. '86, £1,400.

    An exceptionally good price, considering three figures are duplicates from another set. A complete set could realize over £2,000.

12. *A pair of export polychrome candlesticks, Qianlong (damaged).* 7½ in. Nov. '85, £1,700.

12

Soapstone and Lesser Hardstone Carvings

In this article I am leaving aside jade, about which a whole book would be more appropriate, in order to outline briefly the many other Chinese stone carvings which one comes across regularly at antique fairs, in shops and in auctions worldwide.

Probably the largest of these groups is soapstone, or to call it by its less common name, steatite. Because of its softness, which obviously makes it much more easy to carve than other stones, and its great abundance in China, the native carvers have used it copiously over the years. Although soapstone carvings are known which are thought to come from the Ming dynasty, the earliest and best seen on the market with any regularity are from the 18th century. These, in comparison with many of their later counterparts, are very well carved, with good use of the stone colour, and as a result are greatly sought after. In 1984, a set of eight 18th-century soapstone Immortals, some with damage, each standing approximately 10 inches, realized £3,500. The appearance of these was not unlike the figures in the group shown here (No. 1).

As the 19th century arrived, however, and the quantity of carvings grew, so the quality deteriorated. Although there are good figures to be found from this time and later (Nos. 2 and 3), the vast majority became very stylized and have a mass-produced feel. Brush-pots and vases (No. 4) are extremely common, and can be bought at very low prices, as can any number of small pots and animals (No. 5).

Quartz is another group seen regularly around the country. This stone, however, is not as easy to carve, and quality tends to vary much less, practically all carvings being 19th or 20th century in date. Colour, therefore, plays an important part in value, and pink and amethyst have shown themselves to be more popular than green or smoky quartz (Nos. 6 and 7).

Many other stones were, of course, used by Chinese artists. Agate with its different tones and structures is reasonably popular (No. 9), and bowenite, which generally resembles most people's idea of what jade should look like (No. 10), is one of the most common and is therefore on the whole cheaper. All the other stones used would be too numerous to mention, but the most common include turquoise, sodalite (No. 8), tigerseye, rock crystal and crocidolite. A word of warning to potential investors, however, is that all these stones are still being used for decorative carvings, and modern examples appear in our shops and markets in large quantities, having been imported from the Far East. Damage must be looked for too. If a stone develops a flaw through being knocked, or is broken or chipped (No. 11), it will, in most cases, be rendered virtually valueless. An agate deer similar to No. 9, for instance, but with one ear missing, was unsold at £25 in Apr. '86.

Nicholas Pitcher

1. *A sectional soapstone group of a kneeling man making an offering to an Immortal, 18th/early 19th century. 8 in. wide. Apr. '86, £320.* The figures are well above average in the combination of colour-use and carving, and are typical of the 18th century. The base and surrounds have, however, assumed a more stylized 19th-century look.

2. *A mottled brown soapstone carving of Guanyin, 19th century. 7½ in. Mar. '85, £100.*

3. *A small brown soapstone carving, 20th century. 5¼ in. Dec. '85, £100.*

4. *A pair of late 19th-century soapstone brush-pots. 8 in. Dec. '85, £25.* There are literally thousands of similar carvings on the market. Note the stiffness of the work compared to Nos. 1, 2 and 3.

1

2

3

4

6

8

9

5. *A group of seven small soapstone carvings, late 19th century and later, the horse 6 in. long.* Mar. '86, £65.

6. *A rose quartz carving of Budai and three boys, late 19th century. 6 in. wide.* Mar. '86, £120.

7. *A pair of green quartz carvings of Buddhistic lions, late 19th century. 5 in. wide.* Dec. '85, £100. Although these are a pair, which should help the price, the colour of the quartz and the stiffness of the carving ensured a lower price than No. 6.

8. *A mottled blue and white sodalite carving of a duck, late 19th century. 6 in. wide.* Apr. '86, £90.

9. *A small brown agate figure of a recumbent deer, 20th century. 3¾ in. wide.* Mar. '86, £95.

10. *A green bowenite figure of Guanyin with a hare, early 20th century. 9½ in.* Mar. '86, unsold at £90. A common type of 20th-century bowenite carving, and the reserve, on this occasion of £150 proved too optimistic.

11. *A small rock crystal carving of Buddha seated, 19th century.* 4 in. May '86, £50. This piece had been broken in half and repaired, which accounts for the price. In perfect condition, it could have realized up to £150. Although a stiff and unimaginative carving, rock crystal in general is one of the more popular stones used.

10

11

Earlier Japanese Ceramics

An article on Japanese Ceramics in last year's *Popular Antique's Yearbook* (pp. 56–7) concentrated on the decorative wares of the 19th century, some of which have realized even more this season than last – not least Satsuma ware.

I feel, however, that some mention must be made of earlier Japanese ceramics, particularly those in the lower to middle price range. Most people with an interest in this subject will know or have heard of fine pieces of Kakiemon, Ko-Imari or Nabeshima making large sums of money (No. 1). There are, however, many examples of late 17th and early 18th century Japanese porcelain, some in my opinion delightful, which do not make headline prices.

Arita blue and white pieces of this period, because they are often of mediocre quality in terms of colour, which tends to be a rather muddy and fuzzy blue, are a good example (No. 2). Of course, as in many areas, exceptionally large specimens or examples with unusual subject-matter will command much higher prices (No. 3). The same applies to Arita polychrome wares; there are fewer of these on the market than the blue and white Arita, and this, combined with their greater decorative qualities, does tend to make them relatively more expensive, but still not out of reach for the enthusiast of more limited means (Nos. 4 & 5). Late 17th- and early 18th-century Imari (predominant colours iron-red, underglaze blue and gold) is distinguished from the 19th-century copies by a rather bluish-grey glaze and again, as in the case of Arita blue and white, that muddy, inconsistent blue crops up. It is worth noting, incidentally, that the Japanese virtually stopped exporting porcelain between about 1720 and 1840, and so Imari and other export wares are not normally found between these dates. With prices, though, in spite of the 150 years or so difference, the gap is not as wide as one might expect. Pre-1720 Imari is generally more expensive than that of the 19th century, but the variation in some cases is much less than for other types of porcelain (Nos. 6 & 7).

Animal subjects, as with most Chinese and Japanese wares, are very much in demand. Although in the main they are rare, they too vary in quality. The prices for Kakiemon enamelled animals, even the more modest ones, will easily run into the thousands (No. 8). Less decorative but rare examples will create much interest even when heavily restored (No. 9). However, in my experience blue and white Japanese animals from this period are very seldom seen, and therefore it is a fairly safe assumption that any one comes across will be 19th- or 20th century.

Finally, although my conscience tells me I should not advise the purchase of damaged wares, it is a fact that good examples can be had at relatively modest prices (No. 10).   *Nicholas Pitcher*

1. *A Kakiemon shallow dish, late 17th century, 8¼ in. diam., and a pair of Kakiemon ewers, late 17th century, 5½ in. Nov. '85, Christie's King Street, £1,944 and £864 respectively.*

2. *An Arita blue and white jug, late 17th century, 6¾ in. Nov. '85, £300.* A relatively common type of early Arita blue and white. The painting is not particularly good and the blue rather dark and muddy.

1   2

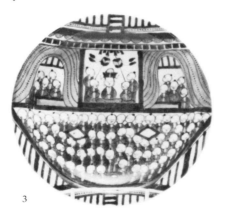

3   4

3. *One from a set of four rare Arita blue and white plates painted with 'The Hall of One Hundred Children', c. 1700, 8 in. diam. Nov. '85, £1,400.*

4. *An Arita polychrome stem-bowl and cover painted in green, yellow, aubergine and iron-red, c. 1700, 7½ in. wide. Feb. '86, £200.* An unusual piece, but the price was perhaps halved by slight damage to one handle and the cover.

5. *An Arita polychrome dish, the colours similar to No. 4, late 17th century,* 14 in. diam. Nov. '85, £850. The larger size and more displayable qualities render this dish much more saleable than No. 4 The only defect is a chip to the underside.

6. *An Imari dish, late 17th century,* 13 in. diam. Jul. '85, £380. An example of typical mediocre quality. A 19th-century Imari dish of good quality and similar size would not realize a great deal less today.

7. *An Imari deep-bowl, early 18th century,* 7½ in. wide, Dec. '85, £350. A type of better-quality Imari, which is reflected in the price, bearing in mind that this is a relatively small bowl and is lacking its cover.

8. *A rare Kakiemon water-dropper modelled as a hare, late 17th century,* 3¼ in. long. Christie's King St., Mar. '86, £14,090.

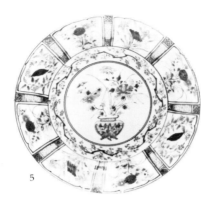

5

6

7

8

9

10

9. *A rare Arita iron-red decorated figure of a cat, late 17th century,* 10 in. Dec. '85, £3,200. The rarity of the figure and the popularity of animal subjects were the influential factors here, even though the piece was appallingly restored.

10. *A Kakiemon stem-cup,* c. 1680, 5½ in. Dec. '85, £160. This is a perfectly good example of what, at its best, has been called the best porcelain in the world, but it was purchased at this low price because of two cracks.

Champlevé Enamel – The Rise and Fall?

First used by the Chinese during the Qianlong period (1736–1795), the name actually comes from a type of enamel work evolved by the French in medieval times.

Many people today still confuse it with cloisonné enamel, although the techniques are different. Cloisonné is the filling in of wire cages on a metal base, champlevé simply gouging out the metal base (usually bronze) to a pattern and filling with coloured enamels.

The Chinese only began to produce much champlevé work in the 19th century, and towards the end of the century, as its popularity increased, many examples were even made in Japan. Most of the examples seen on the market today come from this period, and nearly all have the same particular style of decoration in the form of archaic Chinese designs, taotie (stylized masks) and formal foliage.

Towards the end of 1985 I was given the idea for this article by an increase in demand for rather ordinary examples of champlevé enamel. Alas, this has not lasted and prices have appeared to slump again. Although the market in this country has always been good for the large or unusual piece (No. 1), the smaller vases and figures of crude form and design can on occasion still make as little as £10–£30 (No. 5), and even the best single examples rarely exceed £500.

Although it is more versatile, appearing on almost anything from vases, figures and incense-burners to bookends and altar sets, champlevé enamel is not as popular as cloisonné. One similarity is, however, apparent, and that is the importance of damage, which will lower the price of both dramatically. Thus it is important to scrutinize the enamelling carefully before any purchase.

Nicholas Pitcher

1. *A large Chinese champlevé and bronze circular dish, early/mid 19th century*, 22 in. diam. Mar. '86, £220. An earlier and better example than usual.

2. *A large Japanese champlevé enamel stick-stand, late 19th century*, 25 in. Apr. '86, £170.

3. *Two champlevé and bronze vases, mid/late 19th century*, 16½ in. and 11 in. Dec. '85, £90 and £60. These are typical of the many average quality vases seen on the market every week.

4. *A bronze and champlevé incense-burner, c.1900, probably Japanese*, 13 in. Mar. '86, £90. A more unusually shaped piece than No. 3.

5. *A Japanese champlevé and bronze vase, c. 1900*, 7 in. Apr. '86, £20. The bronze surface being slightly polished certainly did nothing to help the price of an already poor specimen.

1

2

3

4

5

19th-Century Japanese Bronzes

Interest in Oriental bronzes generally has shown a marked increase over the past year, not least for 19th-century Japanese bronze figure and animal subjects (see *The Popular Antiques Yearbook*, Vol. 1, pp. 73–5). Some notable pieces and prices were seen at auction last season, a selection of which is shown here (Nos. 1, 2, 4, 5). Smaller Japanese bronze articles of good quality, especially with metalwork and enamel decoration, have also been received with great interest (No 3). Other more commonplace and inferior bronzes have, however, not made a great impression on the market. All items illustrated on this page were made during the Meiji period (1868–1912).

Nicholas Pitcher

1

1. *A bronze group of six tigers.* 14½ in. wide. Jan. '86, £1,300.
   Although tigers are a common subject individually, this particular model is rare.

2. *An unusual bronze group of five hares.* 13 in. wide. Feb. '86, £1,300.

3. *A fine bronze koro and cover decorated in silver and enamel.* 10½ in. Mar. '86, £4,800.
   The combination of silver filigree, coloured enamel and virtually no damage made this koro one of the best examples of its type.

4. *A bronze figure of a seated man, on rootwood base.* 12½ in. Mar. '86, £900.

5. *A large bronze standing elephant with ivory tusks.* 27 in. long. Apr. '86. £1,500.
   A very common subject, but in this case unusually large which is probably why this doubled the price of a slightly smaller example.

2

3

4

5

Shibayama

To most people the word 'Shibayama' suggests any piece of Japanese ivory which is inlaid in any way, but theoretically nearly all these works of art should be termed 'Shibayama-style'. The name in fact comes from a family who in the 1820s or 1830s supposedly devised the idea of encrusting pieces of ivory and wood with such decorative substances as coral, turquoise, tortoiseshell, horn, colour-stained ivory and, most common of all, mother-of-pearl. All these early examples were probably *inro* (a small case which was hung by a cord from the belt) or *netsuke* (the ivory or wood toggle which kept it in place on the cord). Around forty years later, however, when the export boom descended on Japan, numerous craftsmen started to create a wide variety of objects using these extremely decorative techniques. Signatures reading 'Shibayama' are sometimes found on Meiji period examples (1868–1912), although they are very unlikely to have been made by descendants of the original family. They were simply made in the same style, using the same techniques, and this accounts for the broad modern usage of the word.

The technique was applied to a wide variety of shapes and sizes, some of the finest and most expensive seen today using bases other than ivory, such as lacquer (No.1), or mounting the ivory panels in silver. Perhaps most representative of the finer pieces produced, however, are vases made from inlaid tusk sections (No.2), which always seem to be popular, despite being turned out in relatively high numbers. Of course the quality of the inlay is an important guide to value, as is the variety of materials used. The inclusion of coral, tortoiseshell and turquoise will usually augment the price realized. In addition, perhaps obviously, the rarer the shape of the piece, the more it will fetch. There are many small and relatively common Shibayama-style items on the market today which do not necessarily sell very well unless the quality of the decoration is unusually fine. These include card-cases, game markers (No.3), paper knives, small boxes and even knife handles (No.4).

As mentioned earlier, this style of work was used on *netsuke* and also on ivory figures, although it does not seem

1

4

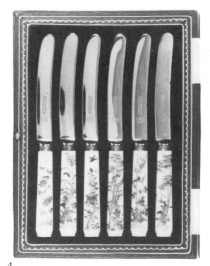

2

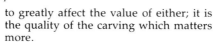

3

5

to greatly affect the value of either; it is the quality of the carving which matters more.

Inlay often comes away and is lost over the years, and this can have a very detrimental effect on the values of certain objects. Replacing a small intricately carved piece of tortoiseshell or mother-of-pearl is both a skilled and expensive business. It did not dramatically lower the price of the ivory and gilt-metal vases (No.5), however, because they are impressive and unusual, making them well worth the trouble of restoring.

Nicholas Pitcher

1. *A fine pair of large gold lacquer vases, late 19th century.* 14½ in. Christie's King Street, Mar. '85, £7,560.
    Work of this type on such good gold lacquer is very rare.

2. *A large inlaid ivory tusk vase on elaborate wood stand, late 19th century.* Overall height 35 in. Christie's King Street, Nov. '85, £2,160.

3. *An inlaid ivory game marker, late 19th century.* 3½ in. wide. Feb. '86, £75.
    A small tortoiseshell bird was missing from the inlay, which did not help the price of a good quality, but otherwise fairly common object.

4. *A set of six knives with lacquered and inlaid ivory handles, probably early 20th century.* Mar. '86, £190.
    They are not very displayable or decorative, hence the rather low price despite good work.

5. *A pair of gilt metal two-handled vases, each with four inlaid ivory plaques, late 19th century.* 9½ in. May '86, £700.
    An unexpectedly good price considering the amount of inlay which was missing.

and other Ivories

It has been a somewhat fluctuating year for Oriental ivories. Prices for good quality or unusual Chinese examples have risen to a certain extent. For more commonplace Chinese articles and for most Japanese ivories, they seem to have taken a small drop. Standard Japanese figures, from the better carved 'one-piece' immortals (No. 1) down to badly worked sectional farmers (No. 3), are certainly realizing less than a year ago, although the dollar exchange rate may have something to do with this. Netsuke, on the other hand, remain popular, especially 19th-century examples of above average quality, a selection of which is shown here (No. 4). This market is, however, not helped by the numerous modern netsuke which constantly appear and which, at first glance, look reasonably well carved.

The subject of Oriental ivories is covered extensively in *The Popular Antiques Yearbook vol. I*, pp. 76–9, and this page should serve as a useful update and reminder.　　　*Nicholas Pitcher*

1. *A Japanese marine ivory immortal with dragon, late 19th century.* 11 in. May '86, £160 (unsold).
    Previously, this would easily have reached its estimate of £200–£300.

2. *A Japanese figure of a standing immortal, late 19th century.* 8 in. May '86, £220.
    This would probably have made over £300 a year before. The subject is good and the carving competent.

3. *One of five Japanese sectional figures, late 19th century.* Each approx. 7 in. May '86, £260.
    Standard sectional figures of this type are down from around £80 to about £50 each.

4. *A selection of six above average quality 19th-century ivory netsuke.* Feb. '86, (left to right, top to bottom) £280, £380, £250, £220, £380, £300.

5. *A Chinese ivory tusk-vase with gilt lacquer decoration, mid/late 19th century.* 8½ in. Dec. '85, £130.
    An unusual treatment for Chinese ivory, probably an effort to simulate the Japanese 'Shibayama' work (see opposite page). It is nevertheless, in my opinion, a fairly dull object and obviously most of the buyers on the day agreed.

6. *A Chinese ivory box and cover carved as a quail, early/mid 19th century.* 4 in. wide. Feb. '86, £550.
    A good example of an unusual and intricately carved piece of Chinese ivory doing well in spite of a crack. Small boxes are always in demand, and the bird subject is charming.

Later Decorative Chinese Ceramics

By the early part of the 19th century, the amount of Chinese porcelain being produced for the Western market was at its height. Even more was turned out than in the already very prolific 18th century, and consequently the quality of much of it suffered terribly.

Over the past year, 19th-century Chinese ceramics have, in the main, retained their immense popularity, but only the better or more unusual examples. This is a predominantly American buyers' market, and the dollar rate being less favourable than a year ago has meant that poorer quality wares have suffered slightly. In short, American collectors are having to be more choosy when buying in London. For instance, a very ordinary pair of Cantonese 18 in. vases which would have made perhaps £700–£900 in 1985 is in 1986 realizing more in the region of £400–£600 (No. 1), whereas top quality Cantonese jars have retained or in some cases increased their value (No. 2).

Good Cantonese and particularly *famille verte* porcelains (No. 4) are still the most popular of the decorative 19th-century wares, with competent bird decoration and large jars with covers seeming to be top of most buyers' shopping-lists. I have also noticed that 19th-century *wucai* copies of 17th-century originals have been in demand (No. 5) as an alternative to the *famille verte* palette.

Prices for blue and white examples do not seem to have moved a great deal in the last year (No. 6), even for the more popular shapes such as pilgrim bottles and tulip vases. Those who read the *Popular Antiques Yearbook*, vol. 1, will have seen two such objects illustrated on p. 68 – a pair of large pilgrim bottles at £950 and a tulip vase at £150. I would certainly not expect them to exceed those prices this year.

As mentioned earlier, the less exciting pieces seem to have dropped slightly in price. Examples include standard crackleware (No. 7), lesser quality and everyday Canton (No. 8) and 19th-century gingerjars of almost every type.

Finally, it is imperative to be aware of modern copies. These are plentiful at the moment, turning up in country auctions, some shops and many antique fairs.

1

2

They range from massive *famille verte* fish bowls, Canton-type and *famille verte* vases (No. 14) to such small items as sauce-tureens, soap-boxes and figures. Look out for bright enamelling, an unusually glossy finish and smooth, shiny glazed bases. In comparison to the pieces they are copying, they actually look modern, but the unwary could purchase one by mistake. Indeed, I know of experienced dealers who have done so.   *Nicholas Pitcher*

1. *A pair of Cantonese vases, mid-19th century.* 18 in. Jan. '86, £500.
   A fairly standard shape with medium quality decoration, these would perhaps have made a little more on a better day.

2. *A pair of Cantonese baluster jars, c.1830.* 18 in. Mar. '86, £1,700.
   Good decoration and an extremely popular shape contributed to the price, despite restoration to the necks, which matters much less on jars of this type.

3. *A large and very unusual Cantonese hexagonal moulded stick-stand, c.1840 (chipped).* 24 in. Feb. '86, £480.

4. *A famille verte baluster jar and cover, late 19th century.* 18 in. Feb. '86, £260.
   A reasonable price for a late and by no means top quality example. Of course, a pair would much more than double this price.

5. *A wucai baluster jar, underglaze blue and famille verte enamels, mid/late 19th century.* 11½ in. May '86, £300.
   Not a large example of its type, but nevertheless a good price, which shows the increasing popularity of this palette. Covers seem to make a great difference to jars such as these, although this particular one was not intended to have a cover, the rim being fully glazed in brown.

3

4

5

7

9

6. *A large blue and white prunus-pattern baluster jar and cover, mid/late 19th century.* 17½ in. May '86, £260.

   Although a good size and shape, the prunus-pattern is one of the most common.

7. *One of a pair of* famille rose *crackle-glazed vases, mid/late 19th century.* 17 in. May '86, £190.

   These are common and poorer quality wares, and as a result have become less saleable.

8. *One of two Cantonese teapots and covers, mid/ late 19th century.* 6 in. and 5 in. May '86, £60.

   At the height of the market a year ago, these might have made up to £60 each.

9. *One of a pair of Cantonese jardinières and stands, mid-19th century.* 14½ in. diam. Dec. '85, £1,800.

   Very much the same decoration as the teapots (No. 8) and the vases (No. 1), but, as jardinières, far more unusual and popular.

10. *A Cantonese oval food-warmer and cover,* c.1830. 16½ in. wide. Sept. '85, £850.

    A rarer and earlier example of Canton, this was still a remarkable price considering the piece had a large crack.

11. *An unusually shaped Cantonese teapot and cover,* c.1810–20. 9½ in. Oct. '85, £420.

12. *A powder-blue glazed oviform jar with gilt decoration, late 19th century.* 15 in. May '86, £380.

    Late examples of powder-blue wares seldom sell very well, but the gilding here was completely unrubbed, which is rare.

13. *A Cantonese vase painted in brown, gilt and white on a blue ground, mid-19th century.* 17 in. May '86, £180.

    A more unusual type of Canton, always reasonably popular. A pair, however, would perhaps have made three times as much.

14. *One of a pair of modern* famille verte *black-ground square tapering vases.* 16½ in. May '86, £180.

8

10

12

11

14

15

13

15. *A famille verte square tapering vase, mid/late 19th century.* 20½ in. Feb. '86, £500.

    Very much the sort of vase which No. 14 is copying. Even in these black and white photographs, the overall clumsiness of the fake should be obvious.

Chinese Ricepaper Paintings

Why on earth, you might ask, would anyone want to paint pictures on a brittle, edible, paper-like substance made from the pith of an Oriental tree called *Tetrapanax papyriferum*, or the ricepaper plant? A good question, and one which technically only the Chinese artists in and around Canton in the early 19th century could answer. However, paint on it they did, and profusely from around 1820 until the end of the century, as anyone who has ever spent hours leafing through scrap albums of late 19th-century travellers will know; for along with Indian mica paintings, European etchings and ink studies of various exotic scenes, there is often a ricepaper painting or two, usually of the type shown in No. 1, although a traveller of good taste earlier in the century may have tucked away a few like No. 2.

All ricepaper paintings were originally in album sets, normally of around twelve, and often with embroidered covers. They were painted not for the Chinese themselves, but specifically for foreign visitors or tradesmen. This is why so many travellers to China returned to Europe with ricepaper albums as postcard-like souvenirs of their visits, and it explains their abundance today. It is in their original albums that they seem to command the highest prices at auction, and not when the albums have been split and each painting framed.

The quality and subjects vary, some of those most in demand being sea and shoreline scenes (No. 2), such as the harbour at Canton, showing the 'Hongs', or warehouses, of the European and American merchants, and sets showing the process of tea or rice growing (No. 3). In these subjects the paper area is completely painted, leaving no white. The others, mainly painted with the subjects on plain white backgrounds, vary from exotic birds (No. 4), butterflies and flowers (No. 5), which when of good quality can command high prices, to fish among waterplants, ancestors in splendid interiors (No. 6), figures in processions (No. 7), ceremonial river-boats and, commonly, rather gruesome punishment scenes (No. 8). These last two categories in particular, as well as the simple single-figure subjects (No. 1), have not been too popular over the last year.

Although used in great quantities, ricepaper is not a very satisfactory medium for pictures since it deteriorates so easily. It can crack and split by being in the wrong atmosphere, and even turning the pages of an album must be done with the utmost care to avoid damaging the paper. Therefore even the most sought after of these delicate paintings will only realize a high price if in good condition, the treatment of foxing and repair work being expensive.

Nicholas Pitcher

1. *Two from an album of 12 paintings each with a single costumed figure, mid/late 19th century.* Nov. '85, £110. One of the most common types and small in size. These made the price only because the paper was in unusually good condition.

2. *One from a set of 9 paintings, each of a port scene with European and American flags, c.1830, sold in an album with a further three much more common subjects.* Nov. '85, £1,300. Although rare subject-matters, the quality of the painting is not as good as the best, which could make as much as £2,000. The China Trade Exhibition which opened at Brighton in spring 1986 is likely to push prices in the area still further.

1

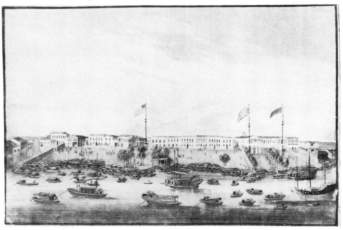

2

3

4

3. *One from a set of 6 paintings showing the production of tea, c.1835, sold in an album together with 6 paintings of figures among furniture.* Dec. '85, £1,400. The greater part of this price was undoubtedly made by the first six. The example shown here is the last in the series, where the tea is finally being drunk.

4. *One from an album of 12 paintings showing different birds among flowers and rockwork, c.1850.* Nov. '85, £380. Bird subjects can make much more than this, but these were of mediocre quality.

5. *One from an album of 10 paintings with butterflies among flowers, c.1840.* Jan. '86, £1,300. Butterflies and flowers are very popular and these were top-quality examples.

6. *One of 3 paintings of ancestors in interiors, mid/ late 19th century.* Apr. '86, £60.

7. *One from a set of 10 paintings with processions of figures, mid/late 19th century.* Jan. '86, £100. A common subject, and of mediocre quality. These were unframed, but had been removed from their album.

8. *One from an album of 12 paintings of punishment scenes, late 19th century.* June '86, £95. Predictably, these rather gruesome scenes are not in great demand.

6

8

4.   Silver

Introduction
by James Collingridge

To our predecessors, silver was a means to display wealth and still retain an easy method of raising cash at short notice. In times of war the table silver would quickly disappear into the melting pot, to make coins to pay the troops. Although prized by the owners, it was also subject to fashion and easily melted to restyle in an age when craftsmen were paid little for their work.

It follows therefore that the bullion price of silver has always been related to the cost of the made up item. So much so, that the older reader may well remember the days when silver items were offered for sale by auction at 'per ounce'. The auctioneer's clerk would be armed with his ready reckoner calibrated in grains, penny weights and ounces. What a boon today's calculators would have been! In *Values of Antiques*, published by J. W. Caldicott in the 1930s, a sample of a typical auction catalogue is reproduced. Perhaps one of the most interesting descriptions is lot 7: 'a silver coffee-pot with a moulded dome cover, foliage and strapwork by Paul de Lamerie, London hallmark 1728 – 25 ounces at 150 shillings per ounce.' The £187.10*s*.0*d*. that it realized would have been close to the annual salary of a labourer in that depressed time. However, one cannot but help comparing it with today's prices (Nos. 1 and 2).

While today the weight of silver still has a bearing on the ultimate price, it has become more a guide to quality and less of a deciding factor to the prospective purchaser than even two or three years ago. It appears that good items are at last beginning to be appreciated for what they are, rather than for what they weigh. A good example of this can be seen in No. 3, a dog collar weighing less than two ounces and yet realizing £700. The appeal of such an item is not only the rarity of a well-documented piece of silver, but also the historic interest to a collector of theatrical memorabilia. A further example can be seen in the opaque glass claret jug

1. *A George II coffee-pot by Paul de Lamerie, 1735.* 9½ in. 37 oz. Christie's New York, Apr. '86, $16,500 (£10,375).
   Although heavy for this size pot, the patched repair near the lower part of the handle accounts for the relatively low price. The arms are those of Stuart impaling Elphinstone for Francis (Stuart), 7th Earl of Moray, (1673–1739).
2. *A fine George II coffee-pot by Paul de Lamerie, London, 1749.* 9⅞ in. 31 oz. Christie's New York, Apr. '86, $55,000 (£35,458).
   The arms are those of Osbaldeston, probably for Richard Osbaldeston (1690–1764).

tastefully decorated with a minimal amount of silver (No. 5).

As stated earlier, fashions do change. However, with workmanship (and the additional burden of VAT) costing more today than in the past, it is no longer viable to put the unfashionable into the melting pot. Perhaps the most notable victim to fashion in the past year has been that old favourite 'Kings pattern' tableware, which has been edged out, no doubt temporarily, by less ornate styles such as the thread and bead edge 'Old English' tableware, resulting in a slight decrease in the price of the former, to the advantage of the latter. Notwithstanding this, some of the better makers, such as George Angel, whom we mentioned in last year's *Popular Antiques Yearbook* (p. 97), appear to be still very much sought after and have proved to be a good investment.

Wine decanters and coasters have maintained their

3. *A rare George IV Irish dog collar engraved 'Theatre, The World', with the crest of the celebrated actor Edmund Kean, to whom it belonged, James Fray, Dublin, 1828. 3½ in. Oct. '85, £700.*

4. *An unusual Victorian parcel-gilt centrepiece formed as a pond, Stephen Smith, London, 1871. 21½ in. 167 oz. Oct '85, £3,400.*

5. *A good early Victorian frosted glass claret-jug with plain mount and applied silver-gilt vine decoration, Mortimer & Hunt, London, 1841. 12¼ in. Oct. '85, £1,600.*

6. *One of a pair of Edwardian silver-mounted cut-glass cologne bottles, William Comyns, London, 1905. 5½ in. Mar. '86, £700.*

popularity, as have corkscrews (see pp.84–5). The demand for the unusual is still on the increase and accounts for the prices paid for such things as the dog and goat creamers (see pp. 82–3.) The undeniable quality of the cologne bottle (No. 6) accounts for the high price the pair realized, although the interest in all scent bottles has been quite marked. Items of modern domestic tableware, such as tea sets and trays, have not shown any noticeable sign of movement and the prices have remained fairly static.

Pride of place for a silver-plated item sold during the year must go to the toast rack designed by Christopher Dresser and made by James Dixon & Sons of Sheffield which was sold in a sale of Decorative Arts at Christie's King Street in Jan. '86 for £3,400 (No. 7). It is interesting to compare this price with the £3,200 paid for the unusual Victorian pond centrepiece by Stephen Smith with a silver weight of 167

ounces (No. 4). While the simplicity of the toast rack cannot be denied, the centrepiece does have a considerable intrinsic value.

In the *Popular Antiques Yearbook*, Vol.1, we devoted a section to a subject on which really a book should have been written – the alteration and faking of silver. During the last year a number of such items have been rejected for sale by us. However, for ingenuity, the piece that really must be commented on is the swing-handled basket (No. 8). The mind boggles, perhaps not so much at the owner who was so disenchanted with what was a delightful pair of wine coasters, as at the so-called silversmith who desecrated them by refashioning them into a sugar basket. By sweating them together and adding a base and a swing handle, he may have well pleased his client but has reduced a very saleable piece to one that is totally unsaleable. It should, however, prove a relatively easy task to dismantle and restore it to the original coasters with turned wood bases.

It does prove the point made earlier that while it may no longer be worthwhile to melt down and refashion, silver is an easy medium with which to work, particularly for the unscrupulous.

7. *A James Dixon & Sons electroplated toast rack, designed by Dr Christopher Dresser, stamped marks EP JD & S, facsimile signature Chr. Dresser. 7¼ in. Christie's King Street, Jan. '86, £3,800.*

8. *This basket started off as a pair of wine-coasters made in London, 1789, by a silversmith FPP. Today, if left alone, they would be worth £600–£800. Sadly, by adding the feet, base and handle, a later silversmith has made a rather ugly object, which cannot legally be sold in England today.*

Candle Holders

In a nuclear age the candle seems completely outmoded and yet its reliability has ensured that it has retained its place as the best standby in the event of a power failure. As a basic form of lighting it has been with us for hundreds of years, during which time it has been consistently used in religious ceremonies where the flicker of the flame is a symbol of life itself, and certainly no good Jewish home would be without its Sabbath candlesticks.

However it is the romantic appeal that accounts for the popularity of candlelight. Few can resist the candlelit dinner, and the Victorians even designed their jewellery to show it at its best on such occasions. Small wonder, then, that the candleholder should be designed to complement the candle, particularly as a table centrepiece.

Few candlesticks seem to have survived the destruction of the Civil Wars when so much silver was melted down for cash, but good examples of the late 17th century are still to be found. Although chunkier in appearance, they are generally much lighter than the cast examples of the 18th century and were often weighted with pitch (No. 1). With the appearance of the cast candlestick at the end of the 17th century, much more silver was used, giving a more solid feel to the construction.

Casting continued throughout the early 18th century until about 1770 when manufacturing from sheet metal became a viable proposition. By 'loading' with plaster of paris and pitch, it became possible to use less silver and still retain the overall weight. This became even more attractive when the tax of sixpence per ounce on silver weight was imposed in 1774. While casting was used, and indeed still is today, it is the exception rather than the rule.

Since the sheet metal on a filled candlestick is very finely rolled, it is essential to examine the 'highspots' of the decoration closely, as this is where the stick is likely to show the most wear, and holes are likely to appear. After the base, the most vulnerable spot is the narrowest part of the stem, which suffers most if the candlestick is dropped or knocked,

and it is this area which should be examined for evidence of repair. Repairs and removal of bruises can be costly as any work involves the extraction of the infill and its subsequent replacement.

Cast candlesticks on the other hand, contain a sufficient thickness of material to stand the handling and polishing over the years and are only likely to show the passage of time by general wear. A word of caution is required at this point, since it is a common practice to recast the candlesticks. This is not illegal provided that the new model is submitted for assay. However, all too frequently one finds an example where the original hallmarks have been recast and left to deceive the unwary. It follows that careful examination of the hallmark should be made for the telltale casting marks.

It is surprising how many sets have become mixed over the years, and it is not uncommon to find two identical candlesticks with different date letters and makers, which will obviously make a vast difference to their value (No. 5).

James Collingridge

1. *A pair of William and Mary candlesticks on octagonal bases, London 1691, maker's mark TA, between pellets. 7 in. 17 oz. 16 dwts.* Christie's King Street, Nov. '84, £3,672. A typical example of the chunky appearance of the English candlestick of the 17th century.

2. *A set of four William III candlesticks, each on moulded octagonal base, by Joseph Bird, London 1699. 6 in. 50 oz.* Christie's King Street, Nov. '85, £28,080. The dished octagonal bases shown here are still used today, although the more favoured stems are those on illustration No. 5 rather than the inverted bell shapes on this set.

3. *A set of four George II candlesticks, the octagonal bases cast and chased, by Edward Wakelin, London 1757. 12½ in. 187 oz.* Christie's King Street, Jul. '85, £56,160. The good solid design of this set is matched by the amount of silver employed and the price realized.

4. *A pair of George III fluted candlesticks, John Scofield, London 1792. 11¼ in. 41 oz.* Christie's King Street, Sept. '85, £3,024. For my money and taste, these are the finest design and made by one of the best silversmiths – beautifully balanced, and in first-class condition.

1

2

3

4

6

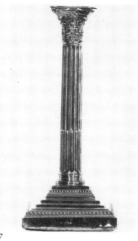

7

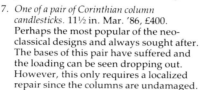

8

9

5. *One of a matched pair of George II cast rococo baluster candlesticks engraved with crests, John Cafe, London 1752, and John Priest, London 1753, the nozzles by John Roberts & Co., Sheffield.* 10½ in. 42.5 oz. Mar. '86, £800.

6. *One of a pair of William IV baluster candlesticks in the 18th-century taste, T.J. and N. Creswick, Sheffield, 1835.* 9½ in. Mar. '86, £750. It is interesting to compare this pair of loaded candlesticks with the cast sticks (No. 5). While they are a copy of the cast originals and of a later date, they realized almost as much as the matched originals.

7. *One of a pair of Corinthian column candlesticks.* 11½ in. Mar. '86, £400. Perhaps the most popular of the neo-classical designs and always sought after. The bases of this pair have suffered and the loading can be seen dropping out. However, this only requires a localized repair since the columns are undamaged.

8. *One of a pair of George II style candlesticks, William Hutton and Sons Ltd., London 1910,* 12 in. Feb. '86, £520. Like the Corinthian, a very much reproduced design. The originals would be cast and worth over £1,000.

9. *One of a pair of George III candlesticks, Matthew Boulton, Birmingham 1793,* 6 in. Mar. '86, £550. Although these are of small size, they are an uncommon design and the maker has a great bearing on the price realized.

10. *One of a pair of late Victorian candlesticks, Walker & Hall, Sheffield 1895.* 5¾ in. Mar. '86, £320. Although the large capitals appear to be out of balance with the slender columns, these are of pleasing design, and somewhat reminiscent of the chimneys on Elizabethan houses.

11. *One of a pair of Victorian gadrooned piano candlesticks, TS, London 1875.* 5½ in. Mar. '86, £480. Although more squat, these are a reproduction of the style of the early 19th century, much used by Matthew Boulton. Designed to stand on a piano, the large bases would ensure stability, no matter how spirited the playing of a rousing tune.

12. *One of a set of four George IV rococo baluster candlesticks, S.C. Younge & Co., Sheffield, 1825.* 11 in. Mar. '86, £1,150. Appearance can be deceptive. By comparison with No. 6, this set of four should have realized at least £1,500. However, close examination of the high spots show the tell-tale sign of wear from over-zealous cleaning, and the pitch can be seen through the resulting holes – hence the price is lower.

13. *A modern cast candlestick showing how much heavier the silver needs to be to stabilize the stick. As the hallmarks are struck in an area not subject to polishing, they should remain crisp.*

14. *The base of a 'loaded' candlestick with the weighting removed showing clearly the thinness of the silver used and the metal reinforcing rod set in resin running through the stem. The hallmarks on these sticks would be on the rim around the base where they will be subject to wear.*

11

12

14

Buckles and Buttons

Silver has always maintained a decorative as well as a functional value, and perhaps no better example of this can be found than in dress accessories.

Very early on, silver was prized as a sign of affluence and was flaunted whenever possible. Buckles became notably popular in Roman times, but very few have survived as they were often either melted down to provide emergency funds or remodelled to keep pace with ever changing fashion – a situation which has continued over the centuries.

Buckles were probably most highly prized in the 18th century when fashion demanded they be worn on shoes, on breeches at the knee, on sashes, belts, cravats and even hats. At that time, it is estimated that 2½ million buckles of various shapes and sizes were manufactured in Birmingham each year. Nearly all had steel pins and fittings, and fell prey to rust, so that comparatively few remain in good condition, making an original pair in its fitted case an exciting find for the collector.

Buttons had also become very important at this time, having been used purely for decoration before the 16th and 17th centuries. Thousands of people became involved in the manufacture of buttons of all shapes and sizes, the sheer variety of which gives the collector great scope and pleasure. Not only were there many different designs purely to please the eye, but also special buttons for hunts, regiments and societies. Servants' uniforms were embellished by several rows of buttons which were normally engraved with a crest – many spurious, as middle-class families without crests simply designed their own. Many buttons were made up from other items such as hat pins, brooches and coins.

Towards the end of the 19th century, both buttons and buckles were greatly influenced by the Art Nouveau movement (No. 14), and a new surge of interest and enthusiasm kept production high. Tradition dictates that when a nurse is given promotion, she should wear a silver belt buckle, and such continuous demands have ensured a continuous rise in price.

Buckles and buttons were worn by both men and women, but there are many dress accessories which were used only by the fairer sex. A charming example is the posy holder (Nos. 2–8), particularly popular in the 19th century, and now avidly sought after by collectors. These can command what might seem high prices for things of little or no practical use in today's society. Posy holders were mostly made in silver (although usually unmarked), silver plate or gilt metal, sometimes combined with other materials. Many had mother-of-pearl or ivory handles, often carved in high relief, and they might even incorporate small mirrors in their design.

Most holders are about 5 inches long and designed to be hand held with a finger loop and chain for suspension when necessary. Some were specially made with handles that opened to form a stand, enabling the newly married bride to stand her wedding bouquet in front of the cake at the reception. The guests may well have worn smaller posy holders pinned as brooches to the bodice, and even the gentlemen wore a small cone-shaped holder in the buttonhole.

From around the middle of the 18th century, chatelaines became commonplace (Nos. 9–11), until superseded by the pocket. They consisted of a brooch or a clip suspended from a belt, from which many attachments could be hung. Normally used by housewives or housekeepers, they could carry a vast variety of essential items, such as keys, notebooks, pencils, pillboxes, penknives, vesta cases, scissors or etuis (small cases for objects too small for individual suspension, such as sewing and manicure items).

Hair combs, slides and grips date from the mid-17th century, with long-toothed crescent shapes and two- or three-tined hair ornaments introduced in the following century. These were often of delicate filigree design, becoming more solid and stiff in form in the late 19th century (Nos. 1 and 13).

Hat pins developed on the same lines as combs, but were made extensively after 1900, with steel shafts and either commemorative or purely decorative die-stamped silver terminals. Sets could be purchased with perhaps two pins and several interchangeable heads. Prices for combs and hat pins vary, with only the unusual achieving high prices.

The vast range of dress accessories provides the collector with ample scope for excellent buys in areas not yet fully collected – with the added bonus that most can also be used.   *Sally Everitt*

1. *A small collection of belt buckles and a hair comb, mostly cast late Victorian examples and still fairly common.* Apr. '86, £100.

2. *A gilt-metal part filigree posy holder with applied turquoise decoration and filigree handle. Sold with No. 5, Oct. '85, £140.*

3. *An unmarked silver posy holder in the Gothic taste.* Oct. '85, £100.

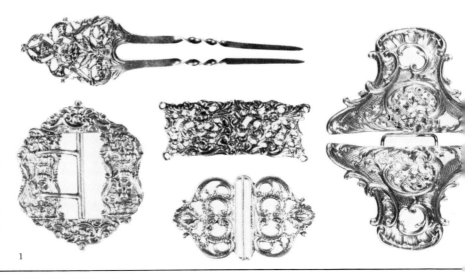

1

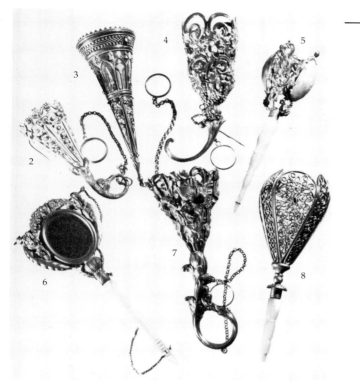

4. *An unmarked silver posy holder,* Oct. '85, £90.

5. *A gilt metal posy holder with two applied mother-of-pearl shells and turned mother-of-pearl handle.* Sold with No. 2, Oct. '85, £140.

6. *A gilt-metal posy holder with mirror and turned mother-of-pearl handle.* Sold with No. 8, Oct. '85, £95.

7. *An unmarked silver posy holder.* Oct. '85, £100.

8. *A gilt-metal filigree posy holder with mother-of-pearl handle.* Sold with No. 6, Oct. '85, £95.

9. *An American chatelaine illustrating some of the attachments found: a mesh purse, pencil, and two notebooks, each containing ivory leaves for each day of the week.* Apr. '86, £100.

10. *A chatelaine with a matching belt, in the Dutch style, English, London 1900.* Apr. '86, £190. *The matching belt is unusual.*

11. *A chatelaine in the Dutch taste, showing how some were used almost entirely for carrying keys, London 1900.* May '86, £85.

12. *One of two filigree brooch posy holders.* Mar. '86, £75.

13. *A George III filigree hair comb, Birmingham 1808.* Mar. '86, £130. *A good example of its kind, it doubled its estimate.*

14. *One of a pair of Art Nouveau buckles of typical flowing design.* Mar. '86, £40.

15. *The button bottom left is one of a set of 4 and the button on the right one of a set of six, sold together with the others illustrated as one lot,* Mar. '86, £85.

12

13

14

15

Scottish Provincial Silver

Collectors of provincial silver are few but enthusiastic, and while this article refers to Scottish provincial, there are equally enthusiastic collectors of the English and Irish varieties.

'Provincial silver' means articles produced in small towns by individual craftsmen for local needs, normally utility items of unpretentious design (No. 1). It is not primarily for aesthetic quality that such items are keenly sought after, although their simplicity has undoubted appeal.

In addition to the recorded makers' marks, there are total obscurities, flowers, animals, insects or initials. Such marks are, we believe, those of tinkers or gypsies whose craftsmanship often equals that of urban silversmiths, although their designs may be 'countrified'. These can be frustrating, in that one can never make a definite attribution and can only describe them as 'possibly by Joe McBloggs'.

As with silver in general, most early pieces were made for the Church, and therefore take the form of Communion cups, ewers, baptismal bowls, etc. These date from the early 17th century.

A tiny proportion of the silver which is sold is provincial, and therefore rare and collectable, and of that small quantity, most is flatware. This term covers all cutlery from teaspoons to toddy ladles. The collector with limited resources can gather a collection of makers and places at reasonable cost. Teaspoons by the more prolific makers (Keay, Cameron and Jamieson) from the larger towns such as Perth, Dundee or Aberdeen can be bought for as little as £15–£25.

With hollow-ware – snuff boxes and mulls, nutmeg graters, sporran mounts, quaichs, wine funnels and stands and tea and coffee ware – prices move into top gear.

There can be great variation in prices for similar items, depending on provenance and maker. A teaspoon by Robert Keay of Perth or A. Cameron of Dundee might be £20, but one from Stonehaven, Cupar or Tain perhaps ten times more, because of rarity. An example of the difference in prices between makers in the same town can be illustrated by the work of Peter Lambert of Aberdeen, which might make twice as much as a similar article by James Erskine, a fine but more prolific craftsman

Provincial silver never carries the Sovereign's head duty mark, which might seem surprising, as most of it was produced when duty was payable. Briefly, the law was as follows: an Act of 1555 required that all silverware should bear the maker's and town marks. In 1687, James VII and II reconfirmed an earlier Act, giving the Edinburgh Incorporation of Goldsmiths the right 'to search and test' all silverwork. All smiths in Scotland would have been sent a draft of this.

The 1719 Act imposed a tax of 6d per ounce on all silver plate bought in Great Britain, and required that no person shall put on sale "any plate until it shall be touched, assayed or marked" in accordance with the law. The Act of 1555, therefore, still applied, and all provincial centres were affected. However, collection of the duty was difficult, and the Act was later repealed.

A 1784 Act re-imposed duty on silver, but only on plate which had been assayed. Unlike the 1719 Act, it did not apply to plate already covered by the Act of 1555 and thus did not touch provincial wares. The 1836 Act which required silversmiths to have their wares marked at an established assay office such as Edinburgh, Glasgow or London, did much to kill off the provincial smith, particularly in the smaller towns with a small output. The delays of sending wares to the city and the very real risk of highway robbery were an irritation they could not afford.

Those working in the larger towns, and particularly those with retail shops, continued to produce reasonable quantities, and one frequently encounters, say, an item inscribed 'A Cameron $\frac{DUN}{DEE}$' and bearing a London hallmark of the late 19th century. These are still classified as provincial, but there is no doubt that enthusiasm is much diluted by the addition of another city's hallmark.

Glasgow and Edinburgh silver of the same period is entirely different from provincial, designs being much more influenced by London. By Scottish definition, we do not, therefore, classify them as 'provincial', although early pieces from either city are sought after with an equal enthusiasm.

Provincial silver collecting is relatively new. It is unlikely to avoid the peaks and troughs, but in time it is a market which can only strengthen.   *Arthur J. H. McRae*

All the items illustrated here were sold at Christie's Scotland.
1. *Thistle-shaped dram mug by William Scott the Younger, Aberdeen, c.1720. Nov. '85, £860.*
2. Provincial marks on flatware, top to bottom: Perth, Inverness, Greenock, Aberdeen.

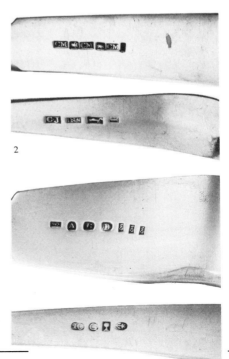

1

2

3. *Gold snuff box by Benjamin Lumsden, Montrose, 1791–4. Mar. '85, £11,600.* This box was presented to the 1st Viscount Melville by the town of Montrose "for the Abolition of the Tax on Coals in Scotland" according to the inscription inside the lid. This association helped to make a worthwhile price for the American owner who had returned it to Scotland.

4. *Wine funnel by James Sinclair, Wick, c.1810.* Mar. '85, £1,350.

5. *The marks from a set of Old English Pattern table spoons by Robert Keay the Elder, Perth, c.1810.* Mar. '85, £320.

6. *Marks from an oar end toddy ladle by Robert Robertson, Cupar, c.1820. Mar. '85. £165.* Cupar is much rarer.

7. *A small, plain George I quaich by Colin Mackenzie, Inverness c.1720. Mar. '86, £650.* These marks are in accordance with the 1515 Act.

8. *A plain oblong snuff box by Robert Keay, Perth, 1800. Jul. '85, £280.*

9. *A navette-shaped snuff box by William Scott, Dundee, c.1780. Jul. '85, £390.*

10. *A cowrie shell snuff mull, maker not traced, AD, Dundee, c.1800. Jul. '85, £225.*

11. *A cowrie shell snuff mull by James Erskine, Aberdeen, c.1795. Jul. '85, £380.* Seemingly similar things vary in price according to rarity of maker or town of origin.

12. *A tobacco box of cushion outline by Robert McGregor, Perth, c.1830. Jul. '85, £250.*

13. This mark complies with the Act of 1836 whereby all items had to be hallmarked at an established assay office. It bears the marks of Rettie & Sons of Aberdeen along with Edinburgh hallmarks for 1839.

14. *A pair of George III sugar and cream baskets, together with a salver, all by Peter Mathie, Edinburgh, 1785. Mar. 86, £800 (baskets); £580 (salver).* These items perfectly illustrate the more refined taste of the Edinburgh silversmiths, and their quality is certainly equal to that of the best London makers.

15. *Bullet-shaped teapot by Alexander Forbes, Aberdeen, c.1735. Mar. '86, £2,450.* This Aberdeen teapot is beautifully proportioned and decorated to a high quality, proving, together with the price, that provincial wares are not necessarily 'countrified'.

3

4

5

6

8   9   12

10   11

14

15

Silver and its supporting role

Silver has long been combined with other materials in the form of mounts. lids and feet. At first it was used primarily to enhance exotic rarities such as ostrich eggs, rock crystal and even carved or polished coconuts, creating vases and vessels of greater beauty than practicality (No. 1).

In the 18th and 19th centuries, craftsmen still favoured silver-mounting as a form of decoration, exploiting contrasts of colour and texture with the whiteness of the polished silver. Certainly after examining many pieces of silver in each working day one can become a little bored with the sheer sameness of finish. It is sometimes a great relief to encounter the precious metal combined with another substance.

The list of possible materials to combine with silver is endless, the 19th-century silversmith in particular stretching his imagination to create charming articles, many of which I have tried to illustrate here. One of the most common is glass in its various forms, and many Victorian and Edwardian homes would have contained much-prized examples, including scent and cologne bottles, claret jugs, bon-bon dishes and massive epergnes (or table centrepieces), designed to display fruit, sweets and flowers and often incorporating candle holders (Nos. 2–4).

Drawing rooms were often cluttered with massed displays of photograph frames, and one even finds massive silver-mounted dressing-table mirrors, the mounts elaborately stamped and pierced with fluting, flowers, cherubs and birds. These are delightfully extravagant in design, often showing a Victorian over-exuberance in the rococo style, and invariably they find much favour in the saleroom today. Sadly, while many of them are impressive from a distance, these mounts were normally made from thin sheet silver. Cleaning over the years has generally resulted in the appearance of holes as the silver has been worn away; this obviously reduces the potential price considerably.

Pottery and porcelain were also frequently combined with silver, and any sale of objects of vertu will contain examples of scent bottles and pill boxes, some of the former delightfully painted to simulate the eggs of wild birds. Many of these were made by the London firm of Samson Morden, a specialist in pens, pencils and other novelties, while others display import hallmarks suggesting manufacture in Germany or Holland.

Other small pieces of silver such as boxes were enamelled in bright colours (Nos. 13, 15, 17), their value today depending largely on the subject. Animals, sporting scenes and mildly erotic subjects are especially sought after, as are those with puns or jokes, usually of a particularly unfunny nature. Indeed, some unscrupulous manufacturers are buying pieces of plain silver, and putting them back on the market with modern enamelling in the Victorian or Edwardian style. These are often very difficult to detect, but their colours are usually too hard and unsubtle, the quality of painting rather stilted and the general condition is too pristine for a hundred or so years of use. Examination of genuine pieces with a magnifying glass will often reveal a web of tiny scratches on the surface of the enamel caused by contact with watch fobs and even loose change!

In my opinion the most attractive material frequently to be found in combination with silver is tortoiseshell (Nos. 10, 11, 18, 19), the rich dark browns providing an ideal contrast in colour and adding warmth and life to an essentially cold metal. Desk equipment and sewing accessories are particularly collected today, and even the commonplace dressing-table sets with mirrors and brushes have recently come into their own after many years of total neglect. One factor affecting this sudden upsurge of interest in tortoiseshell must surely be the recent protection of the Hawksbill Turtle, ironically the source of this material named after his land-bound cousin. One may speculate that many dressing-table sets are being broken up by purchasers, providing an invaluable source of raw materials for repair and manufacture.

Other materials to be found combined with silver include velvet (No. 7) horn, bone and ivory (No. 6), wood and even ostrich and emu eggs, the latter often covered with Australian scenes in low relief giving a cameo effect (No. 1), the dark green outer shell shading into a cream inner shell. *Stephen Helliwell*

1. *Two examples of the art of the Australian silversmith, combining silver with olive green emu eggs.* These were probably made by Wendt, the vase bearing his impressed mark, and were offered in sales along with pictures of Colonial interest. The Australian market is strong at the moment, hence the prices of £1,600 and £800 respectively when offered in May 1984.

2. *A Regency style silver and cut-glass cruet by William Hutton and Sons of London, 1930s.* Mar. '86, £480. An excellent reproduction of the rather ornate style much favoured around 1815.

1

2

3

4

5

6

3. *A pair of dessert stands and a decanter stand, 19th century.* Dec. '85, £1,300 and £260 respectively. Cut-glass combined with electro-plate to create a very impressive effect. Until recently, Victorian plate was of little consequence, but over the last decade prices have soared as collectors have come to appreciate the exuberance of 19th-century design.

4. *A double spirit or ginnel flask with festooned clear and milk glass body by Heath and Middleton, Birmingham 1896;* (centre): *a liqueur bottle designed to hold four different spirits, London 1896;* (right): *an unusual conical decanter with ribbed body by Middleton, Birmingham 1892.* Oct. 85, £130, £300, £360.

5. *An unusual Edwardian cigar box made of cedar-lined silver, the hinged cover inset with a fine water-colour by Charles Dixon, 1903, of H.M.S. Majestic entitled – 'The Royal Salute June 26, 1897',* Oct. '85, £1,050. Despite the ink stain on the watercolour, a good artist, a much collected subject, and an unusual combination of silver cigar-box and watercolour ensured a good price.

6. *A silver-gilt cigarette box made in Germany and imported by Dunhill in the 1920s.* Oct. '85, £360. The contrast of black and white guilloche enamel and the finely-painted ivory inset is most attractive, the coaching scene taken from an aquatint by George Havell, 'The Blenheim Coach leaving the Star Hotel, Oxford'. Of very fine quality, the inside of the lid had another ivory plaque, also engraved with a coaching scene.

7. *A Victorian visiting card case of silver-mounted burgundy velvet charmingly decorated with a huntsman and his dog and made by S B, London, 1889.* Jan. '86, £95.

8. *A Victorian silver-mounted crocodile purse made in Birmingham, 1900.* Jan. '86, £65.

9. Sadly this pair of Victorian wall sconces by F. B., London, 1886, had been drilled for conversion to electricity. Nevertheless they sold for £850. The large mirror in the centre was made in London, 1899. 17½ in. high, it reached £260, Nov. '85.

10. *A silver and tortoiseshell tea caddy, late 19th century.* Nov. '85, £280.

11. *A silver and tortoiseshell trinket box, late 19th century.* Nov. '85, £280.

12. *A charming tea set made by Spode Copeland, with silver mounts, spoons and tongs by Walker & Hall, Sheffield, 1911.* Mar. '86, £280. The fitted case has kept the set in excellent condition, hence the good price.

13. *A silver and enamel bull mastiff vesta case made in Birmingham, 1886.* Mar. '86, £150.

14. *A polished stone and silver vinaigrette made in Birmingham, 1812.* Mar. '86, £100.

15. *A silver and enamel 'visiting card' vesta case by S. Morden, London, 1888.* Mar. '86, £180.

16. *A polished stone and silver vinaigrette made in Birmingham, 1858.* Mar. '86, £170.

17. *A silver and enamel life-belt scent bottle, possibly made in Birmingham, 1896.* Mar. '86, £220.

18. *A silver and tortoiseshell sewing box, late 19th century.* Nov. '85, £480.

19. *A silver and tortoiseshell letters clip, late 19th century.* Nov. '85, £180.

7 8

10 11

9

12

13

14

16

17

15

18 19

Silver Models

Over the centuries silver has primarily been used in the manufacture of useful domestic ware. The versatility of the metal, and the many different methods of working with it, have, however, made it ideal for the creation of models and sculptures, some of which combine usefulness with delight and charm.

Sculpting in silver has a long history, and European craftsmen of the 16th and 17th centuries made vast figures of animals and birds, both actual and mythical. These were finely cast and chased, and frequently studded with precious stones or decorated with bright enamelling. Many were life-size and almost certainly made purely for ostentatious display, demonstrating the wealth and taste of the patron who commissioned them.

Here I will concentrate on models made in the 19th and early 20th centuries, which range widely in quality and consequently in price. British silversmiths of the 1850s were much admired for their naturalistic pieces, usually combining marvellously solid workmanship with a large dose of delightful Victorian whimsy. They were usually extremely well made, each hair or feather chased or engraved by hand to capture the nature of the beast or bird. Many were made for practical use, the Hennell brothers and the Fox brothers in particular making charming cruets, inkwells, matchstands and cream jugs in the form of pigs, owls, apes and even a basket of kittens and puppies. Over the last 10 or 15 years these examples of Victorian craftsmanship have become much sought after, appearing only rarely at auction and attracting much interest and high prices.

Towards the other end of the spectrum of quality come the vast quantity of model birds and animals made in both Germany and Holland in the last decades of the 19th century and at the beginning of this one. These were primarily for export to Britain and are usually found bearing import hallmarks to show that they were assayed and found to be of British sterling standard, along with the initials BM for Berthold Muller who sponsored their importation, hallmarking and subsequent distribution to retailers throughout Britain.

The majority of these pieces were mass-produced, stamped out from sheet silver and show little attention to detail or quality. Most are extremely stilted and unnatural, decorative from a distance but clumsy and grotesque on close examination.

Despite these criticisms, such models found great favour as they were inexpensive compared with the far better work of British silversmiths. Indeed, towards the end of the 19th century the latter found themselves in great financial difficulties owing to the enormous influx of Continental silver and successfully petitioned parliament to withdraw the duty on silver imposed in 1784. This was repealed in 1890.

At the very bottom of the quality spectrum, one must finally discuss the almost brand-new birds and animals made from low-grade silver, usually not more than 800 standard, so without even the saving grace of import hallmarks. Here the workmanship is practically non-existent, and one is reminded of cheap late 19th-century tin-plate toys stamped out of metal and crudely soldered together. Most of these very late pieces were, and indeed still are, made in Italy and Spain, and they are often decorated with bright gilding, thus creating a misleading first impression. Handling will soon reveal that they are light and flimsy, easily damaged, and totally lacking in charm.

Obviously, the illustrations will show these differences of quality only to a certain extent, and I would advise a potential buyer to examine at first hand any pieces offered for sale. As they were made primarily for show, they are bound to create an imposing first impression, but handling will soon reveal vast differences in weight of silver, skill of manufacture and sheer charm and vitality of subject.   *Stephen Helliwell*

1. *This well cast and chased table lighter in the form of a running fox combines usefulness and quality of manufacture with a certain liveliness.* Oct. '85, £290.
2. *This pair of brand-new Italian model pheasants looks quite impressive, but closer examination reveals tremendous lack of quality and substance.* When offered for sale in Feb. '86 they failed to find a buyer at only £70.
3. *Pointer made by George Adams of London, 1861, from an original modelled by Colonel Liberch of St. Petersburg. Weight 38 oz.* Oct. '85, £950. Even in this illustration, the skill of the silversmith who captured this splendid Pointer can easily be recognized.
4. *Two Continental model owls with detachable heads and glass eyes.* Oct. '85, £650. Owls seem to be more appealing and collectable than most birds – psychologists tell us it is because they have large eyes and round heads, giving them a certain humanoid appearance!

1

2

4

5. *An amusing Victorian novelty bear inkstand only 4¾ in. high and made by C.F. of Sheffield, 1885.* Nov. '85, £500. Sold against a pre-sale estimate of £150–£200, this is perhaps another example of the Teddy Bear mania sweeping the salerooms today.

6. *Another Continental model owl, this example bearing import marks for London, 1910, and standing on a Connemara marble plinth with an overall height of 13¼ in.* Sept. '85, £850. Better than most.

7. *A fine quality crocodile made in Birmingham, 1914, overall length 19 in.* Aug. '85, £2,100.

The crocodile was extremely finely chased and moulded and was mounted on a fossil marble base. It weighed only 33 oz., but sold for a staggering price.

8. *A pair of Continental model foxes with gem-set eyes.* Of better quality than most modern pieces, and probably made in Germany, but unmarked, they failed to sell, reaching only £320 in Jan. '86.

9. *A pair of good-quality model knights imported by Berthold Muller in 1911 and based on 17th-century originals; and a Victorian model of an equestrian knight made by Stephen Smith London, 1870. 9 in.* Christie's King Street, Mar. '86, £2,376 and £1,026. In this case the faces were carved in ivory, although some copies use plastic.

10. *Cow cream jugs are relatively common, but here we have rarer jugs formed as a pug dog and a nanny goat. The first was made of unmarked Continental silver, the second by Joseph and John Angell, London 1840.* The quality and workmanship of the goat produced a bid of £2,000, the dog made only £280. Mar. '86.

5

6

7

9

8

10

Corkscrews

The Romans first discovered the practical use of cork, but it was not until the turn of the 17th century, when it was realized that wine could improve by bottling rather than being kept in a cask, that the use of cork oak, *Quercus suber*, came into its own. The air-filled cells of cork were ideal for wine stoppage, being watertight and odourless and allowing the wine to mature for many years without leakage or evaporation.

No one knows exactly who invented the corkscrew, but the first examples known are believed to date from 1690. Towards the end of the 18th century, however, the corkscrew became an essential item in every gentleman's dining room and travel bag. In 1795 the first patent for a corkscrew was taken out by the Reverend Samuel Henshall, and this cleared the way to a period of invention and inventiveness in the 19th century when the age-old problem of extracting the cork from a bottle by the most efficient means possible was vigorously pursued by an enormous number of patentees.

In fact it is well known that well over 300 patents and 100 registered designs were taken out in the 19th century, when English craftsmanship reigned supreme as it did in so many other aspects of industrial inventiveness and endeavour.

The production of corkscrews was not confined to these shores, but was naturally found in the European wine-producing countries such as France, Germany and Italy, while the Dutch specialized from an early date in producing small silver corkscrews mainly intended for the use of ladies to uncork their scent bottles.

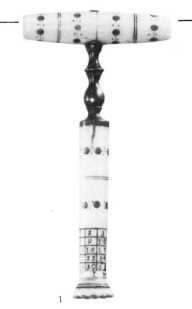

1

This activity in corkscrew production did not go unnoticed on the other side of the Atlantic, although it took some time, and the first American patent was applied for in 1860. This fired the imagination of many inventors and entrepreneurs, who had the advantage of a large home demand, and modern production line techniques, to flood the market with cheap but effective corkscrews.

It is with this background that the present great interest in corkscrews has made them very much a 'collectors' item', and examples which only a few years ago would sell for a pound or two can now command hundreds!

As in all lines of collecting, the price is governed by the laws of supply and demand. Some of the most effective examples which were commercially viable to produce are still to be found in great numbers, and their prices reflect their frequent appearance on the market. Other, rarer, pieces were very often of flimsy and inefficient design, or just too expensive for commercial production – even though their patent papers were lodged with the patent office. It is these elusive and perhaps one-off items which are today ardently sought by collectors all over the world.

In an age when economics dictate that cheaper alternatives should be found in every sphere of our lives, it would be a pity if the cork were entirely overtaken by plastic, which could be unstopped by hand, and the challenge of inventing the 'perfect' corkscrew lost forever.

Francis Hutchinson

1. *An English ivory and steel corkscrew combined with an inscribed day and month calendar, mid-18th century. Aug. '85, £650.*
2. *A folding steel bow compound tool, including a corkscrew, early 19th century. Aug. '85, £150.*
   No doubt this also included the traditional implement for removing stones from horses' hooves, and it was in fine condition.
3. *A Dutch silver corkscrew, unmarked, 19th century. Aug. '85, £500.*
4. *An early open-frame king-screw with bone handle. Feb. '86, £240. Here is a narrow ratchet driven by a bone winding handle through an open frame.*
5. *An English king-screw, the collar marked 'GR' and stamped with maker's name 'G Palmer', early 19th century. Aug. '85, £280.*

5

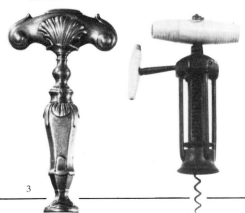

3

4

6. *A brass, iron and bone king screw marked 'Wilmot Roberts & Co.' and with the royal coat of arms, c.1850.* June '86, £80.
7. *A Thomason patent brass and steel corkscrew, the barrel with Gothic architectural decoration, c.1850.* June '86, £150.
8. *Small silver corkscrew made by Cocks and Bettridge, 1800.* June '86, £160.
   These small corkscrews were usually made in Birmingham between about 1760 and 1820 and were designed for travellers, with the steel screw fitting into the case. They normally have just a maker's mark.

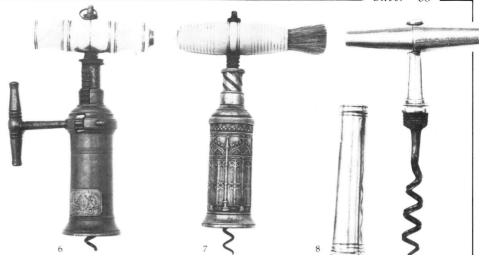

. . . *and Wine-related Items*

Items of an alcoholic nature are popular with our buyers and we are still holding bi-monthly sales of wine related items, mainly of silver and silver-plate, as well as corkscrews.

This year has seen consistently buoyant prices, especially for the larger, more showy pieces. Cut-glass claret jugs are particularly collected along with coasters in silver or plate, wine funnels and sets of goblets. The one exception to this are wine labels, which appear to be somewhat in the doldrums along with other small collectables such as vinaigrettes or snuff boxes. Examples appearing recently in the saleroom have generally failed to live up to expectations based on past experience in valuing.

Stephen Helliwell

A selection of silver, silver-plated and glass claret jugs and decanters, all sold April 1986.

1. *French style rococo claret jug with silver-plated mount.* 12¾ in. Apr. '86, £220.
2. *A good example of a Victorian novelty claret jug by A.C., London, 1881.* 11 in. Apr. '86, £2,700.
3. *A pair of Victorian plain wine bottles by W.S., Birmingham, 1884.* 11¼ in. Apr. '86, £650.
4. *An Edwardian claret jug of standard form by the Goldsmiths and Silversmiths Co., London, 1902.* 6¾ in. Apr. '86, £180.
5. *A pair of continental decanters with white-metal mounts.* 7½ in. Apr. '86, £420. Usually less popular but very decorative.
6. *An Edwardian claret jug by Elkington & Co., Birmingham, 1902.* 8¾ in. Apr. '86, £190.

5. *Jewellery*

Introduction
by David Lancaster

1

She was a delightful young lady, enormously excited by the imminent announcement of her engagement and bursting with plans for the future. She had come to South Kensington in search of an engagement ring, a very specific ring, exactly like the family heirloom which had been stolen from Grandma. She described it to me in detail, the typical delicate gold work and soft-hued pink and green stones arranged in a cluster, and showed me a carte-de-visite of a matronly lady wearing an indefinable blob on one finger. Would I find her a replacement in the three weeks before the announcement?

Hardening my heart to the appeal of those enormous eyes it was my sorry task to explain that this is entirely the wrong approach to buying jewellery at auction. The range of goods that we offer is determined by what was brought in for cataloguing some three or four weeks before, and thus sales are a merry mixture of old and modern jewellery in various qualities and states of repair. Thus I recommended that to find exactly what she wanted in the short time available she should approach shops specializing in antique jewellery. She complained that such shops were too expensive, but she failed to appreciate that the need to tie up large amounts of capital in carrying a wide choice of jewellery entitles the jeweller to his profits.

The auction room is at a disadvantage in supplying particular requirements unless the client has the time to wait until the item turns up, but for the buyer willing to look through a sale for attractive pieces the chances of purchasing a desirable addition to the jewel case at a reasonable price are excellent.

Having said that it does not do to start with too fixed an idea of what is required; it is also important to realize that one of the great advantages of jewellery is that the materials can be constantly remodelled. To take an example: the

typical 19th-century diamond solitaire was cut in a deep, steep-shoulder style, which reacted well with the prevailing gas- and candle-light, creating a display of spectral colours, but modern neon and bright spot lighting does little for such stones. The cost of re-cutting such a stone to modern dimensions is surprisingly modest and the sudden increase in brilliance can be quite startling. Similarly, to dismiss a diamond solitaire ring because the setting is not to your taste is to ignore the fact that ninety per cent of the purchase price for a diamond ring of one carat or more is for the stone—so it is well worth considering buying the ring and having the stone remounted. A surprising number of people worry about the finger size of a ring, but this is a minor correction with the average solitaire or cluster, only becoming a problem when a ring spreads right across the finger, and a near impossibility with an eternity ring.

There are of course many pieces of jewellery which should not be altered, such as antique items in original condition or good quality jewels in their fitted cases. The latter are the ideal purchase if they appeal, for the fact that they have retained their original case normally implies that they have seen little wear and have been well looked after.

1. *A foiled sapphire, diamond and rose diamond open scrollwork brooch/ pendant with diamond-set pendant loop, c.1880. May '86, £1,000.*
   This very pretty pendant is quickly converted into a brooch by unscrewing the pin and hook and sliding the diamond-set loop from its serpentine hook. A sign of the quality of manufacture is the exact alignment of hook and pin when screwed into their setting. Many items of this nature have lost their fittings and the original condition of this one made it very desirable.

2

3

4

Even so, not all jewellery must be taken at immediate face value, for many Victorian brooches were made to serve several purposes. With their exquisite engineering, the brooch fittings are often detachable, with alternative pendant mounts and even hair-slide fittings concealed in the base of the case. Chandelier earrings which appear far too ostentatious for normal wear often unclip into two or three sections to provide an entire range from casual to grand ball jewellery. This sort of adaptation can be carried forward into many fancy pendants, where pieces can be made detachable to increase the versatility of the necklet, whilst long chains can have two discreet catches inserted so that a part of the chain can be worn alone as a choker.

When next you view a sale of jewellery, consider the pieces from the point of view of content and alternative use, and quite possibly you will realize that great potential is being masked by poor presentation.

2. *A continental gold and diamond pendant with diamond drop, diamond-set loop and detachable brooch mount, c.1900.* May '86, £900.
   A heavier example of a similar theme; in this case, the hook is hinged to fold away behind the pendant. The greater bulk and polished gold make this a more difficult piece to wear and consequently bidding was slightly less than enthusiastic.

3. *A pair of diamond drop earrings, c.1920.* May '86, £1,600.
   This pair of dramatic evening-wear earrings could easily be converted to a more adaptable form by altering the links to hooks, thereby enabling the entire centre section to be removed, leaving the drop-shaped clusters suspended from the upper fittings.

4. *A diamond double-clip leaf cluster brooch, c.1920.* May '86, £950.
   Although the double dress-clip was a standard item of Edwardian jewellery, this example is unusually neat and compact. The two clips make charming ornaments to highlight the classic little black dress, whilst the combined unit is still not too ostentatious.

5. *A ruby and diamond marquise cluster mounted as a bar brooch, c.1900.* Feb. '86, £300.
   An item which has already followed the dictates of earlier fashions when it was converted from a ring to a pin, this cluster is now ripe for a relatively simple alteration back to a ring, which would immediately enhance its value.

6. *A gold, enamel and pearl ribbon brooch decorated in blue and white, housing a pair of detachable cloak pins, c.1880.* Feb. '86, £260.
   An interesting double-use brooch from which the pair of pins can be removed to hold a light cloak in position.

7. *A Victorian gold mesh bracelet with twin snap fittings, the chrysoprase and garnet cluster clasp detachable for use as a brooch or pendant, c.1850.* June '86, £420.
   By fitting two clasps instead of the normal one, the versatility of this piece of jewellery has been greatly increased.

5

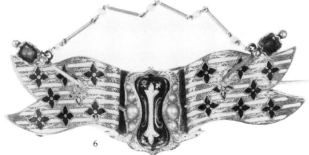

6

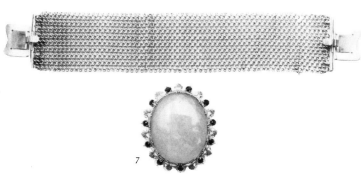

7

Jewellery: What's in a name?

One of our directors appeared on the Money Programme on BBC Television recently, discussing various items he considered to be of good investment potential. One of these was a small gold enamel and pearl pendant signed by Fabergé (No. 2). The response to this brief item was immediate, with phone calls pouring into the office from people who had always wanted to own an item of jewellery by the master Russian gold-smith but could not afford the more important pieces offered in specialized sales. The eventual price realized by this little pendant was some ten times the figure it would have achieved had it not borne the Russian initials which Fabergé used on smaller pieces.

Why is it that collectors will pay such a premium for a signature? Often it is because the signatory was the first to establish a new fashion, in Fabergé's case the breakaway from traditional diamond and brightly-coloured gem-encrusted jewels to his own emphasis on delicately shaded hard-fired enamels, intricately worked varicoloured golds incorporating small gems, and constant insistence on the highest standards of workmanship.

This meticulous care with the assembly and finish of all the products of the workshop is also the hallmark of two 19th-century companies specializing in the then fashionable reproductions of antique jewels. Both these families signed with initials, the entwined Cs of Castellani, or the various initials of members of the Giuliano family ensuring quality and desirability. No. 3 is an excellent example of the delicate goldwork set with tumbled gem beads of minor value used by Castellani to re-create antique styles, and it bears his stamp (No. 4) on the reverse. Even more man-hours are required to execute the saw-fretting of the design in No. 5, with an interesting combination of colours achieved by the central green tourmaline with ruby-set gold border. The back of this pendant bears the applied oval plate C.G., the mark of Carlo Giuliano, and it is contained in its original case stamped with the London address of the workshop.

Original cases are an important part of the appeal of named jewellery, and are often the clue to changes of address or amalgamations of companies, as well as being the ideal way to present interesting jewels. The designer Sibyl Dunlop is best known for Arts and Crafts pieces combining gold and silver with such gems as amethyst and moonstone in floral pierced and engraved mounts, so the pair of very plain cabochon amethyst cuff-links (No. 6) is an interesting revelation of the more commercial stock carried by the Kensington Church Street shop. On the subject of cases, and returning for a moment to Fabergé, his demand for quality was also evidenced by the fitted cases supplied with his objects of virtu, and the icon (No. 7) is in the traditional pear-wood case with radiused corners, the silk lining stamped with the company symbols.

The Art Nouveau and Art Deco movements promoted many famous names in a period when designers became recognized as an important influence. The finest jewel houses such as Cartier, Liberty and Tiffany produced distinctive house styles which can still be recognized on sight. The styles were of course part of a total package for jewellery, fashion accessories, clothing, furnishing, etc., and the powder compact (No. 8) is from a range of gold-inset, silver-and-gem receptacles ranging from lipstick holders to evening bags produced by Boucheron, a French company famous for the highest-quality goods. Another name rising to prominence in the Art Nouveau era was the Danish designer Georg Jensen, who specialized in motifs from nature adapted to a stylized design and mostly produced in silver. No. 9 is distinctively a Jensen design and is a wearable brooch at an affordable price.

Looking at the names which command high prices it becomes clear that innovation, a distinctive recognizable style, and an emphasis on high quality are necessary ingredients for lasting fame. What of today's fine jewels, the products of such names as Garrard, Asprey, Cartier and the designer/retailers like Andrew Grima? It is perhaps inevitable that in our cosmopolitan society styles have tended to become less distinctive with retailers stocking a wider range to cater for the varied tastes of their clients, while the recent angular and abstract designs, although striking, often have little sympathy for the delicate materials to which they must be attached.

No. 10 is of excellent quality and bears the prestigious signature of Kutchinsky, but is the product of the casting mould and polishing machine, lacking the appeal of the personal involvement of a craftsman which is such a feature of the previous examples.   *David Lancaster*

1. *A Russian wave-textured gold pendant with central cabochon sapphire and half pearl set suspension, the ring signed with Fabergé initials, c.1895. Dec. '85, £420. This little piece exemplifies the delight Fabergé and his employees took in using the malleability of gold to its maximum extent.*

2. *A Russian gold, green and white guilloche enamel circular pendant with half pearl centre, signed on suspension ring with Fabergé initials, c.1895. Dec. '85, £350. The term 'guilloche' implies enamel which has been fired on to an engraved or engine-turned surface, so that the decoration is visible through the enamel, an art raised to superb standards by the Fabergé workshops.*

3. *A gold necklace modelled after Roman 2nd-century* AD *examples, set with cabochon emeralds and pearls in rope-work collet mounts with a fringe of tumbled gem beads, c.1870. Dec. '85, £950.*

1

2

4

5

4. *The applied entwined Cs mark of Castellani on the reverse of necklace 3.*

5. *A gold, ruby, green tourmaline, pearl and enamel pendant, the central tourmaline with a floral pierced ruby-set border, with pearl and enamel drop attached, the reverse with affixed plate signed CG for Carlo Giuliano, in a fitted case, stamped 'C. Giuliano, 115 Piccadilly, London', c.1880. Feb. '86, £2,000.*

6. *A pair of 18ct. gold cabochon amethyst cuff-links signed Sibyl Dunlop, in maker's case, c.1925. Dec. '85, £380.*

7. *A Russian silver-mounted bell-shaped icon with a chased foliate and scroll surround inset with two cabochon sapphires, with a pencilled inscription on the wood back – 'Save and cherish Mamma 1912' – the mount and the fitted case signed Fabergé, c.1912. Dec. '85, £1,550.*

8. *A French silver reeded powder compact, the lid inset with a gold pierced mirror-backed panel set with cabochon sapphires, signed Boucheron Paris, with suède slip case, c.1930. Apr. '86, £140.*

9. *A silver pierced circular brooch signed Georg Jensen Denmark. Design c.1930. Dec. '85, part lot, approx £80.*

10. *A pair of 18ct. gold abstract nugget cuff-links signed Kutchinsky, 27.2 grams, c.1970. Apr. '86, £220.*

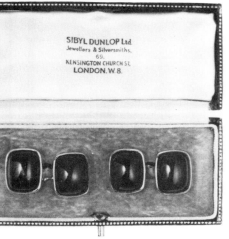

SIBYL DUNLOP Ltd.
Jewellers & Silversmiths.
69,
KENSINGTON CHURCH ST.
LONDON. W.8.

7

9

10

Enamelled Jewellery

If one were to consider the evolution of jewellery design only in terms of variations in shape and combination of gem stones and minerals such as gold and silver, an important complementary feature would be overlooked.

In theory, it might seem unlikely that the application of fired coloured glass (enamel), juxtaposed with diamonds and rubies for example, would enhance the beauty and quality of an article of jewellery. However, the art of combining these materials successfully can be traced as far back as the Egyptian period – approximately 900 BC. In 1922, when the archaeologist, Howard Carter, prised the last of the three lids from the coffin of the Pharaoh Tutankhamun, he revealed the now famous gold death mask. The only added decoration to this mask was the blue enamel inlay, which made an essential contribution to its striking appearance. The discovery of this particular tomb triggered off a new revival in Egyptian style jewellery, the vast majority of which included some enamel work, representing vultures, sphinxes, hieroglyphics, etc.

There had been earlier imitations of older European designs; examples of work by the 19th-century Italian jewellers Carlo Giuliano (No. 1) and Alessandro Castellani, who emulated the designs of the Renaissance and incorporated enamel to great effect, frequently appear in the salerooms today.

The earliest technique of enamelling was known as *cloisonné*, the inlay of molten glass into a wire-backed framework. *Champlevé* was a later and more advanced technique of pouring enamel into cut grooves previously engraved in the gold or silver and then polishing it down to the same level as the metal. *Champlevé* enamelling was extensively used during the late 18th and 19th centuries, and the preoccupation with death during this period encouraged the production of large quantities of black or white enamelled mourning jewellery (No. 2), the white normally signifying unmarried, adolescent or, more commonly, infant mortality. It was a custom for the bereaved to have a wedding ring converted for mourning.

A modification to the *champlevé* process was a translucent enamel, *basse taille*, applied over the engraved or cast metal, the colour appearing stronger where the metal was deepest cut. This style was popular during the Art Nouveau period and put to good use by designers such as Charles Horner, Theodore Fahrner and Child & Child (No. 3). A further refinement is *guilloche* (No. 4), similar to *basse taille*, but with the metal surface engine-turned. Carl Fabergé employed this technique for a wide variety of jewellery and objects of virtu.

The stained-glass effect of *plique à jour* (No. 5) was the method discovered in the 15th century of filling a backless metal frame with coloured enamel, sometimes referred to as 'cell enamelling', which proved particularly effective for evoking natural forms in Art Nouveau jewellery.

Mark Bowis

1. *A 19th-century gold, champlevé enamel and pearl caduceus (Greek messenger) brooch signed Carlo Giuliano. Mar. '86, £400.*
2. *A George III white enamel knife-edge pattern mourning ring, the inscription reading 'In Memory of Major Fra C. Peirson killed at Jersey 1781 age 24'. Mar. '86, £380.*
   Major Peirson was Commander of the British garrison and the Jersey Militia when the French under Baron Rullecort attacked St. Hélier, Jersey, in 1781. He is commemorated in a painting by J.S. Copley, *The Death of Major Peirson* (1783), in the Tate Gallery.
3. *Late 19th-century Art Nouveau design spreading-wing brooch of basse taille enamel (producing a shaded effect), with aquamarine drop attached, by Child & Child. Mar. '86, £200.*
4. *An Edwardian pearl-set pendant with guilloche enamel and central diamond-set initial. Apr. '86, £110.*
5. *An Art Nouveau cabochon sapphire, cabochon ruby, rose diamond, pearl and plique à jour enamel wing pendant. Feb. '86, £750.*

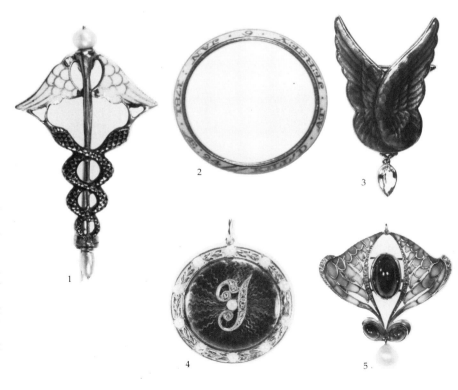

Cameos

The art of gem engraving developed in ancient Egypt and spread by way of Greece to Rome. Any striated stone or agate could be used, because the outer layer could be cut back to leave a miniature carved relief of one of the classical heroes standing out against a darker background.

Although there was something of a revival during the Italian Renaissance, real interest in cameo production started again in the early 19th century when Napoleon in Imperial mood had his portrait carved in cameo in the style of a Roman emperor by Beneditti Pistrucci, whose patron was Napoleon's sister. With the coming of the Victorian era this French neo-classicism gave way to the gothic romanticism that surrounded the influential figure of Queen Victoria herself. This change in taste stopped the demand for the finest stone cameos, but Victorian shell cameos (No. 3) with romantic female figures became a popular item of decorative jewellery until well into the 1880s. No Victorian jewellery collection is complete without one.

Although shell cameos have been carved since the 15th century, quantity production using the helmet and green conch shells started in Sicily about 1805. By the 1830s workshops had been set up in Paris and London, although the work was still supervised by Italian specialists. To satisfy demand the process was inevitably automated with cameos being machine-cut from templates. The buyer therefore needs to be careful. Most of the cameos within the reach of the average collector will be 19th-century, and Victorian shell cameos can represent both the best and the worst of 19th-century craftsmanship.

A little experience and an instinct for quality will soon tell you whether a cameo is good or bad, hand-made or machine cut. Composition, gentleness of execution and good detail are points to look for. Run a thumb over the surface, and if the lines feel sharp and overprecise, it is more than likely machine-cut. If the edges are more gentle and fluid it is most likely hand-carved.

As with all jewels buy the best you can afford. *Claire Ayres*

1. *A helmet conch shell, carved for display purposes with a large cameo, demonstrating the use of high points in the shell contour to provide depth of material for the hair ornament. Italian, late 19th century. 8 in. Apr. '86, £80 (unsold). Had this been mounted as a brooch it would easily have reached its estimate of £120–£180.*

2. *A white on grey banded agate cameo carved in high relief with the head of Achilles, the stone signed Isler, for Luigi Isler, second half of the 19th century. Dec. '85, £950. This finely carved cameo was probably purchased in Italy as an unmounted cabinet piece and was subsequently mounted as a brooch by Robert Phillips, who had a shop in* Cockspur Street, London, from 1851 to 1885. The mount is an excellent example of the archaeological style; the applied bead and wirework is in the manner of early Etruscan jewellery, and complements the cameo perfectly.

3. *A late Victorian shell cameo with stylized profile and blank torso. Feb. '86, £120. This is a typical example, although demonstrating skill in the detailing of floral head-dress and ringlets. The mount is affected by the mixture of mass-production and hand-craft, with an unpleasant saw-tooth setting edge bordered by well engraved scrolls.*

4. *A twentieth-century shell cameo cut on a template, producing a harsh, stilted profile with no depth and economically mounted in 9ct gold. Sold as part of a lot, Dec. '85, approximate value, £30.*

5. *A well-detailed cameo of a classical male head carved in malachite, mid-19th century. Feb. '86, £150. Although of undoubted quality, the choice of material is not ideal, as the stone is a mottled green throughout, allowing no definition between figure and background, and is also soft, so that regular use as a stick pin would soon result in damage.*

6. *A typical late Victorian pale pink on white coral cameo with lifeless standardized profile set in a machine-stamped gold mount, subsequently hand-engraved. Feb. '86, £400. Although not of superior quality, this large brooch has the attraction of being in mint condition with its complete tassel fringe, geared locket back and contemporary inscription dated 1873.*

Pendants, Brooches and Bracelets

1

2

3

Pendants are always popular items of jewellery as they are so easy to wear, and versatile examples from many periods can be worn with today's fashions (Nos. 1–3). Meanwhile, the brooch market has been fairly quiet over the last few years, but as with all categories of jewellery, the more unusual and well crafted items are eagerly sought after (Nos. 4–7). By contrast, bracelets enjoy a constant demand (No. 8) and hinged stiff bangles (No. 9) are particularly sought after. Prices, however, are often dictated by appeal rather than bulk. This also applies to lesser diamond rings, where the size of the stones themselves is not of vital importance (No. 10). Finally, Victorian ivory jewellery appears to be a good buy at present (No. 13).   *David Lancaster*

1. *An antique pink topaz and yellow chrysoberyl cannetille gold drop pendant with belcher link chain, c.1840.* Feb. '86, £300.

   Cannetille gold work uses spiralled wires and beads to occupy a considerable area with little weight, and it was much in vogue in the early part of the 19th century. The pink and lemon-yellow stones are also typical of the period, combining to produce a bright, bold and very attractive drop.

2. *A Victorian cabochon garnet solitaire pendant suspended from a snake link neckchain, c.1880.* Feb. '86, £170.

   As in the previous example, maximum use has been made of the minimum of gold, with a lightweight scrolled stamping brought to life by the continuous movement of the suspended fringe. The correct period chain adds considerably to the appeal of this pendant.

3. *A diamond and drop cut aquamarine pendant with diamond floral cluster suspension, c.1905.* Feb. '86, £500.

   This delicate pendant, typically Edwardian in style, is equally at home worn with casual clothes or evening dress. Such versatility ensures a ready market.

4

4. *An antique gold mounted eye miniature with half pearl border, c.1840.* Feb. '86, £350.

   During the first half of the 19th century many miniaturists earned their bread and butter painting expression-filled eyes for use in jewellery. The more exotic examples incorporated diamond teardrops and frames, but part of the appeal of this example is its charming simplicity.

5. *A late Georgian diamond and gem brooch, c.1820.* Feb. '86, £550.

   An interesting souvenir brooch, the centrepiece is typically Indian, the garnet cabochon carved and inlaid with gold, set with a rose diamond and rubies, presumably brought home after service and mounted with the diamond border by an English jeweller.

5

7

Compared with the simplicity of No. 8, this bangle represents excellent value but it is a difficult piece to wear.

10. *A diamond marquise cluster ring with ruby border and rose diamond three stone shoulders, c.1930.* Feb. '86, £300.

   The marquise shape continues to grow in popularity and this cluster, although small, would be ideal for a long, slender finger.

11. *A diamond bracelet of five open-work panels separated by diamond-set rectangular links, c.1925.* Feb. '86, £2,500.

   Only a few years ago such bracelets were regarded merely as a source of diamonds for remodelling, but they are now desirable items in their own right. Here again restraint is desirable and this bracelet is not too ostentatious.

12. *A seed pearl bracelet with a cabochon garnet and half pearl clasp, c.1860.* Feb. '86, £200.

   Seed pearl jewellery was a favourite of the Victorian ladies but, being strung on silk, few pieces survive in good condition. The price paid for this little bracelet reflects how few good pieces are available.

13. *A carved ivory demi-parure of a ribbon-tied sheaf-of-wheat brooch and matching earrings, in a case, c.1860.* Jan. '86, £95.

   The conservation movement, while laudable, has had some strange side effects, including the condemnation of Victorian carved ivory, despite its craftsmanship. This brooch and earring suite must represent excellent investment potential at current depressed prices.

6. *A gold and enamel laurel wreath brooch set with a hardstone intaglio, c.1870.* Feb. '86, £500.

   The 19th century witnessed a revival of interest in cameos and intaglios, and this brooch incorporates a fine agate example, with the romantic theme so dear to Victorian hearts.

7. *A rose diamond arrow sûreté pin, c.1920.* Feb. '86, £130.

   A simple piece of jewellery, using the economical flat-backed faceted rose diamonds. The arrow head twists off to reveal the pin, making this ideal for wear through a scarf.

8. *A Victorian snake design bracelet with turquoise-set head and tail, c.1850.* £380.

   Victorian snake bracelets come in a range of qualities, many with detailed flexible bodies and diamond-set heads. This example has obviously been made for the then emerging middle-class market who wished to follow the fashion of the period at a reasonable price.

9. *A diamond pearl and green enamel hinged bangle, c.1900.* Feb. '86, £650.

   A large flamboyant bangle which restricts its own market by its size.

8

9

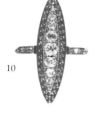

10

13

6.   *Clocks*

Introduction

by Santiago de Barry

This past year has seen a continuing stability in the clock market in general. Prices for the better examples do appear to have improved – but not dramatically; and those in the middle range have perhaps declined – but not dramatically. In comparison with 1984–5 there does seem to have been a healthy interest from overseas and from private buyers in Britain, especially with regard to longcase clocks (see pp. 96–7).

As a result, now should be a good time for a bargain hunter with an eye to the future. The clock may no longer play the vital role in the home that it once did, challenged as it is by wrist-watch, television and the appalling quartz, but few homes feel complete without at least one decorative timepiece.

Since the middle of the last century, many mass-produced clocks have been loosed on the world, but among them are well-made and decorative types, which are now often to be found at very reasonable prices. For instance, 'black marble' – actually Belgian slate – mantel clocks from the 1880s onwards can both look good and keep good time (No. 6). Twenty years ago they seemed expensive at a fiver or so, but now they are hardly expensive at up to £50. Equally, many German, spelter and even American clocks of the turn of the century still sell for between £50 and £100. These can all be of excellent workmanship, but they seem to be damned purely because they were mass-produced for the middle classes. If one seeks out the decorative and reliable examples, they can fit almost any present-day room setting.

At the upper levels of the 'everyday' rather than the specialist horological market, standard Regency and Victorian bracket clocks now usually sell for between £300 and £500 (pp. 98–9). However, in overall terms there seems to have been a slackening in demand for ormolu, with standard Empire clocks making between £200 and £500 – but Sèvres plaques and quality may help (Nos. 1–3).

1   2

Last year we included articles in *The Popular Antiques Yearbook*, Vol. I, on carriage clocks and wrist-watches. There has been little change in the first market, but the second has seen both something of a depression and a remarkable new auction record price. This is in no way a contradiction. In many ways the market is subject to fashion – and a 'men only' fashion at that, good lady's watches generally being far cheaper than the male equivalents – and it is no bad thing that some of the dross, which had been making good money, should be revalued – downwards. On the other hand, No. 8, which sold back to its makers in Geneva, was a superb piece of craftsmanship and engineering.

1. *A French ormolu and blue ground Sèvres pattern porcelain mounted mantel clock surmounted by a massive urn.* 22 in. Mar. '86, £1,400.
    A rather impressive clock and an unusual size and design of case.

2. *A French ormolu and blue ground Sèvres pattern porcelain mounted mantel clock.* 17 in. Mar. '86, £800.

3   4   5

3. *A French ormolu and blue ground Sèvres pattern porcelain mounted mantel clock.* 23 in. Apr. '86, £3,400.

   A superb quality clock of its kind, with attractive finely chased ormolu mounts.

4. *A Regency library timepiece in rectangular black marble case, signed 'Barraud & Lund, Cornhill, London, 1735'.* 10½ in. Feb. '86, £380.

   This is an interesting clock to compare with the more common French black marble clocks, which regularly sell in the £30–£50 bracket. This example, with the simple unadorned lines of its case, fine gilt and engine-turned dial and English chain and fusee movement could be said to be the 'king' of black marble clocks!

5. *A French Empire ormolu and bronze mantel clock formed as a dolphin ridden by a cherub.* 17 in. Mar. '86, £950.

6. *'Black marble' mantel clock in architectural case.* 17 in. wide. May '86, £25.

   The decoration of this is good, but the superior quality of No. 4 can be seen by comparing the dials and bezels of both clocks.

7. *An Edwardian satinwood, parquetry and tortoiseshell inlaid wall timepiece in the Sheraton style.* 25 in. Apr. '86, £800.

   Although not of great age, the case is extremely attractive and elegant.

8. *A very rare gold-cased gentleman's perpetual calendar bracelet watch with split-seconds chronograph, by Patek Philippe, Geneva, 1955.* Christie's Geneva, May '86, £102,500.

   Only three of these remarkable instruments were made, and this was bought back by the makers for their museum. The illustration shows the intricate dials.

7   8

Longcase Clocks

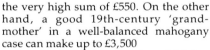

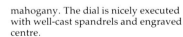

1   2   3   4   5

As already stated, prices have been very stable, but possibly longcase clocks are the one section in which a slight upward change might be noticed. As usual, the good mahogany George III longcase clocks have been selling well, anywhere between £1,500 and £4,000.

Oak cases, always difficult to sell, have proved more so in recent months – unless they have brass dials. It is interesting to compare two relatively similar 'grandmother' clocks of very similar date. No. 7, with an oak case, realized £100, and No. 8, which had a good figured walnut veneered case, realized

the very high sum of £550. On the other hand, a good 19th-century 'grandmother' in a well-balanced mahogany case can make up to £3,500

It is this side of the market which has produced the most interesting prices in relation to last year, and I would assume will continue to do so in the immediate future.   *Santiago de Barry*

1. *A George III mahogany longcase clock, signed 'John Crouch, Knightsbridge'.* 94 in. Feb. '86, £4,000.
   A high-quality clock in all respects, with a well-balanced case in finely figured

mahogany. The dial is nicely executed with well-cast spandrels and engraved centre.

2. *A George III mahogany longcase clock.* 102 in. Feb. '86, £2,700.
   A similar clock to No. 1 but with no maker's name and in need of repairs.

3. *An Irish Georgian mahogany longcase clock, signed 'W. Henry Nugent, Dublin'.* 90 in. Mar. '86, £580.

4. *A George III mahogany alarm longcase clock, signed 'Jno. Murch, Honiton'.* 90 in. Mar. '86, £450.
   A disappointing price for a rather elegant clock.

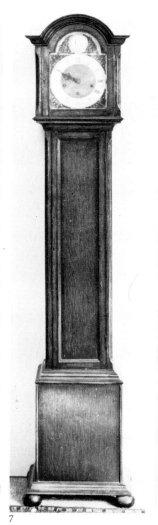
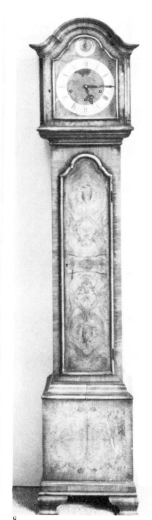
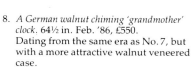

7

8

9

5. *An 18th-century pine longcase clock, signed 'Peter King, Long Acre, London'. 80 in. Feb. '86, £600.*
Although one may think this a high price for a pine clock, the price was actually for the movement. A standard pine clock would realize in the region of £150–£250.

6. *An oak and mahogany longcase clock, signed 'John Cousens, Langport'. 82 in. Feb. '86, £350.*
A rather unattractive case, the door to the trunk probably a later addition to enhance its decorativeness, which seems to have paid off to a certain extent, judging by the price realized.

7. *A German oak chiming 'grandmother' clock. 76 in. Feb. '86, £100.*
One of many produced in the early part of this century.

8. *A German walnut chiming 'grandmother' clock. 64½ in. Feb. '86, £550.*
Dating from the same era as No. 7, but with a more attractive walnut veneered case.

9. *A late Victorian mahogany chiming longcase clock, the case carved in the Art Nouveau style, inscribed 'Maple & Co., London'. 96 in. Apr. '86, £2,400.*
Although there are a fair number of these chiming clocks, the unusual carved case with its attractive foliate motifs typical of the Art Nouveau period helped it to realize its final bid.

10. *An early 19th-century small mahogany longcase clock ('grandmother'), signed 'James Munk, Tenterden. 56 in. Mar. '86, £3,500.*
Rather unusual to find this type of clock at auction – very much a collector's piece.

10

Mantel and other Clocks

This is not the most exciting of times to be observing the mantel clock market, and changes, if any, have been of no great importance.

It is interesting to notice that whereas over a year ago ormolu was in quite a healthy state, now it has become rather difficult to sell, possibly because of the lack of interest from the Middle Eastern market. Similarly champlevé enamelled clocks continue their drop in price. Bracket clocks remain stable, with the more out of the ordinary realizing higher prices.

In the more encouraging group are the four-glass bracket clocks; perpetual calendar examples; and good early 19th-century French and English clocks in bronze and ormolu, which continue to increase in value, but it must be said at a rather slow pace. *Santiago de Barry*

1. *A French white marble and ormolu mantel clock of lyre form. 28 in. Nov. '85, £700.*

2. *Regency rosewood four-glass mantel timepiece signed 'Gravell & Son, Charter Square, London No 4166'. 11 in. Nov. '85, £400.*

   It is interesting to note that No. 2, being a timepiece, realized half the price of No. 3, which is a striking clock.

3. *A Regency rosewood four-glass mantel clock signed 'Birch, Fenchurch St, London'. 9¾ in. Nov. '85, £950.*

4. *A French Empire bronze and ormolu mantel clock surmounted by a Greek warrior. 23 in. Nov. '85, £500.*

5. *A French Empire bronze and ormolu mantel clock surmounted by Venus seated on a shell and drawn by swans. Aug. '85, £2,800.*

   A more interesting and attractive case than the angular design which is more commonly found.

6. *A French ormolu mantel clock in lyre-shaped case, signed 'Chaude HR Du ROI'. 18 in. Aug. '85, £900.*

7. *A French lacquered brass and champlevé enamelled mantel clock. 16 in. Aug. '85, £450.*

7

8

8. *A French Empire ormolu mantel clock surmounted by a classical figure depicting the 'Sciences', signed 'Cronier Jeune, Rue de la Monnaie, No. 6'. 15 in. Aug. '85, £650.*

9. *A French rosewood and floral marquetry mantel clock in waisted case. 16½ in. Aug. '85, £550.*

10. *A French Directoire white marble and ormolu mounted portico clock, signed 'Gravella à Paris'. 18 in. Aug. '85, £600.*

11. *A French ormolu four-glass perpetual calendar mantel clock signed 'Boxell, Brighton'. 22 in. Dec. '85, £1,800.*
    Perpetual calendar clocks are always popular at auction. In addition, this one is attractively cased. Boxell, incidentally, was a retailer, not a maker.

12. *A French Empire ebony and ormolu mounted mantel clock in lyre-shaped case. 20 in. Dec. '85, £700.*

13. *A French black and green marble perpetual calendar mantel clock with Brocot escapement beating half seconds and dead centre second hand. 18 in. Dec. '85, £1,500.*

14. *Detail of escapement of No. 13.* Clocks of this type usually make between £500 and £800, but this one, with its more unusual escapement, has proved more desirable.

9

10

11

12

13

14

7. Decorative Objects and Sculpture

Introduction
by James Dick

'Objects', whether 'of art' or merely 'decorative', is a portmanteau term coined to embrace all the small European items in almost all materials which do not fit comfortably into any of the established antique categories. A dealer in such things must be a master of all trades and a jack of none if he is to survive.

However, because of this limitless scope and diversity, 'objects' provide the best possible training for a good eye. An expert will look at a bronze, say, and notice at once and almost without thinking whether it has been well cast or not. He must look at the small details, often the giveaway, to see if they are well defined and designed or merely muzzy and crude ornaments. Has a wood carver, in making a tray, done justice to the balustrade gallery (No. 1)? There is a commonly heard and sarcastic comment, 'Oh, that was carved with a fork and a knife.'

Glass pictures also come under the 'objects' umbrella. So, is a painting on a mirror really a painting, or just a transfer print? With such a vast field for a collector to choose from, and for a dealer to cultivate in the attempt to supply the wants of as many different collectors as possible, it is obviously vital to know what is selling at present and what is not. Changing fashions and habits of collecting play their confusing parts as ever. Papier mâché, for instance, is sought after, but it seems that the large prices are reserved for only well-painted tea trays and Regency wine coasters (see pp. 112–14).

In theory quality should always sell an object of any kind. However, some types of object are only now beginning to recover from a slump in popularity and prices. A good example is the increasing interest in the 19th-century French animalier bronzes by such artists as Mène, the Bonheurs and Moigniez. The very high prices paid for such things in the early and mid-1970s are only just being matched again after a dramatic fall at the beginning of the present decade.

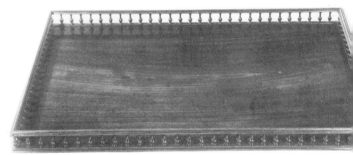

1. *A George III mahogany rectangular tray with well-carved balustrade gallery.* Feb. '86, £600.
2. *A Viennese gilt metal and enamel musical box formed as a grand piano, with stool.* Feb. '86, £250.
3. *A Viennese gilt metal and enamel draught screen incorporating a watch movement.* Feb. '86, £230.

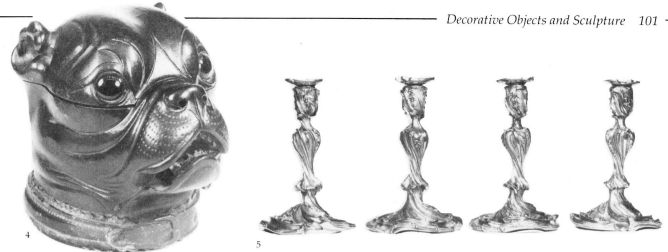

4

5

English enamels can be a minefield, even for the wary. Generally speaking the safe and non-committal term 'Staffordshire' is used. Bilston, which is in the county, is only one of several places in the Midlands which were known for their enamelling work. Then, Battersea in London was rightly famous in the 17th and 18th centuries, and examples from there were, and still are, highly prized. Added to this are the vast numbers of enamelled items from Continental European centres (Nos. 2–3).

There are great numbers of enamel boxes about – pastel boxes, snuffs, nutmeg holders and so on ad infinitum. Many of them, especially in the 19th century, bear the legend 'a present from . . .' or a more intimate, affectionate message. Tourist trinkets in their day, certainly, but now much collected. With modern techniques enamel can be repaired, although it is still fairly expensive, and this explains why even defective items can now find buyers.

Small items of treen remain well to the fore, notably Tunbridge ware and Mauchline ware from Scotland. But it is the unusual (No. 4) which attracts serious and keen collectors.

Dummy boards (No. 6) are certainly decorative objects, and they remain firm favourites with collectors. Apart from the obvious, that many were portraits, I have heard three explanations for their manufacture. They could be used as screens from the heat of the fire, to provide an illusion of company for lonely ladies, and if placed before a fire in an empty room, they would create moving shadows to deter burglars. Take your pick of one or all. Ordinary needlework polescreens are also in demand once again (No. 9, overleaf).

7

8

4. *A stained wood inkwell in the form of a bulldog, 19th century. 4 in. Mar. '86, £220.*

5. *A fine set of four ormolu candlesticks in the rococo taste, early 19th century. Jan. '86, £2,000.*

6. *An 18th-century style dummy board painted with a Cavalier. Jan. '86, £240.*

7. *One of a pair of Regency giltwood wall brackets supported by storks. Feb. '86, £650. Very nice, clean carving.*

8. *A pair of French silver and gilt metal mounted glass jars and covers. 7 in. Mar. '86, £480.*

Queen Anne and later brass candlesticks have been sought after again during 1985 and 1986 (No. 10), but there is a disappointing falling off of interest in pewter. This is true as much of the Continent as of Britain. When I was asked by a Swiss dealer to place a Bernese 18th-century wine flagon in a London sale because there was no demand at home, I felt that things were not exactly as they should be.

However, while on the subject of metalware, there has been a continuing demand for fireside furnishings, with high prices for Georgian implements, good brass fenders and crisply chased French chenets, or fire dogs. Fire baskets of 18th-century shape – even if not date – are also still climbing in price, and many are now in the £400 to £600 bracket without appearing in any way exceptional (see pp. 106–7).

9. *A pair of Regency or William IV mahogany and parcel gilt pole screens.* Jan. '86, £300.

10. *A pair of brass candlesticks, 18th century.* 6 in. Mar. '86, £500.

9

10

Two objects which are certainly decorative but have little else in common.

11. *A well-sculpted white marble bust of Galileo by Aristodemo Costoli, Florence, 1866.* 32 in. Jan. '86, £450. After many years of neglect the decorative qualities – and quality – of many 19th-century busts are beginning to be appreciated again.

12. *A polychrome plaster figure of an Arab warrior.* 32 in. Feb. '86, £420.

11

12

It is difficult to know whether theme collections boost prices by strength of numbers or depress them by providing too much of the same thing. A collection of items of Napoleonic interest, which was offered for sale in April 1986, had the advantage of a royal provenance, since it was sent for sale by H.R.H. the Duke of Gloucester; but this was perhaps offset by the lack of French buyers at the sale. Here we show a selection.

13. *A bronze figure* 12½ in. £120.
14. *A bronze figure.* 11 in. £160.
15. *An equestrian group, after David.* 8¼ in. overall. £350.

13   14   15

16   17   18

19   20   21

16. *Sèvres Parian ware bust.* 10 in. overall. £150.
17. *Staffordshire figure.* 12 in. £50.
18. *Wedgwood black basalt bust.* 9 in. £280.
19. *Circular silver and ivory box.* 3½ in. £280.
20. *An ivory brass-mounted desk seal.* 4½ in. £400.
21. *An ivory card case, showing Longwood House, St. Helena, and Napoleon's tomb.* £340.
22. *A gilt-bronze and ivory bust of Napoleon by E. Bernoud.* 4 ½ in. £160.
23. *A seated and pensive ivory figure.* 4 in. £220.
24. *An ivory bust.* 4 in. £600.

22   23   24

Metalware

Pewter has in the main been something of a disappointment as far as prices are concerned. Of course, some items, such as 9-inch diameter plates, even if they are 18th-century ones, are really very common, but even large-sized chargers, with diameters of up to 24 inches, have often seemed disappointing.

As in most collecting fields, quality is of the utmost importance – and there have been very few takers for items pitted by the dreaded pewter disease. On the other hand, a very good set of six George III pewter plates with deep bowls and wavy edges (No. 1) did extremely well. They were by a good maker, Richard Pitt, dated from about 1780 and were 9½ inch diameter. What produced this really remarkable price was their superb condition and silver-like appearance. In the same sale a similar set, but with shallow bowls, made £900.

A piece such as No. 2 is a prime example of how rarity and condition can produce a splendid price – in this case an auction record. A piece of pewter this early and in such a good state is quite unusual.

Pewter made for religious purposes has always been a specialized field, and there is not much interest in chalices and Nonconformist communion cups unless they are 17th-century. A notable exception is Jewish ceremonial dishes such as the Seder plate (No. 3). An undecorated plate of similar size and date would probably have made about a third of the price.

Brass is another market which is fairly volatile. The endless late copies of Dutch and Spanish candlesticks draw little interest, but then many such things are outright fakes, some cleverly and some crudely executed. An honest pair of Queen Anne brass candlesticks cannot be considered rare, but is always pleasing, with plain lines and satisfying form.

The unusual is always sought after (No. 4). Such things not only appeal to collectors of metalware, but also to the much wider audience who buy pleasing, whimsical or strange objects no matter what the material. No. 5 is a case in point, and it was bought by a collector of general works of art rather than a specialist.

Tobacco boxes (No. 6) have also been a little disappointing, but they too were made in large numbers and engraved with repetitive biblical and secular subjects, animals and figures. Some discerning collectors buy only boxes engraved with bird's-eye views of cities such as Amsterdam and Leyden, which are rarer, so do not be surprised to meet strong competition if you are looking for them.

Brass tobacco dispensers seem to have increased in price over the last few years. These 'honesty' boxes were mainly used in public houses. The drop of the coin released the hinged tobacco compartment. It was up to the individual to limit himself to one pipeful (No. 6).

Metalwork need not always be old to be valuable. The Arts and Crafts brass twin-light wall bracket (No. 7) is an example. It is charming, well engraved and pierced with animal subjects – yet restrained, and so even more appealing.

The Regency brass tea caddy (No. 8) is an unusual and specialized piece – and might be thought too good to use for its original purpose. It is exquisitely engraved with figure subjects, one commemorating the death of Nelson, and with the owner's name and religious mottoes. A new owner would doubtless be just as proud of it. *James Dick*

1. *One of a set of six George III pewter plates by Richard Pitt, c.1780. 9½ in. diam. Jul. '85, £1,300; and a 17th-century Nuremberg brass alms dish, raised with two figures carrying grapes. 16 in. diam. July 86, £300.*

2. *James I pewter flagon of slightly tapering form, c.1620. July '85, £4,000.*

3. *A late-18th-century Continental pewter Seder plate, engraved with a coat-of-arms, Adam and Eve and Hebraic inscription. 12¼ in. diam. July '85, £380.*

4. *An English bronze perpetual taper, the drip pan handles formed as unicorns, c.1700. Feb. '86, £260.*

1

2

3

4

5

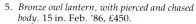

6

7

8

5. *Bronze owl lantern, with pierced and chased body.* 15 in. Feb. '86, £450.

6. *A selection of 18th- and 19th-century Dutch brass tobacco boxes. These can range from £55 to £220 depending on quality and attractiveness. Above them is a 19th-century pub honesty box, or coin-in-the-slot tobacco box.* 9½ in. long. Feb. '86, £400.

7. *Arts & Crafts twin-light candle sconce by Ernest Gimson, pierced and engraved with a fox and rabbits.* 10¼ in. July '85, £650.

8. *Regency brass tea caddy.* 8 in. Feb. '86, £300. This has almost everything in the decoration, from the death of Nelson to religious and masonic mottoes.

9. *Polish pewter Glockenkann decorated with the Royal arms of Poland–Saxony, 1765.* 11 in. July '85, £550.

10. *Swiss pewter Stagkanne, or Bernese flagon, c.1780.* 13 in. Oct. '85, £750.

11. *German or Austrian lidded pewter flagon, c.1800.* July '85, £220.

12. *German straight-sided flagon with cover, early 19th century.* July '85, £130.

9

10

11

12

Fireside Equipment

Fire has always played an important part in society. Apart from the obvious advantages as a means of cooking or forging utensils for the household and the hunt, its main function has been to provide warmth. Even after fires moved from the centres of halls to walls with chimneys, the room with the fire was the nucleus of the family's social and domestic comings and goings and it became 'adorned' with various fittings in the form of fire surrounds, grates, fire dogs, fire irons, fenders, spark guards, coal scuttles and pole screens, which emphasized its importance.

With the advent of electric and gas fires and then central heating, plus the introduction of smokeless zones during the 1950s and 1960s, many fire openings were blocked up. The less troublesome and cleaner gas and electric fires need none of the fittings produced during the previous centuries – except when people insist on the 'olde worlde' look.

In the last ten years there has been a remarkable revival of the 'real' fire thanks to the change of fashion, and made possible to some extent by the introduction of smokeless fuel. Now many house owners renovating their Georgian and Victorian houses choose to unblock their chimneys and reinstall as best they can the original fittings. However, beware, some smokeless fuels are too hot for old cast-iron grates and cause them to crack and warp.

Sets of old-fashioned fire irons (poker, tongs and shovel) in brass and steel regularly sell in the £50–£100 bracket (No. 15), with earlier Georgian sets making as much as £250.

Pierced steel and brass fenders, which are in phenomenal abundance, range equally widely in price, from as little as £50 for the unadorned, up to £1,500 for the more momumental and extravagent examples (Nos. 10–14). Club fenders, which are a cross between a fender and a bench, regularly sell for between £200 and £300 (No. 9).

Also very saleable are the cast-iron fire backs (ideal for inglenook fire places, but much copied), which range from £50 for a plain example to £300 for an earlier dated one. Basket grates have always been popular and have been increasingly so (No. 6). Typically these are of Adam style, elegantly decorated with urns and oval paterae, with pierced aprons echoing the fenders which would usually be matched with them. Good examples of moderately recent manufacture regularly sell in the £300–£500 bracket. Victorian cast-iron register grates are still about in fairly abundant quantities, and they tend to sell for as little as £50.

Coal scuttles in copper and brass usually fall into the £50–£150 range (No. 4). The 'helmet-shaped' type is the most popular. At a more formidable price are the Georgian mahogany peat buckets (No. 8), with fine patinas and polished brass fittings. They can realize over £1,000.

Fire surrounds in a variety of marbles, pine, oak and other woods now turn up everywhere from junk yard to interior decorator's shop. They too come in a wide variety of styles: from the plain Queen Anne by way of the outrageous and sometimes over-the-top mid-18th-century rococo, to the elegant and delicate Adam style. All these styles one can find 'reincarnated' and 'cross-bred' in the 19th century at more affordable prices than the originals (Nos. 1 & 2).

Santiago de Barry

1. *A Victorian pine and composition fire surround.* 68 × 51 in. Oct. '85, £520.
2. *A Victorian pine fire surround.* 71½ × 59 in. Oct. '85, £360.
3. *A George III style steel fire grate.* 31 in. wide. Oct. '85, £680.
4. *A Victorian brass coal scuttle with associated shovel.* Mar. '86, £80.
5. *An early 19th-century brass trivet with iron superstructure and turned wood handle.* 16 in. Apr. '86, £140.
   Usually, £100 is the average price, but this one had the addition of engraving.

1

2

3

5

4

6. *An early 19th-century brass fire grate of Adam design.* 36 in. wide. Mar. '86, £1,100. A superb quality piece.

7. *One of a pair of 17th-century brass andirons.* 22 in. Oct. '85, £450.

8. *A George III mahogany and brass banded peat bucket.* Sept. '85, £650. A good quality piece.

9. *A late 19th-century brass club fender with leather-covered seats.* 72 in. wide. Apr. '86, £240.

10. *A late Regency brass rectangular fender* – 51 in. wide. Apr. '86, £90.

11. *A Regency steel rectangular fender* – 43 in. wide. Jan. '86, £80.

12. *A late Georgian steel serpentine fender.* 39¾ in. wide. Apr. '86, £110.

6

7

8

10

1

12

14

15

16

13. *An early 19th-century steel serpentine fender.* 47 in. wide. Mar. '86, £130.

14. *A 19th-century French ormolu sectional fender of Louis XVI design.* 55½ in. wide. Apr. '86, £280.

15. *A set of late Victorian brass fire irons.* Feb. '86, £35.
These show the most common type although a fine set of Georgian irons in steel can make £150 plus.

16. *A modern steel and brass electrical fire grate.* 28 in. Dec. '85, £45.
A good price but probably due to the cold December we had.

Sculpture and Stained Glass

Overall prices for bronzes have increased slightly from last year (see *Popular Antiques Yearbook*, Vol. 1, p. 134), but the only remarkable advances have been for the most obvious subjects – Arabs, pretty and preferably naked girls, and horses. Ivory items have been much sought after this year – Nos. 13 and 14 are outstanding examples. Stained glass has also seen a revival of interest, especially for non-religious subjects (No. 16).   *James Dick*

1. *French gilt bronze and ivory group of an Arab on a camel, after the model by Agathon Leonard, 19th century.* 9½ in. Feb. '86, £600. Camels are surprisingly rare in Orientalist bronze sculpture, as is the combination with ivory.

2. *Bronzed spelter figure of an Arab, early 20th century.* 26 in. Dec. '85, £1,400. This comparatively undistinguished figure was not even in bronze, and the subject-matter was all important in making the price.

3. *Russian bronze equestrian group of an Arab with falcons, after the model by Lanceray, 19th century.* 18 in. Dec. '85, £2,000. Very similar in taste to the Lanceray group illustrated in last year's book, which made £750. The hawking subject no doubt helped to boost the price.

4. *Bronze group of a young man bound to a wild stallion, 19th century.* 8½ in. wide. Feb. '86, £110. A pity, from the commercial point of view, that this was not a young woman. It was also unsigned.

5. *Bronze group of 'Vainqueur de Derby' after P.J. Mene, dated 1863.* 17 in. Feb. '86, £4,000. A fine example of Mene's ever-popular craftsmanship, but the composition is hardly imaginative.

6. *Late 19th/early 20th century. Bronze of a girl draped over a rock by Albert Toft.* 13 in. wide. Jan. '86, £1,000. A good sensuous subject by a known artist. Toft (1862 – 1949) was a Birmingham man. This is a good contrast to No. 4.

7. *French bronze bust of a girl with cherries, 19th century.* 8½ in. Jan. '86, £380. Pretty, witty and Art Nouveau.

1

2

3

4

5

6

7

8. *A pair of French spelter figures of Peter the Great and Louis XIV, 19th century.* 36 in. Dec. '85, £1,000. Once again, spelter can command at least as much as bronze.

9. *Bronze figure of Robert the Bruce after the cast by W. Beattie, 19th century.* 18 in. Oct. '85, £380. Poor chap. He should have been an Arab.

10. *One of a pair of French parcel gilt figures of male and female water-carriers by H. Dumaige, 19th century.* 21 in. Jan. '86, £800. Pretty and appealing, and at £400 each, not really expensive.

11. *One of a pair of Louis XVI ormolu figures of Bacchantes on plinths.* 28 in. overall. Jan. '86, £2,000. Fine quality, decorative and 18th century.

12. *Bronze figure of Florence Nightingale, 19th century.* 17½ in. Oct. '85, £250. Virtue unrewarded. This price can be compared with those for nakedness, such as No. 15 – despite the differences of material.

13. *Carved ivory bust of a cleric, 19th century.* 5¾ in. Dec. '85, £1,600. This little piece was of very high quality. It is in fact signed 'Cheverton', and it has also been identified as a portrait of a notable pastor of Huguenot descent. Although 1985 was very much the year of the Huguenots, with the exhibition to celebrate the 300th anniversary of the Revocation of the Edict of Nantes, this information did not appear in the catalogue and is unlikely to have greatly influenced the price.

14. *French carved ivory figure of a nymph, 19th century.* 11½ in. Dec. '85, £900.

15. *Marble figure of Eve, by Frederic Brou, c. 1900.* 48½ in. Feb. '86, £600. Eve's state of nature made her price, despite her smashed hand.

16. *Four early Victorian stained-glass panels of the Arts,* each 60 by 20½ in. Oct. '85: 'Architecture', £350; 'Inigo Jones', £325; 'Joshua Reynolds', £280; 'Sculpture', £450.

8

10

11

12

13

15

16

Light Fittings

Lighting, naturally the most important element in a room, whether for itself, to give atmosphere, or to highlight a particular feature, can be found in a vast variety of forms. To a certain extent, these can be grouped into four main categories – wall lights, hanging lights, table lights and floor-standing lights.

Wall lights seem to be the most popular at the moment, and are mostly found in the French 18th-century styles of Louis XV and XVI. Pairs of these regularly sell at auction in the £150–£250 bracket, and they can also be found in larger sets of multiples of two. The price escalates accordingly. Most of these have been converted to electricity and are more desirable than those specifically manufactured for it. It is always a good sign to find examples with drilled nozzles or drip-pans and the wiring following the outside of the candle branch, as it is a possibility that they may be earlier examples. These, of course, are much more desirable and can realize several hundreds or thousands of pounds.

Because of the great demand at present, from both individuals and interior designers, prices are high even for relatively recent examples which can be bought in any modern light fitting shop. A pair of 1930s wall lights in the Louis XV style recently sold for £150!

Following the trend for Victoriana, wall oil lamps are also proving to be popular, but are not yet as highly priced as wall lights. Pairs of oil lamps with decorative glass shades regularly sell in the £50–£100 bracket – although one must be careful as copies abound.

Large chandeliers have always been notoriously difficult to sell at auction, but while those suitable for use in a ballroom may only have a limited market, smaller examples which are more practical for a present-day house sell for anything between £800 and £3,000. One type stands out in particular: the Dutch 18th-century style brass chandelier, with its bulbous baluster centre stem and spidery S-shaped candle branches. These regularly sell in a wide £200–£2,000 bracket. They were reproduced throughout the 18th and 19th centuries – and still are – and weight is always a good guide to go by.

Hall lanterns are also popular. Most examples are in the 18th- or 19th-century styles. Small decorative examples sell regularly for as little as £100, but larger 19th-century pieces can make as much as £1,500 or £2,000.

Candlesticks, which come in a variety of shapes, styles and, of course, prices, would seem to be the only category which one could still use in the original manner – with candles – without seeming uneconomical or wilfully anachronistic. A wide range is regularly found at auction, especially of the typical Victorian brass examples, which can be bought for as little as £30–£50. The earlier 18th-century examples are much more desirable and sometimes run as high as £500. Although they usually come in pairs, sometimes one can find sets of four. These are rarer, and recently a set of four early 19th-century ormolu candlesticks in Louis XV style sold for £2,000.

The candelabrum, a cousin of the candlestick, is equally varied, and equally popular at auction, and a fine pair of French Empire ormolu and bronze candelabra can realize £1,500 or more. However, this is not a regular occurrence; less monumental and decorative examples can regularly be bought in the £200 to £400 bracket.

Many of the above are very sculptural pieces in themselves, and can be appreciated for their fine casting and chasing, but an interesting phenomenon is the 'figure lighting', that is, sculptural works which happen also to be light fittings. Because of this double function, they realize considerably higher prices than if they had just been decorative pieces of sculpture.

Victorian table oil lamps have long been popular, and the better quality designs, such as brass Corinthian columns (No. 9), can bring £100–200. Even the less appealing and poorer quality examples can make up to £50.

An extension of these, literally and metaphorically, are standard lamps, which follow the same rules in pricing, with the Corinthian columns selling in the £200–300 range. Less popular types go for as little as £50. More unusual are the wonderfully elegant Venetian 'Blackamoor' torchères which realize anything from £5,000 to £10,000. Also uncommon are floor-standing candelabra which, depending on their quality, can range between £800 and £3,000.

As in all areas of the art market where there is a large choice, rarity plays an important part in price. This is exemplified by a lantern which we recently sold. It was formed as an owl in bronze, and although it lacked its side door it still realized £450 (see p. 105).

Santiago de Barry

1. *One of a pair of 19th-century twin-light wall appliqués of Louis XV design.* 16 in. Dec. '85, £280.

2. *One of a pair of early 20th-century ormolu three-light wall appliqués of Louis XV design.* 17¼ in. Mar. '86, £160.

3. *One of a pair of late Victorian gilt brass three-light wall appliqués.* 18 in. Feb. '86, £180.

4. *One of a pair of late 19th-century brass chandeliers of Dutch 17th-century design.* 21 in. Apr. '86, £450.

4

9

5

6

7

5. *One of a pair of Italian late 17th/early-18th century painted wrought iron five-light candelabra. 26½ in. Mar. '86, £650.*

6. *One of a pair of early 19th-century bronze and ormolu candlesticks, the stems formed as putti. 14½ in. Feb. '86, £650.*

7. *One of a pair of French bronze and ormolu twin-branch candelabra. 38 in. Dec. '85, £3,000.*

8. *A Victorian oil lamp with iron base. 13 in. Apr. '86, £35.*

9. *A Victorian brass Corinthian column oil lamp. 16 in. Apr. '86, £95.*

10. *One of a pair of ormolu three-light candelabra of Louis XV design. 15½ in. Apr. '86, £150.*

11. *One of a fine set of four early 19th-century ormolu candlesticks of Louis XV design. 10½ in. Jan. '86, £2,000.*

12. *One of a pair of George II brass candlesticks signed on the reverse, W.M. LEE. 7¼ in. Nov. '85, £850.*

13. *One of a pair of ormolu three-light candelabra of Louis XV design. 15½ in. Apr. '86, £150.*

10

11

12

13

Papier Mâché – Market Trends

1

Most items sold at auction are subject to the dictates of fashion, quality and design, and papier mâché is no exception; but prices often seem influenced less by rarity than by the faddishness of the market. Over the last fifteen to twenty years papier mâché has fluctuated in popularity – reflected in the way the Victoria and Albert Museum has handled its collection – at times displaying it generously and at others showing only a few items.

In general terms trays and wine coasters have always been popular, while small pieces, furniture and pictures have tended to be undervalued. However, from about mid-1984, interest in and demand for papier mâché has grown beyond belief, and some of the prices achieved now would not have been conceivable only a year ago.

In May 1985, two pictorial trays made £2,600 each (No. 1), and July saw records of £750 and £800 achieved for two pairs of bright red Regency wine coasters (No. 2). These could be compared to a pair of shaped rouge wine coasters of the same period (illustrated in the first *Yearbook* p. 131) which sold in October 1984 for £650, and which would now be likely to realize nearer £1,000 – a clear indication of the dramatic rise in prices.

Even the fields hitherto unnoticed have done well, providing the quality is there: i.e., no cracking, chipping, cutting, good decoration, whether painted, gilt or mother-of-pearl inlaid. If an item is stamped by a reputable maker such as Clay, Ryton & Walton, or Jennens & Bettridge, this is an additional bonus. For example, in July 1985 an outstanding tea caddy by Jennens & Bettridge sold for £900. This could be compared with an attractive but not so outstanding example which only made £120. This was not stamped by the maker, nor fitted with cannisters and mixing bowl, and the overall quality of the painting and gilding was not as high as in the previous example. The discrepancy in the prices realized at auction underlines how discerning the buyers have become.

The market for papier mâché is currently very buoyant, with the traditional favourites continuing to do well. 1985/6

has seen greater interest in other areas whose potential in terms of price and understanding may not yet have been fully realized.   *Alison Scott*

1. *19th-century papier mâché tray, painted with 'The Happy Meeting', after George Morland, stamped B. Walton & Co. Warranted.* 31in. wide. May '85, £2,600.

2. *Two pairs of red Regency wine coasters: (left) with gilt frieze decoration of flowers and foliage,* 5¾ in. wide; *(right) with reeded sides surmounted by old Sheffield plate mounts,* 5¼ in. wide. Jul. '85, £750 and £800 respectively.

3. & 4. *A Victorian papier mâché red ground wine and supper tray, decorated with gilt vine leaves and inset with two wine coasters, the reverse stamped R. Redgrave, Regd. Dec 10th 1847, Jennens & Bettridge, Makers to the Queen.* 28½ in. wide. Jan. '86, £280. This was a disappointing result for a rare and unusual piece, while high prices continue to be paid for fashionable wine coasters.

5. *A fine mid-nineteenth-century papier mâché games box, fitted with five boxes, the base stamped Jennens & Bettridge Patent Pearl.* 11 × 10 in. Jan. '86, £1,100. This sale result was produced by a combination of a fine-quality papier mâché box and a collection of mother-of-pearl gaming counters bearing the arms of Robert Stewart as 1st Earl of Londonderry (from 1796) and as 1st Marquess (from 1816).

2

3

4

R. REDGRAVE
REGD DEC 10TH 1847

JENNENS & BETTRIDGE
MAKERS TO THE QUEEN

5

Papier Mâché Pictures

In many ways paintings on papier mâché panels represent an underdeveloped and unappreciated area of the market. They have been sold in the past in picture sales without anyone even realizing the substance of the panel they are worked on. Conversely, in a papier mâché sale where the material is known, the competence of the artist is not perhaps fully recognized; and prices therefore tend to be low for the quality of the workmanship involved. A buy within this field could represent a sound investment for the future.

Not as much research as one might wish has been done on these panels. Opportunities to learn more have been considerably restricted by the fact that no artist ever seems to have signed his work. One finds either a stamp on the reverse for the firm who made the papier mâché panel, or their name in tiny painted script, on the front of the picture, often included with the title. The glory of these works seems to go to the manufacturing company who produced

the overall commission, rather than the individual artist concerned.

Another curious aspect of this field is the purpose for which many of these works were commissioned. While today many panels are found in lavish gilt frames, given the treatment of an oil painting on canvas, it is believed that in the 19th century they were designed as panels to be inserted into the interiors of houses and ships, as the *Illustrated Birmingham Times* indicated in a report they produced on Jennens & Bettridge in 1854: 'This firm has just completed some of the finest specimens of Paper Machee that is possible to conceive for panels in ships' saloons.' The shape of the three painted papier mâché panels (Nos. 1–3) suggests that they were originally designed to be inserted into interior fittings.

Finally, it is always difficult to predict

how these pictures will sell at auction, for unexpected outside interests may inflate prices remarkably. For example, while a finely painted pair of pictures of wooded river scenes (Nos. 4 and 5) made £550, against a pre-sale estimate of £500 – £800, a pair of Victorian paintings depicting an Arab hunting scene and a classical ruin sold for £1,200 against a pre-sale estimate of £400 – £600. Technically, these were less competent than the previous examples, but the Arab interest pushed the price up. *Alison Scott*

1, 2, 3. *Three painted panels depicting Ross Trevor Pier; Devenish Island, Loch Earn; and Powerscourt Fall, all with 'Jennens & Bettridge' painted beneath the title. Each 13½ × 31½ in. Feb. '86, £900.*

4, 5. *A pair of pictures depicting wooded river landscapes. 12½ × 17½ in. Jan. '86, £550.*

Papier Mâché Furniture

Owing to the fragile nature of papier mâché furniture, perhaps fewer examples have survived today than might otherwise have been the case. It is not therefore often realized just how many different pieces were made; for example – tilt-top, nests and dressing tables, games and work tables, chairs, sofas, stools, cabinets, pole screens, fire screens, canterburies, teapoys, davenports and beds.

In form many of these items were modelled on their wooden counterparts. However, because of the delicate nature of the papier mâché itself, other materials were used and then lacquered to merge with the whole, for example on chairs, where the legs are of wood and the backs of papier mâché, or beds, where the head and tail boards are of papier mâché but the supports of lacquered iron.

It is an area of the market that has largely been neglected and has shown poor prices at auction. For while its decorative qualities appeal to, for example, the interior decorator, its lack of strength and thus its impracticality have not endeared it to the general public. Indeed a Victorian papier mâché balloon back chair can still make as little as £30–£40 at auction.

Gradually, however, with the strong interest in other areas of papier mâché, it has been possible to detect a rise in prices. In September £1,200 was achieved for a Globe-shaped worktable, and May saw £2,000 for a set of six balloon back dining chairs stamped Jennens & Bettridge, London (No. 2).

These results were exceptional, and there are still many areas of furniture that are undervalued – tilt-top tables can still be bought for under £100. Then, while £400 was achieved for a papier mâché davenport in September 1985 (No. 5), that is still far from equalling the prices that comparable mahogany and walnut davenports are making in furniture sales. This surely is a better area for both investor and collector, rather than the already over-subscribed tray.

Alison Scott

1. *Two-fold papier mâché Victorian screen, the panels mounted in padouk wood frames and stamped Jennens & Bettridge.* The whole 47½ in. high × 39 in. wide. July '85, £800.
2. *Two of a set of six Victorian papier mâché balloon back dining chairs, each stamped Jennens & Bettridge, London.* May '85, £2,000.
3. *A fine Regency papier mâché teapoy, decorated with gilt chinoiserie motifs, stamped Clay, patent.* 30 in. May '85, £700.
4. *(right) Victorian papier mâché armchair.* May '85, £450. *(left) A Victorian papier mâché oval teapoy.* 29½ in. May '85, £300.
5. *Victorian papier mâché davenport-cum-games table.* Sept. '85, £400.
The top part lifts off to make a lap writing desk, revealing a chess and draughts board below.

1

2

3

4

5

Russian Icons

The word comes from the Greek EIKON, meaning an image. Great confusion exists as to what exactly is meant by an 'Icon', and I can do no better than quote from Konrad Onasch, the East German scholar. 'The Icon forms part of the ritual of the Orthodox Church, in that it not only represents the subject painted, but also partakes of its sanctity, it is thus in itself an object of veneration.'

Eastern and Western Christianity art differ greatly, not least because of the essential mysticism of the Orthodox faith. No. 1 is a very good example of this. It came from the Hann Collection and was sold by Christie's New York in 1980. The subject-matter is the 'Dormition of the Virgin'. Our Lady is on her bier, surrounded by sorrowing figures. Behind, the Saviour holds a baby; this is the soul of His mother.

Among the most common and popular subjects are St. Nicholas, the Virgin and Child, and Christ in Majesty. St. Nicholas the miracle worker (No. 2) is the Santa Claus of the Western child, and judging by the demands made on him at Christmas he would indeed have to work miracles! No. 3 is the much-loved Virgin of Kazan (Kazan is one of the regional schools of painting). Note that in the Russian Church, the Babe is not mentioned, only His Mother. The other most common Icon is Christ the universal Ruler, 'Christ Pantocrator' (No. 4).

Russian Icons are painted in tempera not oil. The legend, often garbled, is written in Old (church) Slavonic. Russian and Greek Icons often portray scenes from the Old Testament. No. 5, charmingly painted in vivid colours, shows scenes from the life of the prophet Elijah. The raven is seen bringing him food in the desert, and he then disputes with the prophets of Baal. Finally God summons him to Paradise, and, as the fiery chariot ascends, he throws his mantle to his protégé, Elisha.

Now a word about the painters themselves. They were usually illiterate, hence the titles are not always accurate; they prayed a great deal for inspiration, and they had to paint within the strict confines laid down by a particular school of Icon painting. At the Revolution, many such artists were set to work painting, among other things, papier mâché boxes.

Unfortunately, many old Icons are extensively damaged. Candle burn is one cause, another is the kissing of the faithful, particularly on a much venerated image. While older Icons do appear on the market, the vast majority of those being offered for sale date from the 18th and 19th centuries, and one can certainly obtain a reasonable icon of a good subject for a few hundred pounds.

James Dick

1. *'Dormition of the Virgin', Moscow school, 16th century. Hann collection*, Christie's, New York, 1980, $130,000 (£58,000).
2. *Russian Icon of St. Nicholas, the miracle worker, 19th century*, Mar. '86, £160.
3. *Russian Icon of the Virgin of Kazan, 19th century.* Mar. '86, £280.
4. *Russian Icon of Christ Pantocrator, 19th century.* Mar. '86, £100.
5. *Icon portraying scenes from the life of the Prophet Elijah.* Mar. '86, £500.

8.   Art Nouveau

Introduction
by Neil Froggatt

In May 1986 South Kensington saw its first £100,000 sale in the decorative arts field, and this peak shows unmistakably that prices for all aspects of 20th-century decorative arts are going from strength to strength. Where once only named pieces fetched anything like substantial prices, today the number of new collectors means that, while a signed item still has a strong market, large and decorative unsigned pieces now get the same attention.

Particularly strong at the moment are bronzes and bronze and ivory figures, especially those from the 1920s and 1930s. For example, a bronze and ivory figùre by D. H. Chiparus showed an extremely good result in reaching £10,000 in May '86 (No. 1). Equally good prices were paid for other artists such as Ferdinand Preiss and Lorenzl.

Egyptianesque items were extremely popular during the Art Deco period, after the discovery of Tutankhamun's tomb in 1923, and a piece of jewellery sold in March '86 for £1,500 shows how sought after this style is again today.

Ceramics made during the 1920s and 1930s have always fetched good prices at auction, but with a steady growth in interest the continental ceramics of Goldscheider, Lenci, and Sandoz and British ceramics of Foley, Shelley and, surprisingly, the Ashtead Pottery, have all benefited from a rise in prices. Clarice Cliff, however, has suffered a different fate . . . (see p. 117).

The glass of the period has always had the strongest market, and this has remained so, with Lalique prices reaching an all-time high.

To sum up, it is to be expected that the demand for items made during so short a period should outweigh the supply, and the auction year 1985–6 for 20th-century decorative arts has seen a noticeable overall price increase.

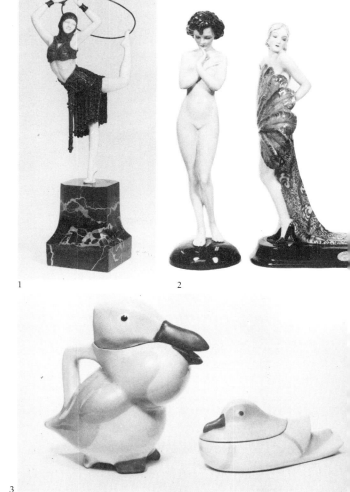

1

2

3

1. *'The Hoop Girl', a bronze and ivory figure, cast and carved after a model by D. H. Chiparus' base engraved.* 19 in. May '86, £10,000.
    Nowadays the condition of the ivory (i.e. cracks) does not seem to affect the prices collectors will pay.

2. *Two Goldscheider figures, both with impressed marks.* 14¼ in. and 13¾ in. Dec. '85, £420 and £350.

3. *Two Limoges boxes and covers designed by Sandoz, both with printed marks.* 6½ in. Dec. '85, £190.

Clarice Cliff – Take care!

The faking of items for personal gain has gone on for centuries, and nearly all major known artists have been treated to the counterfeiter's activities. Just recently, the humble Clarice Cliff's pottery has been accorded the same dubious honour.

As a person who made her wares to brighten up everyday life—wares that ordinary people could afford and enjoy—I am sure that Clarice Cliff would be the first to be surprised at the amount of money her pottery has been making at auction. With a strong American interest, it has enjoyed a price boom for some years. However, as is the case in many areas of the art market, items are highly susceptible to sudden changes of fashion and recently there has been a noticeable fall in prices. It is thus ironic that the fakers have chosen this moment to dupe the innocent with their wares.

The paintings Clarice Cliff used as designs are almost naive in content, and her vivid and garish colours have made her work an altogether too easy target for the faker. This is shown in No. 1, where without experience and knowledge it is almost impossible to tell the difference between the fake (left) and the original (right). However, on closer examination, one can see an unmistakable crudeness in the fake, with the unsteady line of the border and outlining pattern. The fake lacks confidence in the brush strokes, and is very much 'based on an idea by'.

Apart from those mentioned above, there are many other discernible differences between originals and fakes—for example, in No. 2 the undersides of the two vases illustrated show that the fake (left-hand vase) has a patchy glaze, which is brown in colour. This is a definite pointer to a dubious parentage. This streaky brown glaze is also to be found in the interior. At the time of our going to press an individual is helping the police with their enquiries, and it would be injudicious to comment further, but if care and attention are paid when buying Clarice Cliff pottery, the collector should not, one hopes, fall into the faker's trap.

Neil Froggatt

1. *Two Clarice Cliff pieces—or are they?—in one of the more desirable patterns, the 'Summer House' pattern.*

2. *The patchy glaze on the bottom of the left-hand vase gives positive identification of a fake.*

Contemporary British Ceramics

Auctioneers cannot create fashions and markets, they can only follow where dealers and collectors lead. Thus it is only very recently that Sotheby's, Christie's King Street and South Kensington have started to hold sales of contemporary British ceramics, and for those who know their subject it is often cheaper to buy at auction than to go to a dealer or craft gallery. Of course, once such a market exists auctioneers can do much to promote it, and a notable contribution has been made by the Sotheby sponsored show, 'Artist Potters Now' which toured and sold around the country during 1984 and 1985, culminating in an auction in London.

Although the work of the British 'Old Masters', Bernard Leach, Lucie Rie, Hans Coper and Michael Cardew, is well established and has become more expensive over the years, the British market is still very much a poor relation of the American. There, the top contemporary potters can command as much as £6,000 a throw; here, they are lucky if they get a tenth of that. However, the high standing of potters in America is gradually beefing up the British price structure too.

In Britain the history of 20th-century ceramics can be seen as a series of reactions: Bernard Leach against the highly decorated late Victorian and Edwardian pots; the disciples of Rie and Coper, with their sculptural forms, against the functionalism of Leach's 'honest pots'; now, perhaps, a return towards functionalism, albeit in highly decorative forms.

The Leach tradition, stemming from the foundation of the St Ives pottery in 1921, and the influence of his Japanese friend Hamada, produced many fine potters such as Cardew, Katharine Pleydell Bouverie and Norah Braden, as well as his widow, Janet, and their son David Leach, but ultimately it degenerated into the sort of wholemeal craftiness which has given ceramics such a poor name with so many people.

Rie arrived from Vienna, where she was already honoured, in 1938, and worked for many years with Coper, a sculptor turned potter, but as late as 1960 they, and a few other individualists like James Tower, were still working in isolation. The Oriental tradition of Leach

1

(with Cardew's African sub-school) still held sway. However, in 1967 Rie was given a retrospective exhibition by the Arts Council, and Coper, after a period at Camberwell, taught at the Royal College of Art in the early '70s.

It was in that period and at the Royal College that the change of direction may be said to have taken place. Diversity is now the watchword, and the best of the Leach tradition, represented by Richard Batterham, can exist beside the very different styles of Elizabeth Fritsch—who has now virtually acquired Old Master status—Ewan Henderson, Gordon Baldwin, Alison Britton, Martin Smith, Carol McNicholl, Janice Tchalenko, Magdalene Odundo and the Hispano-Moresque lustrewares of Alan Caiger-Smith.

Three names to watch for of the many British potters now emerging are Linda Gunn-Russell, whose forms are not only of high quality but also amusing, Fiona Salazar, who is at the beginning of what promises to be a striking career, and Wally Keeler, whose impressive and imaginative work seems surprisingly underpriced.

Even though the days are past of malfunctioning stoneware teapots which had to be priced to compete with industrial products, it will be some time yet before British artist-potters can compare financially with Americans such as Peter

Voulkos, Betty Woodman, Jerry Rothman and Viola Frey—but some of them certainly deserve to do so.

Huon Mallalieu and Cyril Frankel

1. *A selection of ceramics sold in June '86. a. Stoneware bowl by Lucie Rie and Hans Coper, £130; b. Stoneware Abuja oil jar with screw-cap by Michael Cardew, £75; c. Porcelain bowl by Bernard Leach, £190; d. Stoneware vase by John Ward, £35; e. Stoneware bowl by Rie and Coper, £200; f. Stoneware jug by Rie, £80; g. Stoneware bowl by Rie, £110. The central bowl by Rie was not offered for sale.*

2. *Slip-trailed earthenware baking dish moulded by Elijah Comfort and decorated by Michael Cardew, c.1932. Christie's King Street, Dec. '85, £648.*

2

3. *Porcelain wide bowl by Lucie Rie, c.1967. Christie's King Street, Dec. '85, £4,752.*

4. *Porcelain mallet-shaped bottle by Lucie Rie, c.1967. Christie's King Street, Dec. '85, £3,240.*

5. *Early stoneware bowl by Hans Coper, c.1955. Christie's King Street, Dec. '85, £7,020.*

6. Left to right: *Earthenware cider jar, attributed to the Winchcombe Pottery, £38; Earthenware dish by John Hinchcliff, £38; Stoneware vase by Ewan Henderson, £110. All June '86.*

7. *Handbuilt burnished and polished red clay vase by Magdalene Odundo, 1985. Christie's King Street, Dec. '85, £1,080.*

   Odundo, originally from Nigeria, has combined the African and British traditions to produce work of the highest quality. It is a pity that we cannot give her a colour illustration.

8. *Large stoneware shouldered bottle by Hans Coper, 1970. Christie's King Street, Dec. '85, £5,940.*

9. *Stoneware black bottle by Hans Coper, 1970. Christie's King Street, Dec. '85, £4,320.*

10. *Large stoneware 'egg-in-cup' form by Hans Coper, 1975. Christie's King Street, Dec. '85, £3,240.*

Art Nouveau and Art Deco Glass

During the second half of the 19th century, glass production saw the emergence of individual creative artists, enormously inventive in technique. These artists led the way to the brief Art Nouveau movement in glass and to Art Deco, Functionalist and contemporary glass.

In England, the pioneer work of John Northwood brought about the revival of cameo glass, derived from the Chinese layered and engraved glass of the second half of the 18th century. He worked at the same time with artists such as Joseph and Alphonse Lechevrel. The artists exhibited at the 1878 International Exhibition in Paris and there showed modern cameo glass for the first time. Exhibiting at the same time was Emile Gallé, who was to create and forge a style and technique that was to be admired and imitated by glasshouses from Bohemia and Germany to France, Scandinavia and the United States. Indeed, his work still brings on the whole, the highest of all cameo glass prices (Nos. 1 – 4). Other artists in cameo glass include Antoine Daum, Legras and Le Verre Francais (Nos. 5 – 7).

At the same time, iridescent glass was being used to its fullest decorative possibilities by Louis Comfort Tiffany in the United States, and by Loetz in Bohemia. Loetz and Tiffany influenced, and indeed copied, each other's ideas, and soon inspired a spate of similar products throughout Bohemia, Germany and the United States (Nos. 8 – 11).

Josef Lobmeyr and his brother Ludwig, also working and exhibiting with iridescent glass, later became a very important glasshouse, producing a vast range of fine-quality table and art glass in crystal and coloured glass, which was cut, engraved, painted, enamelled or gilt, often with silver or bronze mounts (No. 12).

The Art Nouveau style and technique went on being used into the 1930s, but really Art Nouveau glass was being challenged as early as 1904 by the emergence of the new Vienna Secession style, with a greater simplicity of line and a rejection of organic forms in favour of geometrism. The Viennese Arts School and its progressive artists, in the main the professors Koloman Moser, Josef Hoffman, later Michael Powolny and Otto Prutscher, were the chief influence in this new field.

In English glass, examples of Art Nouveau are to be found in the work of Harry J. Powell, designer at James Powell & Sons of Whitefriars in London, and the work of Dr. Christopher Dresser, executed by James Couper & Sons, a glassworks in Glasgow (No. 13).

Art Deco glass, or glass manufactured in France between the two World Wars, evolved directly from Art Nouveau with the work of René Lalique. After many years of recognition as a fine goldsmith and jeweller, he experimented with glass, and in 1918, at the end of the First World War, Lalique bought his second glassworks, and this was to become the first to turn to the creation of decorative glass in moulded patterns (Nos. 14 – 16). He was to be imitated by many thousands of glasshouses, in particular Sabino, Ething, Hunebelle and Verlys (No. 17).

The two other schools of thought during the period were to be found in the work of Maurice Marinot who with his freeblown artistic glass found several followers in France, such as André Thuret and Henri Navarre, and with the Swedish glassmakers, mainly the two designers Simon Gate and Edward Hald.

Neil Froggatt

1. *A Gallé cameo glass vase in mauve and etched with stylized flowers on an opaque ground, cameo mark 'Gallé'. 12¼ in. Dec. '85, £500.*

2. *A large Gallé cameo glass vase, overlaid in orange and etched flowering stems on an opaque ground, cameo mark 'Gallé'. 17 in. Mar. '86, £1,600.*

3. *A Gallé cameo glass vase overlaid in mauve and etched with lilies and wild flowers, on a blue to opaque ground, cameo mark 'Gallé'. 11 in. Mar. '86, £1,400.*

4. *A Gallé cameo glass vase overlaid in aubergine and etched with laburnum, on a yellow to grey ground, cameo mark 'Gallé'. 12½ in. Mar. '86, £550.*

1 2 3 4

5

6

7

8

9

5. *A Le Verre Français cameo glass vase, overlaid in mottled brown and etched with large stylized fruit on a mottled yellow ground, incised signature 'Le Verre Francais'. 9¾ in. Feb. '86, £280.*

6. *A Muller Fres. cameo glass vase, overlaid in purple and etched with wisteria, on an opaque ground, inscribed 'Muller Fres.Luneville'. 7½ in. Mar. '86, £480.*

7. *A large Daum cameo glass landscape vase, overlaid in mauve and etched with a wooded riverscape on an opaque to orange ground, cameo mark 'Daum Nancy'. 22 in. Sept. '85, £1,500.*

8. *A Tiffany Favrile golden iridescent glass vase, inscribed 'L C Tiffany Favrile'. 6 in. Mar. '86, £300.*

9. *A Pallme Konig glass box and cover of egg shape on tripod, gilt metal mount. 6¾ in. Feb. '86, £160.*

10. *A J. & L. Lobmeyr lamp-base, richly enamelled with herons and Persian pattern, enamel mark. 20 in. Dec. '85, £480.*

11. *A Loetz iridescent glass vase modelled as a shell. 6 in. wide. Feb. '86, £350.*

12. *A Loetz iridescent glass vase, decorated with silver applique. 5 in. Feb. '86, £260.*

13. *'Ormis', a Lalique opalescent two-handled goblet-shaped vase, inscribed 'R Lalique No 976' 7½ in. Oct. '85, £750.*

14. *Three James Powell & Sons vases. The largest 7⅜ in. diam. May '86, £70. Although James Powell & Sons glass was never marked, it has a very distinctive style.*

15. *'Ondine' Ouverte', a Lalique circular bowl, acid-etched, 'R Lalique.' 12 in. diam. Sept '85, £600.*

16. *'Tourbillons', a Lalique butterscotch clear and frosted glass vase, engraved 'R Lalique No 973.' 8 in. May '86, £3,400. Coloured Lalique pieces have always fetched higher prices due to their rarity.*

17. *A Verlys circular charger, moulded mark. 15¼ in. diam. May '86, £320. This is a very good example of almost straight copying of Lalique's work. See No. 15.*

10

11

12

14

13

15

16

17

British Decorative Arts 1850–1900

'Tons upon tons of unutterable rubbish!' This is how William Morris described the Great Exhibition of London at the Crystal Palace in 1851. Ironically, he was not referring to the actual building, the brain-child of the Prince Consort and Joseph Paxton, which with its simple and startling iron and glass superstructure was in itself a revolutionary step; he was referring to the exhibits.

At the time when the machine was taking over, William Morris was the first to voice disapproval of industrial design and to institute methods of improving the applied arts. He turned his back on the trends of the day, and looked to the Middle Ages for inspiration, when craftsmanship had reigned supreme. The gothic revival, as developed by Morris, is the forerunner and the basis of the Arts and Crafts movement.

In 1861, he founded the firm of Morris, Marshall & Faulkner, later to become Morris & Co., where everything was to be hand-made: furniture, tapestries, wallpapers, fabrics, rugs (No. 1) and pottery. From the 1870s, Morris and his movement seemed to be having a clear influence on contemporary taste and trends, and by now the firm had taken part in international exhibitions. But he did not realize that hand-made products would be far too expensive for the masses, and so his vision was doomed to failure.

It was Morris's theories, rather than his designs, that set the ball rolling, and the generation born around the year 1850—Arthur MacMurdo in 1851, Walter Crane in 1845, C. F. Annesley Voysey in 1857 (No. 2), as well as the younger Charles R. Ashbee in 1863—were all in one way or another associated with Morris or the gothic revival. It was this handful of men and a few others who were to start the Arts and Crafts Movement and who became the leading lights in the various organizations which the movement fostered. It perhaps seems curious that England, a country that up until then was better known as a receptacle for such styles, should be an innovator of them. The Arts and Crafts Movement, in its widest sense, made the most important contribution to an entirely new trend in applied art. Its influence

swept from England to the Continent and America, and gave rise to the Movement's descendant, Art Nouveau.

Walter Crane and Arthur MacMurdo, in their later designs developed a stylistic element based increasingly on the use of floral motifs, an outstanding feature of the Art Nouveau style. Floral motifs were also used in the works of Christopher Dresser, a trained botanist and theorist. At the end of the 1870s, he was associated with the Linthorpe Pottery as Art Adviser, but he also worked in glass and metal (No. 3).

Decorative arts of the period were also greatly influenced by the Orient, with Japan taking part for the first time in 1862 in the World Exhibition in London. A young man called Arthur Lasonby Liberty working as manager for Farmer & Rogers, the firm which sold the Japanese works at the close of the exhibition, went on in 1875 to establish his own firm of Liberty & Co. Here he sold Japanese items, and also sold and encouraged the work of such artists as Archibald Knox, who worked mainly in silver and pewter, and had a definite Arts and Crafts flavour.

From the rejection of the machine by William Morris, the establishment of the

1

Arts and Crafts movement and the beginnings of Art Nouveau in the work of Arthur MacMurdo, British decorative arts went on to include many varied and creative artists and factories: Charles Rennie Mackintosh in Scotland, with his far-reaching influence on the Darmstadt School and Vienna Secessionists; the Martin Brothers (Nos. 5 and 6); William Moorcroft (No. 7); John Ruskin (No. 8) and Elton.   *Neil Froggatt*

1. *A Morris & Co. hand-knotted Hammersmith rug designed by John Henry Dearle, c.1840.* Christie's King Street, Apr. '85, £21,600.

2

3

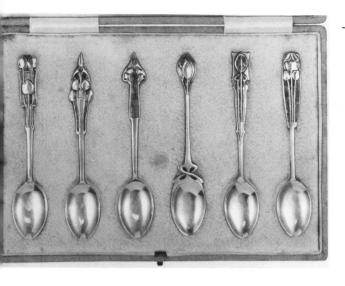

5

6

2. *A C. F. A. Voysey oak music cabinet on stand designed for W. Ward Higgs, 1898.* Christie's King Street, Apr. '85, £32,400.

Voysey produced most of his best furniture designs between 1895 and 1910. This particular cabinet was designed a year before his famous Kelmscott cabinet of 1899.

3. *A Hukin and Heath 'Crow's Foot' decanter designed by Dr Christopher Dresser, 1879.* Christie's King Street, Sept. '85, £7,776.

4. *A boxed set of six Liberty & Co. silver and enamelled spoons, stamped marks, c.1900.* Each 4¼ in. long. Oct. '85, £360.

5. *A Martin Brothers stoneware double face jug, incised marks, dated 1902.* 8¼ in. high. Dec. '85, £800.

The mischievous grin puts us in no doubt as to the factory.

6. *A Martin Brothers stoneware bird tobacco jar, with condescending glare, incised R. W. Martin Bros., London and Southall, 4 May 1911.* 10¾ in. high. Feb. '86, £2,600.

These are probably the most sought after items of the Martin Ware factory.

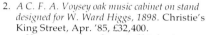

8

7

7. *A Moorcroft vase for Liberty & Co. in 'Claremont' pattern signed in green.* 10 in. high. Oct. '85, £750.

8. *A Ruskin high-fired flambé scent bottle and stopper, with blood-red and white glazed decoration, impressed mark, dated 1928.* 6¾ in. Feb. '86, £420.

9. *A pair of Minton moon-flasks, with painted decoration, printed marks, c.1872.* 16¾ in. Sept. '85, £650.

Dr Christopher Dresser also designed for the Minton factory and if these pieces had been attributed to him they would have fetched a considerably higher price.

9

9.   Costume and Textiles

Introduction
by Susan Mayor

The 1985–6 season certainly saw some interesting objects. As predicted, early needlework was high on the list. The rarest item of all, the burse (No. 1) that carried the Great Seal of England during the reign of Queen Elizabeth I, rightly topped this season's prices and was sold to the V & A Museum at £12,000. Next came a rare pair of 17th-century ladies' shoes (No. 2) embroidered in gold and silver thread, at £8,000. Then, surprisingly, a 19th-century tapestry in the manner of Boucher (No. 3), at £6,000; admittedly, it was very decorative and very fresh. This was closely followed by several pieces of costume: a mid-18th-century 'Banyan', or gentleman's dressing-gown, of crimson damask, in mint condition, at £5,800; and two gentleman's mid-18th-century suits of rust-coloured and cyclamen wool, each £5,000. There were other high-flyers: a fine set of 18th-century English crewel-work curtains of lovely bright colours made £5,200, even though altered; and a 17th-century English needlework casket was sold for £5,000. The first 18th-century hoop (No. 4) to have appeared on the market since we sold one in 1968 realized £4,000 for its sheer rarity.

The Costume and Textiles Department at Christie's South Kensington has found that there is an increasing number of private buyers for the artefacts and material we handle: fine linen sheets, damask and lace tablecloths, lace curtains, Aubusson portières, carpets and seat covers, Victorian and Edwardian silk and woollen curtains, wall-papers, needlework bell-pulls, carpets, cushions and furnishing fabrics. As an example, the quilt sales, which are held quarterly, are well attended. The most charming quilt we sold in 1985 was a patchwork with applied silk animals, which realized £480. A very fine example of a quilt of ivory satin reversing to pink, 100 × 80 in., realized £500 in the same sale. Other, still pleasing, quilts are cheaper (No. 5), although many quilts can be had for even less than this (from £50). We also sell a number of plain Durham quilts.

1

The new departure this season was the sale of the archive of fashion plates and reference books of Mrs Doris Langley Moore OBE FRSL, in April 1986, which realized £34,000 in all. This generated an enormous amount of interest in the press and saw heavy bidding from designers, the National Art Library and museums internationally, as well as book-sellers, print-sellers and costume collectors. The top price, as predicted, was for Lucile's watercolour designs for Autumn 1904 and 1905 (No. 6), which sold to the V & A Museum for £4,400, followed by £3,700 for an incomplete run of *Gazette du Bon Ton* (No. 7). Even loose plates from the *Gazette du Bon Ton* fetched £100 each. Never before had such a costume reference library appeared on the market, but given the enormous interest, we hope to follow it up with more sales.

The number of buyers in this field continues to grow and the market looks distinctly bullish.

2

3

4

1. *The cover of a burse used to carry the Great Seal of England during the reign of Queen Elizabeth I, crimson velvet, embroidered in gold and silver thread with the Royal Arms and ER. 14½ × 13½ in. Mar. '86, £12,000.*

2. *A pair of ladies' high-heeled shoes of royal blue velvet, embroidered in gold and silver thread with dark blue morocco heels, English c.1640. Jul. '85, £8,000.*

3. *A tapestry worked with elegant children playing and picnicking in a landscape, French, 19th century. 68 × 88 in. Nov. '85, £6,000.*

4. *A rare hoop of blue, pink and grey striped linen with bamboo hoops, c.1760. Mar. '86, £4,000.*

5. *A hexagon appliqué patchwork cover, 19th century. 90 × 74 in. Aug. '85, £190.*

6. *Original Lucile designs in watercolour, with samples of the materials and trimmings in which they were carried out for Lucile Ltd, 23 Hanover Square, London. 48 designs for Autumn 1904, 69 for Autumn 1905, 2 vols. Apr. '86, £4,400.*

7. *'Gazette du Bon Ton', eight issues: Nos. 1 & 4, 1912; No. 11, 1913; No. 7, second year, 1914; Nos. 8 & 9, 1915; and Nos. 1 & 2, third year, 1920. Apr. '86, £3,700.*

6

7

Paisley Shawls

The shawls illustrated here are not all necessarily from Paisley, but as Paisley in the mid-19th century was the most prolific manufacturer of these shawls, inspired by the Kashmir ones, the word is now loosely used for the whole type.

In Glasgow there is naturally both an informed demand and a good supply of the products of neighbouring Paisley. In March '86 a fine and rare semicircular woollen shawl, 1860 (130 × 40in.), made £500, while a Paisley plaid of the same date (136 × 64in.) made £300. The second had orange in it, which is popular. Condition does not seem to matter quite as much as it did two years ago.

Even a fold-over shawl *c*.1820 (60 × 62in.), made £70 despite being 'mothed and brittle'.   *Tessa Charlton*

1. *Wool, cotton and silk, 1830s.* 50 × 106 in. Apr. '86, £170. Its size and relatively restrained design help to date it.
2. *Wool 'Kirking' shawl.* 64 × 132 in. Apr. '86, £45. So-called as they were worn for church; the design mainly in blue on a cream ground.
3. *Wool and silk, 1850s.* 60 × 126 in. Apr. '86, £85. Less traditional colours – burgundy brown, dull yellow, blue and palest pink on a cream ground – and the abstracted design are typical of the late 1850s.

4. *Wool and silk, 1850s.* 60 × 126 in. Nov. '85, £180. Also unusual colours – yellow, red, lilac and cream on a dark grey-green ground, with a bizarre, unusual pattern.
5. *Wool, mid-19th century.* 64 × 122 in. Apr. '86, £130. A good lively pattern although worn in places, and the colours are fresh.
6. *Wool, c, 1870.* 66 in. square. Apr. '86, £80. A double-sided shawl – the designs are not very exciting but they are wearable.
7. *Wool, 1860s.* 62 × 140 in. Jan. '86, £130. Although damaged, the stunning *trompe l'oeil* draping design made this a good buy.
8. *Wool, mid-19th century.* 64 × 122 in. Apr. '86, £170. Another good design, the black central field now a design in its own right; also worn but with fresh colours.

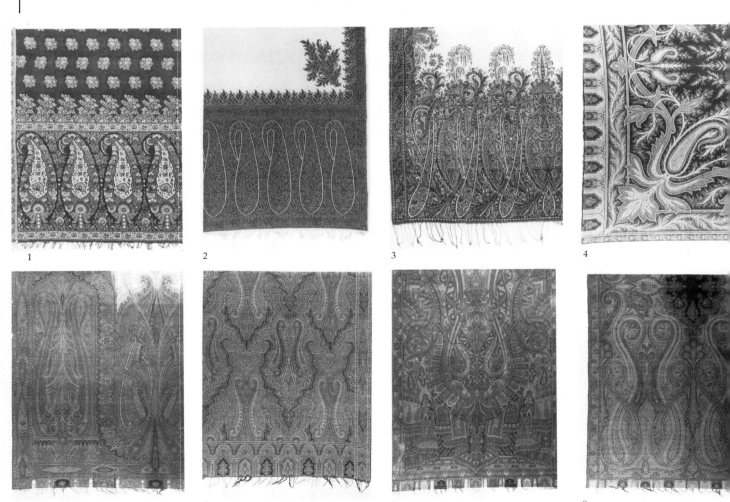

1   2   3   4

5   6   7   8

Kashmir Shawls

Fewer than fifty Kashmir shawls a year are sold at Christie's South Kensington, compared with, say, three hundred European 'paisley' copies. It is rare for a fine early 19th-century Kashmir shawl to appear on the market, the most recent being in October 1985 (No. 1). One of similar quality now would probably realize well over £1,000 at auction. However, stoles or plain *pashmina* shawls (the softest wool from the underbelly of the goat) can still be bought for around £100–£200 at auction — in February 1986 two sold for £65 each.

The majority of Kashmir shawls sold at auction are from the 19th century, although the history of shawl weaving in Kashmir dates back to the 17th century or earlier. The motif that characterizes them and which has become famous in England as the 'paisley' pattern, is the *buta* or *boteh* (in English, 'cone' or 'pine'), which literally means 'flower'. In the 17th century the motif was a flowering plant, a blend of the naturalism of Mughal art and the more formal floral ornament of Persia. By the end of the 18th century the *buta* had developed into a more stylized conventional motif. Then, from about 1830 onwards, with developments in weaving techniques, particularly in England and France (see opposite page), the *buta* became a far more elaborate affair — elongated, swirling, twisting and scrolling, densely filled with flowers and foliage (Nos. 1 & 3).

The Kashmir shawl became a fashionable article of dress in the West towards the end of the 18th century. By 1800 the trade between East and West was well established. The Kashmir shawls were woven from the fleece of the mountain goat, and, unlike their European imitations, they were woven using the twill tapestry technique, only the weft threads forming the pattern. This was a very slow process, and one shawl could take a year and a half to complete. To speed up production, more than one loom per shawl was used and an embroiderer (*rafugar*) joined the parts together.

Another innovation in the early 19th century was the shawl entirely worked by needle, called an *Amli* shawl, much quicker and cheaper to produce. However, these improvements were not sufficient to produce shawls fast enough for the

1

greedy West. Soon the British and French were making their own clever imitations of the real thing at less than half the price. Whereas an original Kashmir cost around £70–£100, a 'paisley' copy cost about £12. In fact the imitations were so successful that British manufacturers tried exporting to India, where their reception was described by Moorcroft: 'At first sight, the Shawl Merchants of this country were deceived, but on handling them, a look of surprise has spread over their countenances, and on closer examination they discovered that the shawls were not of Kashmeeree [sic] fabric. They gave great credit to British artists for their close imitations, but considered them as inferior to the Kashmeeree originals . . . they showed the superior softness, fullness and richness of feel of Kashmeeree over British shawl cloth . . . [which] arises from the greater softness of the goat wool . . .'

Between 1800 and 1860 shawl exports from Kashmir more than doubled. However, this great boom could not last. Not only did fashion change, the shawl no longer being the most treasured article of a lady's wardrobe, but also the average Kashmir was by now not as good as the Jacquard woven ones of Lyons and Paisley — and was more expensive. Today, however the Kashmir shawl is once again the sought after and treasured item it was in the 18th century.

Emma Clark

2

3

1. *A detail of a very fine and large shawl woven in many colours with an unusual, very elaborate arcaded flower-filled curving* buta *pattern around a cream centre field, c.1850–60. 128 × 56 in. Oct. '85, £850.*

2. *One of two pieces of striped and floral patterned* 'jamawar' *each piece 44 in. square, dating probably from the second quarter of the 19th century. Feb. '86, £300.*

   This was the kind of shawl often tailored into men's Court coats or *jamas*. The bright colours and excellent condition together with the very pretty design contributed to the high price for these two pieces.

3. *A Kashmir shawl woven in many colours with curling, flower-filled* buta *and border of cusped arches within semi-circles c.1850–60. May '86, £380.*

   The price realized is about right for this shawl, which is of medium quality wool with a fairly elaborate pattern typical of the period.

Printed Commemorative Handkerchiefs

The first handkerchiefs were printed in Oxford in the 17th century, when the wife of the warehouseman of the University Press was allowed to print off a number of impressions of their annual Almanacks on linen – of which two examples are known.

In the 18th century, the subject-matter became more varied. Silk was occasionally used for maps. Great events like the Peace of Ryswyck, 1713 (No. 1) or the Siege of Gibraltar, 1782 (No. 4) were commemorated, as well as annual events like the Dunmow Flitch – these 18th-century examples are very rare, and all realize something in the region of £600 to over £1,000 unless they are literally falling to pieces.

The 19th century saw an even greater expansion of subjects. Many more were printed on silk – unfortunately, since this becomes fragile with age.

Political satires abound: attacking Napoleon (No. 2), supporting the Reform Bill, praising Disraeli, poking fun at the census or female emancipation.

Royalty and royal events, of course, were popular subjects (No. 5), whether it was the proclamation of William IV (No. 6) or the coronation of Queen Victoria (No. 3). Probably the best-known subjects were the winners of the Derby, published each year, and, the most valuable, the early English cricket teams.

In the second half of the 19th century, there was a return to cotton for cheaper handkerchiefs of greater mass appeal, reaching a crescendo with Queen Victoria's Jubilee and the death of Mr Gladstone. Many new subjects appeared, including the rise of International and Colonial exhibitions, the building of great Town Halls, and trips to the Isle of Man, the three-legged symbol of the Isle of Man lending itself greatly to humorous representations.

With the 20th century comes a decline in the collectability, but not in the production, of handkerchiefs, and only those commemorating provincial exhibitions are rare enough to be of value.

Susan Mayor

1. *A silk handkerchief commemorating the Peace of Ryswyck, published by Charles Weston at the Nag's Head in Bishop's Gate Street near Leaden Hall, 1713. Nov. '85, £260.*
   Although this was the earliest printed handkerchief sold at auction, it was very fragile, hence the price.

2. *The Stage of Europe, December 1812, a commemorative handkerchief printed in rose madder on cotton, numbered in one margin. 35 × 30 in. Nov. '85, £450.*

3. *The Coronation of Her Most Gracious Majesty, Queen Victoria, June 1838, a silk handkerchief, printed in colours. 35 × 36 in. Nov. '85, £900.*
   This was a very high price for a 19th-century handkerchief, but the colours were very fresh and it is the only copy of this version to have appeared on the market.

4. *A view of Gibraltar on the ever memorable 13th September 1782, a linen handkerchief printed in rose madder with portraits of Sir G. A. Elliot and Sir Roger Curtis, English, c.1782. 27½ × 29 in. Mar. '86, £650.*

5. *A faithful representation of the Trial of Her Most Gracious Majesty, Caroline Queen of England in the House of Lords, 1820, a printed commemorative handkerchief on linen. 22 in. wide, framed and glazed. July '85, £400.*

6. *His Majesty's most gracious speech to both Houses of Parliament on Friday 22 April 1831, a silk handkerchief printed in colour. Mar. '86, £400.*

Suzanis

What is a suzani? In the most general terms it is an embroidery from Central Asia. More specifically a suzani (the word itself comes from the Persian word for 'needle') is a large decorative embroidered cover or hanging produced in certain towns in the Soviet Socialist Republic of Uzbekistan – for instance Bokhara, Samarkand, Tashkent, Nuratsa and Shakhrisyabz.

The embroidering of a suzani was a family occupation. First of all the design was drawn on vertical cotton panels by the most experienced embroideress in the family or by a local professional. Then, each girl would embroider a panel or part of a panel (usually three to six panels per suzani, see No. 2). When they finished, the panels were joined to make the final piece – perhaps a bridal bedspread, the most treasured item in a dowry. They were worked in brightly coloured silks, the most common probably being cochineal pink and orange-red, almost always on a cotton ground, but occasionally on silk.

Most suzanis sold at auction are nineteenth-century, although the embroidery tradition in Uzbekistan goes back to the Middle Ages and probably further. The designs used in all the districts are very similar. Flowers (not really identifiable although poppies and carnations are a very likely source of inspiration), rosettes, palmettes, medallions and the leaf trellis pattern are all typical suzani motifs. Nos. 1, 2 and 3 are all most probably from the Bokhara district – indeed these do seem to be more common than any other type. They employ a variety of stitches, usually at least three or four types on one suzani including *tambur*, or chain stitch, and *basma*, a laid and couched stitch.

The combination of the complicated and carefully worked out patterns make these suzanis some of the most beautiful and inexpensive objects on the market today. The ones pictured here realized from £260 up to £700. Smaller ones can make even less (one in an Islamic sale in Feb. '86 realized £100), larger, finer ones even more – as much as several thousand. However, in general these rich embroideries and 'fragments of a way of life' are still undervalued.

1

2

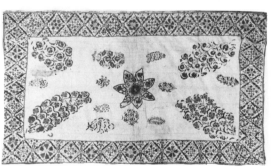

3

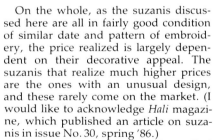

3

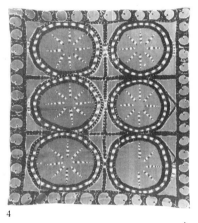

4

On the whole, as the suzanis discussed here are all in fairly good condition of similar date and pattern of embroidery, the price realized is largely dependent on their decorative appeal. The suzanis that realize much higher prices are the ones with an unusual design, and these rarely come on the market. (I would like to acknowledge *Hali* magazine, which published an article on suzanis in issue No. 30, spring '86.)

Emma Clark

1. *A Bokhara suzani embroidered in coloured silks, mostly shades of pale pink and green with palmette type flowers on a joined cream cotton ground, 19th century, probably c.1850–60, 68 × 73 in. May '86, £400.*

2. *A Bokhara suzani embroidered in coloured silks including shades of green, pink, orange and blue with leaves (a design motif common to Bokhara suzanis); the ground of five joined cream cotton*
panels can be clearly seen, second half 19th century, 93 × 60 in. Feb. '86, £550.

3. *A suzani (probably Bokhara) embroidered in coloured silks, mostly pink, orange, aquamarine and yellow, mid-19th century, 94 × 57 in. Feb. '86, £420.* This has a more unusual pattern than Nos. 1 & 2, and the star in the centre and the large corner floral sprays against a less densely embroidered background give it a lighter, more delicate feel.

4. *A Tashkent suzani embroidered in deep magenta, dark blue and mustard silks. Oct. '85. £260.* The large circular formalized flowerheads (possibly poppies), with a border of almost the whole cotton ground and circles hardly resembling flowers any more, are a typical feature of Tashkent suzanis. Although a very strong and bold design it is probably less attractive to the Western eye than the more delicate floral patterns of the Bokhara suzanis. This is reflected in the price.

Eighteenth-century Printed Fans

People tend to refer to fans as painted fans. In fact, a sizeable proportion of fans that survive are printed. In about the 1720s, the fan makers, despite their enormous success at the top of the market, found it necessary to expand their trade and produce cheaper fans in bulk to appease ever-increasing public demand.

In order to do so, they began printing the leaves. They could then duplicate the designs and their products could be sold cheaply at fairs, on stalls and at booths, thus undercutting the cheap Chinese fans that had been scooping the market at the lower end. Printed fans were used to commemorate events. They would have been taken home as souvenirs, and obviously sold by the thousand. Being cheap and ephemeral at the time, they were often not kept – unlike fans of the highest quality made from precious materials. Their sticks are often only of plain wood. As many of these 18th-century printed fans are rare, their prices often rival those for other important fans. For instance, the printed mask fan, *c.*1740, which sold in 1978 for £2,100, stood for some years as the second most expensive fan ever sold at auction. Even today, few fans make over £1,000, let alone £2,000.

The fan printers took advantage of the 1734 Copyright Act, which proved to be of great assistance not only to them, but also to fan collectors and historians later. English printed fans after 1734 may have the name of the publisher, often his or her address, and the date of publication. Sadly, as this was usually at the foot of the leaf, it has often been snipped or guillotined during mounting.

One of the finest collections of printed fans is that formed by Lady Charlotte Schreiber and presented by her to the British Museum in 1891. The catalogue by Lionel Cust is a useful reference book for 18th-century printed fans. The collection contains some 300 English printed fans and 200 French.   *Susan Mayor*

1. *A fan, the leaf a hand-coloured etching of a classical scene with Diana arriving in her carriage at the dais of Hero, the serpentine ivory sticks piqué with silver, and when closed the handle forms a serpent. English, c.1730.* Sept. '85, £180.

2. *A fan, the leaf a hand-coloured etching of a fête champêtre, enhanced with mother-of-pearl and glitter, with ivory sticks, the guardsticks covered. English, c.1740.* 10 in. July '85, £140.

3. *A church fan, the leaf a hand-coloured etching by I. French, 47 Holborn Hill, 1 June 1776, with bone sticks.* 12 in. Apr. '86, £380 There is an example of this fan in the Schreiber collection.

4. *A fan, the leaf a hand-coloured almanack for the year 1794, published 1 January 1794, by John Cox and J. P. Crowder, Wood Street. The reverse is stamped in red with Stamp Duty for the penny, with plain wooden sticks (damaged). Almanacks paid stamp duty.* 11 in., Dec. '85, £180.

5. *The New Charade fan for the year 1798. A printed fan, with wooden sticks, the leaf an etching with a central portrait of Marquis Cornwallis, published by the proprietor of the 'New Charade fan, 22 White Lion Street, Pentonville', 1798.* 10 in. July '85, £180. An engraved text reads, 'Any lady that pleases me send Charade or enigma directed to the proprietor of the New Charade fan post paid before the 10 of Nvr. next with the explanation. If approved it will be inserted. A New Charade will be published every Christmas and every Summer'.

1

2

3

4

5

Nineteenth-century Embroidery

19th-century needlework in any form — carpets, seat covers, pelmets or just fragments — continues to be much in demand. The pieces shown here are mostly brightly coloured and highly decorative, and compared to 18th-century embroidery are relatively inexpensive. Prices can vary from as little as £50 for an embroidered seat cover to several thousand pounds for a needlework carpet.

Emma Clark

1

2

1. *One of a pair of oval pictures finely embroidered in brightly coloured silks with bouquets of roses, tulips, lilies-of-the-valley and other flowers against an ivory silk satin ground, early 19th century, in gilt wood frame, glazed. Each 9½ × 7½ in. May '86, £500.*

2. *A needlework carpet worked in coloured wools with parrots and other exotic birds perched in a leafy tree within a border of trailing leafy cherry branches and outer wide border of lush trailing flowers, probably English, mid-19th century. 70 × 52 in. Apr. '86, £900.*

3. *A needlework rug embroidered in sky-blue, pink and green wools, with stylized peacocks perched among formalized flowering plants, with floral border probably c.1900–30. 56 × 35 in. Feb. '86, £400.*

4. *An unusual embroidered picture worked in coloured silks, mostly in shades of pale green, yellow and white, with a lady lying in front of a villa, exotic trees behind, a man in a sombrero riding a horse on one side, with waving lush floral border against a gauze ground, probably Mexican, South American or Spanish, late 19th century. 19 × 24 in. Apr. '86, £260.*

5. *A needlework carpet embroidered mainly in large and small cross stitches in coloured wools, with a stag lying on the banks of a Scottish loch, a castle and highlands in the background, within border of pink and white roses and outer border of cut pile, c.1850 (some wear). 43 × 82 in. Apr. '86, £780.*

The vendor is a descendant of the Gordon family; the stag's head is the Gordon crest. The castle in the background is probably Inveraray Castle on the banks of Loch Fyne.

6. *A long panel densely worked in coloured beads with flowers. 41 × 9 in. Feb. '86, £160.*

3

4

5

6

Early Needlework

1

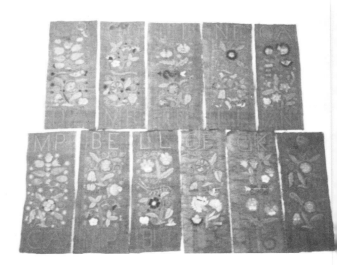

2

1. *A fine beadwork picture worked with a couple standing amid giant flowers and surrounded by a lion, a mermaid, and other emblems, worked in brightly coloured beads against a background of gilt sequins supporting glass beads. English, mid-17th century. 13½ in. wide. Mar. '86, £2,800.*

2. *A rare border composed of eleven panels of green silk embroidered with spot motifs of strawberries, flowers, butterflies, an asp pierced by a dagger, and snails and the inscription 'Sir Colin Campbell of GK, Dame Ieliane Campbell', 1632. Each panel 14 × 15 in. July '85, £3,000.*

    Bought by the National Museum of Antiquities, Edinburgh. This border was from a bed valance that belonged to Sir Colin Campbell of Glenorchy, 2nd Bt., born 1577; he succeeded his father in 1631. In 1594 he had married Juliana (Egidia), daughter of Hugh Campbell, first Lord Louden. Sir Colin died without issue in 1640.

3. *A fine needlework portrait miniature of King Charles I, head and shoulders facing right, wearing a deep lace-edged falling collar, and the lesser George suspended from a blue ribbon, after Van Dyck, in contemporary gilt metal miniature frame, glazed, English, 17th century. 5½ × 4¼ in. Mar. '86, £1,800.*

4. *A fine set of crewelwork bed-hangings, comprising one large panel, a pair of narrow curtains and a valance of linen, embroidered with flowering trees in brightly coloured red, blue, yellow and green wools, English, 18th century. The curtain 88 in. drop; the pelmet 18in. deep × 68 in. long. Nov. '85, £5,200.*

5. *A needlework casket covered in ivory satin embroidered with figures and flowers, partly in stump or raised work, the buildings with mica windows, the figures and foliage embellished with seed pearls and black beads, opening to reveal compartments and drawers lined with olive green silk and velvet and pewter; also an ink bottle and powder container, secret drawers and an etui with padded pincushion, compartment for thimble and another for scissors; covered in pink and silver brocaded silk, in glazed case, English, c.1670. 8 in. deep, 6½ in. wide. Nov. '85, £5,000.*

3

4

6

6. *A rare hanging or valance worked in coloured wools and silks, with a central court scene with figures round a dais and further figures in the countryside in the distance, the reserves embroidered with grotesques and the initials AY against an embroidered blue background, 16th century. (Some repairs, re-working and overpainting.) 88 in. wide. Nov. '85, £3,800.*

It is very unusual to find a secular wall hanging of this period.

7. *A pair of gentleman's carpet slippers of 'Albert' pattern embroidered in blue, brown, black and white wools with a classical design in petit-point on canvas, with leather soles and heels, mid-19th century. Mar. '86, £200.*

8. *A fine linen altar cloth embroidered in red wool with four oval vignettes—King David playing the harp; David and Goliath; Abraham visited by three angels; and the angel staying the hand of Abraham—within spot motifs of tulips, cherries and other flowers and fruit and in the centre two heraldic coats of arms. Danish, Ørtaeklunde, c.1680 (some holes, but otherwise fresh condition). (Part illustrated only.) Nov. '85, £1,100.*

See Georg Garde, *Danske Silke broderede laerridsduge*, Copenhagen 1961, No. 66, pp. 484, 485.

9. *A rare linen stomacher, embroidered in yellow silk with scrolling flowers and foliage enclosing embroidered initials AR or AH and the date 1719, the waistline trimmed with yellow silk braid. Nov. '85, £1,150.*

10. *A fine calash of emerald green silk with twelve wired arches, the front trimmed with a double frill, late 18th century. Mar. '86, £600.*

Susan Mayor

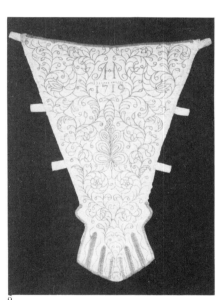

9

8

7

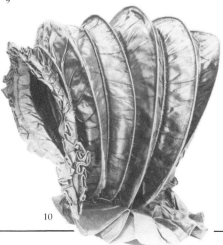

10

10. Photographs

Introduction
by Lindsey Stewart

My optimism of last year has calmed considerably as the demands of collectors and therefore also of dealers have become more and more difficult to satisfy. There is no shortage of photographs generally – it is simply that those which are currently most desirable are increasingly hard to find.

The most exciting area of the market in the last year has been beautiful single images, in excellent condition. Surprisingly, either in negative or positive form – that is where the negatives are of the waxed paper type used during the 1850s. In April '86, a rare mammoth waxed paper negative (No. 1) and contemporary albumen print (No. 2) by Stanley Tytler (1858) sold for £2,400. In the same sale a very good calotype by Hill and Adamson sold for £2,200 (see p. 138, No. 1), against £1,900 for a very special example in June '83, and in June '85 an anonymous English salt print sold for £1,000 – it was a pretty picture and the print was a good colour. Less than perfect examples, even by major figures, have been generally less successful than expected.

Other photographs remain unpredictable. Stereo cards were a disaster in October '85, but picked up again in April '86, with an auction record price of £750 for one important card (see p. 141, No. 1). In many areas interest seems to have diminished, with few but the earliest, rarest or most exotic images attracting more than minimum attention. With wealthy collectors becoming more particular, this could well be the time for those with a more limited income or less extensive collection to add several bargains.

Lindsey Stewart

1. *Stanley Tytler, 'In the hills of Benares, India . . . taken immediately after the Mutiny', paper negative, 16½ × 20¾ in. Apr. '86, £2,400 (with No. 2).*

2. *Stanley Tytler, contemporary albumen print from the above negative.*

Nineteenth-Century Portrait Photographs

Portraiture formed the bulk of the professional photographer's output between 1860 and 1900, when the small carte-de-visite and larger cabinet card were most popular. These were produced in vast numbers and collected in elaborate leather albums reflecting the tastes and aspirations of their owners. The better photographers of the 1860s commanded high fees and were generally only available to those who could afford them. Camille Silvy, Antoine Claudet, J. Mayall and A. Disdéri were among the very best, and their portraits in the familiar small format often exhibit a natural pose, superb detail and a rich print quality. Albums of such portraits, often containing a mixture of aristocrats and leading Victorian personalities, occur regularly – one of only 31 cartes, mainly by Silvy, sold in June 1985 for £100. Unusual subjects or compilations also do well – two tiny albums of 'Les Types Russes' (No. 1), containing 43 portraits by William Carrick, sold for £200, while an album of 50 portraits of professors from Harvard University, including Oliver Wendell Holmes, inventor of the famous 'Holmes-pattern' stereoscope (see page 173), made £400.

However, the skill and sensitivity of the photographers varied, and the majority of surviving family albums from the 1880s and later show generations of anonymous citizens facing the camera with grim determination or blank wooden stares. These albums can often be found for between £5 and £30 – and are rarely worth more.

Other portraits, produced on a less commercial basis, are rarer and may be found pasted in albums or loose. There are many criteria which contribute to the price – identities of the photographer and sitter, date, size, condition and rarity. Again in June, an unusual daguerreotype of a West Country farmer made £180, despite its tiny size and tarnished condition, while a good daguerreotype group portrait of historic interest made £1,500 (see p. 140, No. 1).

However, even satisfying each of these criteria may not make a portrait a great seller, and the far more elusive qualities of a beautiful or powerful image make all the difference. In the same sale, an exotic album of 114 Japanese and Chinese portraits from the 1870s sold for a staggering £5,000 – by comparison an average Japanese portrait album might sell for £150. In this example, the work of Baron Von Stillfried and others, the quality of the portraits was consistently high, with good hand-colouring, and the inclusion of the 57 Chinese studies was most unusual. In addition, several individual portraits were stunningly beautiful (No. 2).

A comprehensive album of approximately 200 portraits from the 1850s and 1860s by Herbert Watkins was unsold at a disappointing £850, again in June 1985. It became apparent that despite the wealth of personalities included, the rather dull appearance of many prints limited their appeal. In October, an album of 48 portraits by the relatively unknown R. T. Crawshay sold for £1,200. Although rather inconsistent in quality, this included many a good image with a haunting presence, not unlike that found in work by Julia Margaret Cameron.

In April 1986 we sold one portrait by an unidentified photographer for £260 (No. 3). In this instance the appeal was possibly the subject – 'The Hairy Family of Mandalay', not an image likely to be found in every family album!

Lindsey Stewart

1. *Portrait, from 'Les Types Russes' by William Carrick, two small cartes-de-visite albums, 1870s.* June '85, £200.
2. *Chinese interpreter, hand-tinted albumen print, approx. 10 × 8 in., from an album of 114 Japanese and Chinese portraits, including several by Baron Von Stillfried, 1870s.* June '85, £5,000.
3. *'The Hairy Family of Mandalay', albumen print, 1860s–70s. 8½ × 7⅛ in.* Apr. '86, £260.

2

3

Popular Nineteenth-century Travel Photography

Although photographers travelled extensively throughout Europe and the Middle East in the 1850s, views from this period tend to be of specific architectural subjects or landscapes selected more for pictorial than topographical interest. Early works which were truly exploratory were published in book form such as Maxime Du Camp's *'Egypte, Nubie, Palestine et Syrie . . .'* of 1852 (see p. 137, No. 1). Individual plates from such books are often available: two mammoth prints by Francis Frith from his expedition to Egypt in 1858 were sold in Apr. '86 for £100 and £420, the higher price being for the better print (No. 1).

During the 1860s, photographers became more commercial in approach, and large numbers of stereo cards were published. British and European stereo views remain inexpensive, typical good examples rarely selling for more than £2–£3 at auction, making this an accessible area for any collector. During this period too, the first commercially available single mounted prints were marketed by George Washington Wilson, through the publishers Marion & Co. These were only approximately 6¾ by 4½ in. and mounted on card with printed captions and photographers' credits. During the later 1860s, an extensive range of views from Britain, Europe and the Middle East was available from Francis Frith's establishment in Reading. In addition to Frith's own photography, this firm printed from negatives by R. Fenton, F. Bedford, A. and H. Rosling, F.M. Good and others. These vary in price, with Fenton's work generally fetching most, individual prints selling between £50 and £180 in the last two or three years.

Other examples tend to sell in groups at auction – 'Gems of Photographic Art selected by F. Firth', forty views of Switzerland, sold in June '85 for only £55. Switzerland is not currently a popular country with collectors, and these might have done better if of Egypt or Palestine.

Photographers were now able to produce acceptable views in conditions which had previously eluded them, most notably Samuel Bourne, who travelled in India and the Himalayas from 1868, producing several hundred images which were distributed through Bourne & Shepherd for decades. Despite being common, these can still achieve relatively high prices. In Apr. '86 an album of 75 Samuel Bourne photographs sold for £350, while another group of approximately 70 loose prints, including five composite panoramas, which are more unusual, sold for £650. These are auction prices and individual prints from these groups may be retailed at widely differing prices, usually dependent on condition and print quality.

By the 1870s the business of selling travel views was well established and firms began selling large quantities of prints in standard sizes, the largest around 8 × 10½ in. These usually had a reference number and often a title and photographer's credit printed on the negative, giving the recognizable white writing which appears within the positive print. This market continued in full force until the early 20th century, and its strength is reflected in the vast number of extant albums dating from the period. With these later 19th-century travel albums, the price depends mainly on the countries included, with Britain or Europe rarely making over £50 while Japan and the Middle East are likely to make more. In Apr. '86, prices for Japanese albums were high, several individual examples selling between £200 and £400. North America and Australasia are in demand, again in April an album of North America, Mexico and the West Indies sold for £300, while a good album, *New South Wales*, made £1,400 (No. 2), although this was more for its strong architectural content. Prices do vary a lot even within these divisions and the popularity of different areas remains unpredictable.

In many cases – for example the Middle Eastern firm of Bonfils – identical photographs were sold over a number of years, although there was often a change in the reference number which may be the only clue to the actual date of the photograph. Of course, the best method of precise dating is by knowing the subject and identifying changes over several years, and this is often where the specialist can pick up bargains, by identifying one rare view of a particular area from an album which may seem quite unremarkable to the less knowledgeable.

Lindsey Stewart

1. *Francis Frith, 'The Mosque of the Emeer Akhoor – Cairo', albumen print, 19¼ × 15¼ in., 1858. Apr. '86, £420.*

2. *Photographer unidentified, 'Lands Office, Sydney Bridge Street Front', gelatin silver print, 11½ × 14¼ in., from 'New South Wales', an album of 50 photographs from 1890s or early 1900s. Apr. '86, £1,400.*

1

2

Photographically Illustrated Books

In virtually every sale of photographs there is a small selection of photographically illustrated books, and these usually cover a wide range of subjects, periods and prices. For example, our April '86 sale included books from 1848 to the 1970s and with estimates from £60 to £40,000.

The few very high prices achieved tend to be for rare examples of early works illustrated with actual photographs. In March '85, Sotheby's sold *Photographs of British Algae, Cyanotype Impressions*, 1843, by Anna Atkins for £44,000. This beautiful book, which predates the publication of the first section of W.H.F. Talbot's *Pencil of Nature*, must be a highly desirable item for any specialist collector in the field, as was No. 1, the first major French book to be illustrated with photographs.

Among less rare works from the 1860s and later, there are a surprising number of bargains to be found, with most prices remaining at the same fairly low levels since their drop from the dizzy heights reached during the late 1970s. Many such books published in the 1860s and '70s can be found for less than £50, particularly those small books of views containing original albumen prints by well-known photographers – in October 1985 a lot comprising *Photographic Views of Dolgelly* by F. Bedford and *Scarborough* by G.W. Wilson sold for £80. Such photographic guide books provide a fascinating record of popular Victorian

Britain and often contain small beautifully detailed images.

Later nineteenth-century books took advantage of the new 'permanent' processes: carbon, Woodburytype, platinum and photogravure printing. Of these, the most expensive is platinum, as this was a true photographic printing method producing unique prints, whereas the others are photomechanical processes. The best-known example of the former is Peter Henry Emerson's *Life and Landscape on the Norfolk Broads* (No. 2). Other volumes by Emerson containing photogravure prints tend to sell for between £500 and £2,000.

Volumes illustrated with carbon prints include the famous *Cabinet Portrait Gallery*, volumes I–V (1890–94), sold together for £60 in June '85. Less common books from the same period and using the same process tend to make more: Thomas Annan's *The Old Country Houses of the Old Glasgow Gentry* made £200 in the same sale, while No. 3 did even better.

Exhibition catalogues and 'art photography' magazines from the Photo-Secessionist period and the 1920s and '30s can attract high prices. Original volumes of *Camera Work* magazine, edited and published by Alfred Stieglitz, sold recently for between £100 and £2,200, the latter for issue XXXVI which was devoted to Stieglitz's own work (April '86). In contrast, the popular magazine of the early 20th-century,

1

Photograms of the Year, tends to average £5 per issue. Although not rare, these include a wealth of illustrations by leading and more obscure photographers together with contemporary advertisements and represent pretty good value for money! *Lindsey Stewart*

1. *Maxime Du Camp, 'Nubie – Ibsamboul, Colosse Occidental du Spéos de Phré', plate 107 from 'Egypte, Nubie, Palestine et Syrie', Paris: Gide et J. Baudry, 1852. Apr. '86, £30,000.*

2. *Peter Henry Emerson 'Taking up the Eel Net', plate VII from 'Life and Landscape on the Norfolk Broads', London: Sampson Low, Marston, Searle and Rivington, 1886. Apr. '86, £10,000.*

3. *Capt. W. de W. Abney, R.E., F.R.S., illustration from 'Thebes and its Five Greater Temples', same publisher as No. 2, 1876. Mar. '85, £280.*

3

David Octavius Hill and Robert Adamson

The partnership of Hill and Adamson lasted only between 1843 and 1847, and yet during this time they produced a body of calotype photographs both of significant historic interest and exceptional beauty. Their best known work was in the field of portraiture, undertaken originally as a means of recording the many members of the newly formed Free Church of Scotland, to be represented by D. O. Hill in his painting *The Signing of the Deed of Demission*. However, after the formation of the partnership it was only a short time before the artist and the calotypist began to appreciate the full potential of their chosen medium, and they extended their scope to other portraits, landscapes and architecture.

Their work has survived well and can be seen in many public collections, most notably that of the Scottish National Portrait Gallery. There are opportunities for the collector, as examples do appear on the market and several have been available at auction over recent years. These vary considerably, not only in their condition but also in the particular printing process used. Prints made during Adamson's lifetime were on salted paper, often 'Whatman's Turkey Mill', and they may have this watermark. At best, these have a warm reddish-brown tone, a very matt surface, and show the rather watery softness associated with calotype prints. They often show signs of fading, usually around the edges. A good example should sell for several hundred pounds. In June 1983, *A Newhaven Fisherman* made £1,900 (No. 3), while in April 1986 *The Tomb of the Family of Nasmyth*, with the artists Thomas Duncan and D. O. Hill, sold for £2,200 (No. 1). Each of these was a good image in very fine condition, and, as such, the prices seem very reasonable when compared with £8,000 for a good calotype by W. H. F. Talbot in 1984. Less interesting subjects or prints in poorer condition generally sell in the lower hundreds.

Shortly before Hill's death in 1870, their studio at Rock House, Edinburgh, was sold to Thomas Annan, and it was subsequently occupied by a series of other photographers. It appears that several of their negatives remained there, and these were used for the production of later prints using other printing methods. The two most commonly found are carbon prints and photogravures. The carbon process produces a permanent print, a dense chocolate

1. *'The Tomb of the Family of Nasmyth, Greyfriars, Edinburgh', calotype, mounted on card.* 8 × 6 in. Apr. '86, £2,200.
2. *'Finlay of Colonsay, Deerstalker', calotype mounted on card.* 9 × 6½ in. Mar. '85, £300.
3. *'A Newhaven Fisherman', calotype, mounted on card.* 7½ × 5½ in. June '83, £1,900.

1

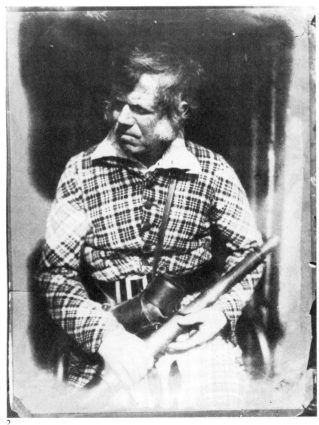

2

brown colour, which shows no signs of fading (Nos. 4 & 5). The image forms in slight relief and it may be possible to see this, especially if the print is not mounted. Carbon prints were produced by the firm of Thomas Annan (*c.*1880) and again by Jessie Bertram between 1919 and 1920, and without a positive credit it is impossible to distinguish which group a particular print may be from. The process allowed for relatively easy mass-production and this, together with the knowledge they were not produced by the photographers themselves, is reflected in their price. The carbon print of *The Artist and the Gravedigger*, an image again including D. O. Hill in a tableau from Greyfriars Churchyard, sold in April 1986 for £80 (No. 4), and *Newhaven Pilot* was bid up to £75 in October 1985 (No. 5).

Thomas Annan's son, James Craig Annan, was responsible for reintroducing the work of Hill and Adamson to the 'art photography' world in the late 19th century. He had been sent to Vienna in 1883 to learn the new process of photogravure from its inventor Karl Klic, a process for which his father bought the rights for use in Britain. In the 1890s J. C. Annan produced photogravures from the original negatives of Hill and Adamson, and these were exhibited in Europe and America, and published in Alfred Stieglitz's influential *Camera Work* magazine in 1905, 1909 and 1912. A photomechanical and again permanent process, the photogravure can be identified by its grey tone and its base paper, which is non-photographic and often tissue, showing the identations of the printmaker's plate. There have been no individual examples sold recently at auction, but copies of *Camera Work*, including photogravures from the Hill and Adamson series, were sold in April 1986 for £500–£600.

In addition to these easily identified and well-documented prints, there are others which appear similar to the original calotypes, but have a very dull appearance by comparison. Little is known of their origin, but it is generally agreed they were printed later than the 1840s. The paper used tends to be thicker than usual and the prints lack subtlety in the range of tones. They have been sold at auction, and do better than either the carbon or photogravure prints, but never as well as a true calotype in good condition.

To me, the photogravure prints capture more of the atmosphere of the originals than do either of the others, and for those who cannot afford a good example of a Hill and Adamson calotype, an Annan photogravure seems to represent a worthwhile alternative. *Lindsey Stewart*

3

4. *'The Artist and the Gravedigger', carbon print, mounted on card.* 8 × 6¼ in. Apr. '86, £80.
5. *'A Newhaven Pilot', carbon print, mounted on card.* 7½ × 5½ in. Oct. '85, £75.
6. *'The Minnow Pool', photogravure from* Camera Work *magazine, pub. Oct. 1909.* Sold with two other issues, Apr. '86, £550.

5

6

Daguerreotypes

In *The Popular Antiques Yearbook*, Vol. 1, I devoted articles to Daguerreotypes and stereoscopic photographs. These two pages show examples from subsequent sales. *Lindsey Stewart*

1. *An interesting and historic early sixth-plate daguerreotype of Professor Justus von Liebig and his students, by Carl Reisser, 1843–4. Accompanied by a contemporary manuscript, signed by each student and dated.* June '85, £1,500.

   Reisser was a chemist from Vienna, who worked in Munich and had inventions published by von Liebig.

2. *Jean Gabriel Eynard-Lullin: self-portrait with family, half-plate daguerreotype, c.1845–50.* Apr. '86, £500.

   Eynard-Lullin, an amateur, is recognized as the first Swiss photographer.

3. *Rare Austrian box thaler containing daguerreotype reproduction of a portrait.* April '86, £650.

1

4. *Ledbury Market Hall, an early sixth-plate outdoor daguerreotype, 1840s.* June '85, £300, despite extensive tarnishing.

5. *West Country farmer, an unusual early sixth-plate daguerreotype, 1840s.* June '85, £180.

6. *'Southern or back view of Rose Cottage', an Australian daguerreotype, sixth-plate, c.1856, sold with a similar ambrotype and two portraits.* April '86, £750.

2

3

4

5

6

Stereoscopic Photographs

1

1. *Thomas Skaife, reverse of stereo view showing the photographer's self-portrait posed with his patent stereoscopic camera, and with affixed label detailing the exact time and place of the photograph, and initialled by Skaife, 1858.* Apr. '86, £750.

2. *A good stereoscopic ambrotype portrait, including a stereoscopic viewer on the table.* April '86, £65.

3. *An amateur stereoscopic autochrome, from a group of fifty, sold with a table stereoscope.* June '85, £1,300.

   Autochromes, early colour slides, are becoming popular and these were particularly good examples, although, being from the 1920s and 1930s, they were not particularly early.

2

20th-Century British Photographers

1

2

3

Few British photographers from the twentieth century have made an impression on the international market. Bill Brandt is one exception, and his work has been appreciated for some time. As yet, other photographers seem to attract limited attention and many bargains are available.

Interestingly, Bill Brandt is one of the few photographers whose 'vintage' prints rarely sell for more than his modern prints. The older examples are generally prints produced for publication, and as such are rarely of the same quality as the exhibition prints produced later in his career.

Lindsey Stewart

1. *Nude, by Bill Brandt, 1956 (printed 1970s), signed.* 13½ × 11¼ in. Mar. '85, £600.
2. *Portrait of H.R.H. the Duchess of Kent, by Cecil Beaton, 1940s.* 10 × 8 in. Mar. '85, £75.
3. *'Maidens in Waiting', by Bert Hardy, 1951 (printed 1970s), published in 'Picture Post'.* 13½ × 10 in. Mar. '85, £160.
4. *Portrait of Marilyn Monroe, by Cecil Beaton, 1940s.* 7¼ × 7¼ in. June '85, £130.
5. *'East End at War', by Bert Hardy, 1940, published in 'Picture Post'.* 9¼ × 14 in. Mar. '85, £110.

4

5

Margaret Bourke-White (1904–1971)

A leading American photographer, Bourke-White is well represented in New York sales, but it is unusual to see examples of her work available in London. These four images indicate to some extent the range of her work, and the variation in price.   *Lindsey Stewart*

1. *'Mohandas Gandhi', 1946, printing date not known.* 13½ × 10¼ in. June '85, £420.

2. *'A New Way to Look at the Statue of Liberty', published in Life Magazine, 1952, printing date not known.* 13½ × 10½ in. June '85, £300.

3. *Industrial landscape, 1930s, signed in pencil on mount.* 8½ × 12½ in. April '86, £1,300.

    This print and the following were purchased from an exhibition in New York in the 1930s by Vera Brittain. Despite some oxidization (or silvering) both were fine

examples of 'vintage prints'. Other than verifying the date, the provenance seems to have had little effect on the price, as the prints attracted considerable attention as striking modern images.

4. *'Plow Blades . . .', torn in three places and with surface indentations.* 9 × 13 in. Apr. '86, £900.

4

11. *Printed Ephemera and Pop*

Introduction
by Carey Wallace

Prices over the last year have shown that Printed Ephemera continues to be popular with collectors. It may well be that the diversity of items embraced by this category accounts for the appeal. The range of articles, from cigarette cards, postcards, valentines and scrap albums to signed photographs, circus posters, Baxter prints and stevengraphs, is so broad that it must appeal to an equally wide variety of tastes. Diversity is a characteristic similarly shared by auctions of Pop Memorabilia. Many imaginations are caught by this new and thriving market in the artefacts of our recent pop culture. Just as Printed Ephemera has a distinctly wide appeal, the broad scope of items – from Adam Ant's jacket to John Lennon's Rolls-Royce, sheltering under the umbrella term 'Pop Memorabilia', must touch a chord with anyone who has ever idolized (covertly at least) a star of popular entertainment.

1. *A Henry Poole & Son weighing machine ticket from the SS* Titanic *with stamped weight 9 stone 5 lb., dated 8.4.12, water stained. 3¼ × 1½ in.* Nov. '85, £500.
   Titanic material is highly popular, and unless she is ever raised, obviously rare.
2. *Poster for the Marilyn Monroe film 'Let's Make Love'.* May '86, £50.
   Original film posters are popular.
3. *W. Duke Bicycle Trick Rides cigarette card,* up to £10 each.

2

3

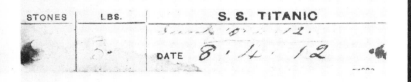

1

Baxter Prints and Stevengraphs

These are two of the more unusual categories that come under the heading Ephemera. Firstly, *Baxter prints*: In the 1830s, George Baxter devised one of the first methods of printing in colour by means of wood blocks and oil-based colours. Baxter was a faithful chronicler of early Victorian life as well as an artist-craftsman of extraordinarily high ability. Usually, the prints are marked, either on the print itself, or with an embossed seal which can be found on the mount (No. 1). The variety of themes can best be illustrated by mentioning some of the titles – 'The Bridesmaid', 'The Lover's Letter Box' (No. 4), 'Victoria, Queen of Great Britain', 'Soldiers' Farewell', 'Grand Entrance to the Great Exhibition' and 'Infantine Jealousy'. Up to about 1843, most of Baxter's work was for book illustrations, sheet music and albums. But from 1843 onwards until the time he discontinued business in approximately 1860, Baxter mainly produced reproductions of paintings for decorative purposes, and this is the period in which we find not only the finest subjects, but also his finest work. Baxter's prints come in various sizes, the largest being 'The Parting Look', 25½ × 18½ in.

Secondly, *Stevengraphs*: This trade name was coined by Thomas Stevens about 1863, and was intended to describe any of his woven articles, but today it is taken only to refer to his mounted silk pictures and portraits. These left the Coventry factory in cardboard mounts, nearly always with Stevens's trade label (No. 5) stuck to the back and with his name and the title printed on the front – e.g. 'Woven in silk by Thomas Stevens, Coventry and London, Registered'. Sometimes this is abbreviated simply to 'Woven in pure silk', particularly on late versions. There is considerable variation both in the size and shape of the silk and the mount, but the identification of a Stevengraph is not difficult. Care should be taken to see that the mount has not been cut down to fit into a smaller frame. Many of the Stevengraphs we see have been remounted or the silk itself is faded. This detracts from the value. Stevens's woven silk pictures and portraits depict a wide variety of themes, including sports, historical and classical subjects, exhibitions, politicians, royalty and ships.

Mark Wilkinson

1

4

3

1. *Baxter's embossed seal.*
2. *River Tiefy, Baxter print,* up to £20.
3. *River Camel, Cornwall, Baxter print,* up to £20.
4. *'The Lover's Letterbox', Baxter print.* Nov. '85, £90.
5. *Stevens's trade label.*
6. *'For Life or Death, Heroism on Land', Stevengraph.* May '86, £35.

Signed Movie Photographs

There is growing interest in a field which has been sneered at by 'serious' collectors for so long. Over the last four years we have seen prices almost double for good-quality items, and there are no indications that this upward trend is not going to continue.

To calculate the price of a signed photograph we must look at a number of important factors. How popular is the subject? For instance, Charles Chaplin (No. 1) would be more sought after than John Wayne. Next, the signature itself, is it by the subject's own hand? This is probably the most difficult to ascertain owing to the fact that photographs of popular stars were sent out in vast numbers from the large studios. Many of the 'signatures' found on them are in fact reproductions on the negative, or copied by means of a stamp or roller, and in some cases they were 'signed' by personal secretaries. It is easier to authenticate when the personality has dedicated the photograph or mentioned something out of the ordinary such as a latest film. A clear large photograph by a known photographer will always add to the price. It also helps if the subject is in one of the roles that made them famous, for example Bela Lugosi as Dracula, or Harpo Marx with his harp.

The rarity of the signature itself is an important consideration. Rudolph Valentino signed very few, and in November 1985 £500 was paid for a single image similar to that shown in No. 2, but with a dedication and date. On the other hand Laurel and Hardy signed numerous photographs, (Nos. 3 and 4), and prices stick around the £100 mark.

Some of the more popular subjects that will always be in demand, other than those mentioned above, are Douglas Fairbanks, Mary Pickford, Marlene Dietrich, Boris Karloff and Judy Garland (No. 5). There is one lesser star who is not now known for his conventional acting, but who still appears on our screen, and whose signed photographs sell for between £40 and £60. That is Ronald Reagan.   *Mark Wilkinson*

1. *Charlie Chaplin, a portrait study, inscribed 'To Jack Palmer, congratulations for your handling of the "Lime Light" premier, Charlie Chaplin, Oct. 18th(?), 1952.'* May '86, £140.
2. *Rudolph Valentino, a portrait study inscribed in ink 'Sincerely Rudolf Valentino'.* 10 × 8 in. This would probably sell for around £200.
3. *Stan Laurel, a portrait study.* 10 × 7 in. Sold as part of a collection. A single Laurel and/ or Hardy might make about £60.
4. *Oliver Hardy, a portrait study.* 10 × 7 in. See No. 3.
5. *Judy Garland, a portrait study.* 10 × 8 in. May '86, £130.

3

4

5

Beatles Under The Hammer

Even today, twenty years later, the sixties tend to be regarded as the golden age of pop culture, and this feeling is reflected in Pop Memorabilia auctions where the Beatles come out as number one favourites. Although items which have a specific rarity or a definite personal connection with the 'Fab Four' tend to be most fanatically sought after by collectors, some of the goods which were originally mass-produced during the period of Beatlemania command surprising prices (No. 1).

Autograph material, has, however, a wider appeal, and owing to its direct link with the artists, is highly collectable. Signed photographs, programmes, record sleeves, books, drawings and letters tend to have a high profile in the memorabilia market. However, there are a number of dangers, as many of the so-called Beatles signatures were in reality the work of their road managers and aides, and to confuse the issue even further, a large number of skilful forgeries also exist. Provenance thus becomes a key consideration with autograph material; it is essential to establish the history of signed items, in order to prove their authenticity. Once it is confirmed that a signature is genuine, its price will depend on the quality and interest of the item which has been inscribed. A good-quality, autographed early photograph of the Beatles, for instance, can realize between £200 and £400 at auction (No. 2). As far as the Beatles music is concerned, auction prices indicate that rare and 'one off' records excite a great deal of interest. Test pressings, and acetates which by definition had an extremely limited circulation, are certainly collectable. These records are particularly valuable if the song recorded is unique, or a variant of the final release, and can make up to £400 and £500 (No. 3). Gold and platinum discs, as the names suggest, should be placed at the top of the Beatles record price ladder. The value of these awards is dependent on two factors, the collectability of the record itself, and the recipient of the presentation (Nos. 4 and 5). Unfortunately a large number of imitations are in circulation, and when prices of gold and platinum dics can exceed £2,000, the danger

of counterfeits becomes acute. Thus collectors of Beatles memorabilia, whether inveterate fans intent on purchasing a symbol of their youth, or astute buyers seeking an investment, should not only look to age, quality, and condition, but wherever possible establish the history of the item, in order to sift the genuine articles from the large quantity of forgeries on the market. If in any doubt, leave well alone!

Carey Wallace

1. *Stockings.* Nov. '84, £65. Once of small value, mass-produced Beatlemania spinoffs, such as these Beatle stockings and Beatle chewing gum cards or tins of Beatles talcum powder, can realize between £60 and £150 at auction.

2. *A good portrait study,* c. 1966, *with each of the four signatures clearly visible.* Nov. '84, £240.

3. *Beatles acetate of 'Across The Universe', a version never released.* Dec. '85, £500.

4. *Platinum disc of 'Let it Be', presented to John Ono Lennon.* Nov. '84, £2,600.

5. *Gold disc of 'My Sweet Lord', presented to Apple.* Dec. '85, £1,000. Not only is platinum a higher award, but the single 'Let It Be' is the more collectable, and the fact that it was presented to John Lennon himself, rather than the Apple Recording Company, increases its value and accounts for the large difference in realized price between Nos. 4 and 5.

Miscellany

Obviously there is no clear pattern to ephemera collecting. Here are some diverse objects which have escaped the waste-paper basket and which now have a price. *Carey Wallace*

1. *A pair of portrait photographs by Dorothy Wilding of HM Queen Elizabeth and HM King*

George VI, inscribed on mount 'Elizabeth R. 1939' and 'George R.I. 1939'. 11 × 9¼ in. and 11¼ × 9 in. Feb '86, £520.
    Photographs bearing royal signatures are among the most highly prized of autograph material.

2. *Unusual cards such as this 'Napoleon Fantasy Head' are worth up to £15 each.*

3. *Raphael Kirchner's Art Nouveau cards, such as 'Geisha', realize up to £25 each at auction. Part of a lot, May '86, £12.*

4. *Harry 'Handcuff' Houdini, a signed postcard of Houdini in chains. May '86, £110.*

5. *'The Sorcerer', c.1920. May '86, £55. Colourful circus, magician and opera posters, apart from being decorative, are collectable.*

6. *A Henry M. Stanley portrait photograph inscribed 'As a souvenir to Little Effie from her friend, Henry M. Stanley 1886'. May '86, £85. Signed photographs of notable sports personalities, explorers, etc. maintain their popularity.*

7. *Highly ornate Victorian Valentines realize up to £30 each.*

8. *Prices have risen in the last year for photographic cards of motor transport, such as this close-up of an electric tram. This would fetch £10–£20 at auction.*

9 & 10. *On a similar theme, photographic cards of unusual incidents, such as accidents, are sought after. If the whereabouts of an accident is also known, this adds to the value. No. 10, for example, is inscribed on verso '. . . accident that happened in Montague St., facing Crescent Rd.', and is post-marked Worthing, 1908. Value £15–£20.*

11. *Unusual items which do not fit into any specific category often appear, and these can be included under the umbrella term 'ephemera'. Sir Harry Lauder's crooked stick, 33.5 in. long, used as a stage prop, and allegedly associated with the song 'The Wedding of Sandy McNab', sold with letters and other related material. July '86, £650.*

12.   Toys

Introduction
by Timothy Matthews

1

This last year has seen the continuing trend of high prices paid for rare tinplate toys. In the January 1986 toy sale, a Carette Open Tourer reached £7,200 (No. 1). Early penny toys made in Nuremburg at the turn of the century continued to catch the eye of the collector. The tinplate toys made by Lehmann continued to be eagerly sought after – in September a 'Panne' four-seater open tourer reached £600. Damaged Lehmann toys did not fare so well – a rusted 'Am Pol' three-wheeled motor cycle only reached £180 in the same sale.

Meccano continued to make high prices too – a 'No. 2' constructor car reached £600 in May '85, and a Meccano Outfit set No. 10 reached £420 in January. However, Meccano that is rusted or worn is not popular – neither are loose Meccano bits. In order to gain high prices, the pieces need to be part of a set, in the original box and with instructions.

Austin pedal cars continued to attract a great deal of attention, the Austin J40 'Joy Cars' still making figures of between £500 and £800. A fine example in white paintwork reached £750 in January '86, and March '86 saw a well-restored 'Pathfinder Special' Grand Prix racing pedal car reach £1,000 (No. 4). These cars were made by the Austin Car Company from the early 1950s. They were beautifully constructed and finished and are fairly scarce. Collectors will therefore pay high prices for them. Other pedal cars, such as those manufactured by Triang, only sell for a few pounds.

Noah's Arks made in Germany c.1880 have also maintained their high levels. Sotheby's sold three in October last year for over £1,000 each. A deep-hulled Ark with approximately 75 pairs of animals reached £650 in July '85 (No. 3) and a set of 48 carved figures, German, c.1880, made £920 (No. 6) on the same occasion.

Rocking horses swing on steadily, especially the late Victorian horses. These steeds have beautifully carved features. Some were constructed on bow pillar rockers and others, more common, on pillar stands. A bow rocker type of about four feet in length reached £450 in November '85. This horse was stripped of its original paintwork, but was still in basically good condition. A later 19th-century horse on a pillar stand reached only £300 in January '86, but this mount was not as unusual. However, it was a good shape and had its original saddle and reins. Even recently made rocking horses will sell (No. 5).

Even biscuit tins are sought after so long as they are in the form of a toy, such as a ship, a train or a delivery lorry! Many manufacturers, like Huntley and Palmer, Crawfords, and Jacobs, marketed biscuits in novelty tins during the 1920s and 1930s. 'General', an early London Transport double-deck bus, reached £1,200 in January '86 (No. 7), and in the same sale, a 'Coronation Coach' issued by Jacobs in 1937 reached £75.

1. *A rare Carette hand-enamelled Mercedes 2-seater open tourer, c.1907.* Jan. '86, £7,200.

2. *A Lehmann 'Dancing Sailor' EPL 535, with original box, Germany, c.1920.* Sept. '85, £150.

3

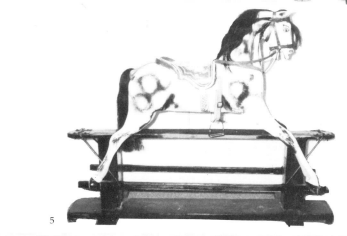

5

6

3. *A deep-hull painted wood Noah's Ark with 75 pairs of animals and people, including Mr and Mrs Noah, German, c.1880. Jul. '85, £650.*

4. *An Austin 'Pathfinder Special' pedal car 'No. 8', c.1949. 63 in. long. Mar. '86, £1,000.*

5. *A modern 'Pony size' rocking horse, on twin pillar stand. 50 in. Nov. '85, £350.*

6. *A painted carved wood fair, by Erzgebirge, Germany, late 19th century (48 pieces). July. '85, £920.*

7. *'General', a rare printed and painted double-deck bus by Huntley & Palmer, with clockwork mechanism and opening roof, c.1928. 9½ in. long. Jan. '86, £1,200.*

Tinplate Toys

The market for tinplate toys has remained very high, indeed it has expanded as more people are becoming aware of the value of tinplate toys. It is not only at South Kensington that record prices are being achieved for rare toys in good condition (No. 1). Sotheby's sold a hand-painted four-seat open tourer by Carette, *c.*1910, for £6,710 in January '86, and Phillips recently sold an early Gunthermann 'Gordon Bennett' racing car for £4,000.

Tinplate toys from the 1890s to late 1920s are creating the most interest internationally, German toys in particular. The toys need to be complete, that is to say, not broken. Prices will be slightly lower if the clockwork mechanism is defective. If the toy has its original box then the price will be higher. A good example of this is No. 7. A 'Stubborn Donkey', EPL No. 425, reached a mere £150 in September '85.

Also collected are French tinplate toys, especially those by A.F. Martin. Planes and airships are collected too (No. 5). Sotheby's sold a fine Tipp 'R.100' Zeppelin Airship for £825 in January '86. Even a smaller airship by the same firm, with

many parts missing, reached £250 in September '85. The early two-funnel liner *Columbia* caused a stir when she sailed into the September '85 toy sale. Many old ships have missing parts, such as lifeboats, or have had a very hard working life, but this fine ship was intact. A Bing four-funnel battleship, *HMS Powerful*, reached £935 in a May sale at Sotheby's.

However, it is not just these tinplate toys from the early 19th century that collectors are seeking—see No. 6. Tinplate toys of the 1930s by Chad Valley may not realize as high a price, but are still eagerly sought after, especially the clockwork racing cars. Schuco clockwork toys of the 1930s to 1950s are selling well too. Japanese toys of the 1950s and '60s need to be in mint condition and in their original boxes. When a small lot can be made up of four or five battery operated toys, collectors and dealers will pay about £100.　　*Timothy Matthews*

1. *A Bing enamelled open-cab two-door limousine, German, c.1908. 9⅞ in. long. Mar. '86, £3,800.*

2. *A Carette lithograph limousine, with chauffeur in open cab. 8½ in. long. Sept. '85, £720.*

3. *'Columbia', a painted metal two-funnel ocean liner by Bing, c.1904. 26¾ in. long. Sept. '85, £3,600.*

4. *Two German toys and one French, c.1910. Left to right: 'Heavy Swell' by Lehmann; A Gunthermann lady with basket; and a F. Martin bear. Nov. '85, £700; £190; £190.*

5. *A hand-painted early 'Blériot' type monoplane, German, c.1903. 5⅝ in. long. Mar. '86, £400.*

6. *An Arnold 'Mac 700' motorbike and rider, US Zone, West Germany, c.1953. 7¼ in. long. Mar. '86, £480.*

7. *A Lehmann 'Baker and Sweep', EPL No. 450, with original box, c.1905. 5¾ in. long. Nov. '85, £1,600.*

1

2

3

7

4

5

6

Tinplate Trains

2

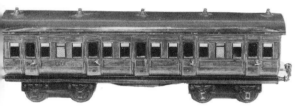

4

This is a market in which prices do not change dramatically from year to year. It is dominated by experienced collectors who are chiefly concerned with quality, and here we look at some of the models which are most likely to excite them.

The most capable and reliable express locomotive that this country has ever seen was undoubtedly the 'Flying Scotsman'. No. 4472 was a Pacific Class locomotive built by Sir Nigel Gresley, and on test runs in 1934 it achieved a speed of 100 mph. This splendid locomotive was faithfully reproduced in miniature by Bassett-Lowke in the late 1930s in gauge O scale. It came in a variety of colours and was powered either by clockwork or electricity. One in British Railways dark blue, sold for £450 in Sept. '84, and a light green LNER version made £550 in July '85 (No. 1). In fact the British Railways blue is the one to look for, as it is rarer. Both of these were electric.

Bassett-Lowke models are among the most highly sought after. Here one might quote No. 2, and, more dramatically, a British Railways Class 5 4–6–0 locomotive which sold for £1,100 in Feb. '86. Electric-powered locomotives in good condition regularly make high prices.

Locomotives generally need something to pull, and carriages and rolling stock of all kinds are equally in demand.

No. 3 is one example, and a Märklin 'Bass' covered waggon in gauge O scale, which made £140 in Jan. '86, another. A quantity of rolling stock by Bing made £480 in the same sale.

A little down the range, gauge O Hornby trains are also doing well. An early pre-war LNER 4-4-4 tank locomotive No. 406 made £190 in Mar. '86, a GWR 4-4-2 tank locomotive together with two carriages made £280 in Jan. '86, and on the same occasion eight Hornby waggons made £120.

There is no discernible price scale for the British railway companies, although British Railways examples tend to be rarer than the independent companies. However, No. 4 introduced another element to the competition, since it obviously attracted collectors from France as well as the home team.

Lineside equipment is also sought after – except for track. This was made in such huge quantities that most collectors are well provided for already. If you do want track, it is often worth looking at flea markets and car boot sales where boxes of it appear.

The quality of No. 5 ensured a high price, but this was no one-off result. In Sept. '85 a Märklin engine-shed made £180, and three months later a set of street lamps reached £150.

Timothy Matthews

1. *Bassett-Lowke gauge O electric model LNER 4–6–2 locomotive and tender, 'The Flying Scotsman,' c. 1936.* July '85, £550. This was a beautiful model of one of the most famous of all locomotives.

2. *Bing for Bassett-Lowke, gauge 1 clockwork L & NWR. 4–4–2 'Precursor' tank locomotive.* Nov. '85, £380.

3. *Märklin gauge 1 GNR teak-finished twin-bogie 1st/3rd class passenger coach (one of a pair).* Nov. '85, £260.

4. *Hornby gauge O 3-rail electric SNCF autorail car with original box.* Jan. '86, £280. This model is distinctly scarce.

5. *Britain's Set No. 158, Railway Station Staff in original box.* Nov. '85, £550. This set was in mint condition, and even more unusually so too was the box. Even the shovel, which has often been lost, was present. In July '84 a similar set did even better, making £600.

5

Dinky Toys

It was only in 1933 that Frank Hornby, of the famous trains and Meccano, launched the first Dinky Toys: a tank, two sports cars, a tractor, a motor truck and a delivery van. These toys were cast in heavy lead alloy and had metal wheels (Nos. 1–4).

By the outbreak of the Second World War the range had considerably expanded; the toys now had white rubber tyres and tinplate radiators, and many had chassis, some of a criss-cross design and others more solid. The range now included many more cars, vans and lorries, army vehicles, ships and aeroplanes, trams and buses, farm animals, road signs and even waterline ships.

Dinky Toys managed to produce some toys throughout the Second World War, many at Christmas time. After the war when full production began in April 1946, the range continued to expand. Many pre-war toys were reissued with improvements or minor changes. 1948 saw the emergence of the very fine range of 'Supertoys' (Nos. 5–10). Many of these models had yellow boxes with coloured pictures of the toy inside. Commercial vehicles had blue and white striped boxes, again with pictures.

Now it is not just Dinky Toys that are being eagerly sought after. The first series 'Matchbox' toys (No. 12) and the 'Models of Yesteryear' (No. 13) by Lesney, introduced in 1956, both with yellow and blue boxes with a black-lined picture, are avidly collected. For example, in January 1986 a group of 25 first series toys reached £160, in the same sale 12 Models of Yesteryear sold for £140. Corgi toys from the 1960s in original boxes are highly sought after too (No. 11). A lot consisting of 24 toys reached £180 in May 1985. Other makers such as Rio, Tekno and Spot On are all just as keenly collected.

Diecast toys in mint condition will reach high prices at auction. If the toys are boxed then prices are even higher. Damaged and scratched post-war toys do not attract much interest. However, pre-war toys, even in worn condition or fatigued, do sell. A group of eight such toys reached £120 in January 1985. Diecast toys from the late '60s and '70s do not sell at all well yet, but collectors are already starting to sniff them out. Some models, such as the Beatles 'Yellow Submarine', can reach £160, as at Sotheby's in August 1985. There is no doubt that since the Dinky Toy factory at Binns Road has now closed down, even the most modern will soon be in demand.   *Timothy Matthews*

1. & 2. *Two early rare pre-war Dinky 22 series vans with metal wheels. Jan. '86, £400 and £420.*

3. & 4. *Two early pre-war Dinky Toy 22 series sports cars, with metal wheels. Jan. '86, £320 and £380.*

1

2

3

4

5. *Dinky Supertoys, part of a lot of 8 commercial vehicles (most boxed). May. '85, £200.*

6. *Dinky Supertoy, 918 blue Guy Van advertising "Ever Ready" (mint, unboxed). Sept. '85, £60.*

7. *Post-war Dinky buses (mint, unboxed). May '85, £130.*

8. *One of a group of 12 Dinky aeroplanes (mint, most unboxed). May '86, £90.*

9. *Dinky post-war roadway accessories (mint, most unboxed), part lot. Jan. '86, £95.*

10. *Post-war Dinky French and British military items (most unboxed, some in worn condition). Jan. '86, £300.*

11. *A collection of 25 Corgi cars (mint and boxed). May '85, £400.*

12. *Lesney Matchbox toys, 1st series, 2 lots of 24 (mint and boxed). Jan. '86, £110 and £160.*

13. *Lesney, Models of Yesteryear (mint, unboxed). Sept. '85, £95.*

6

7

8

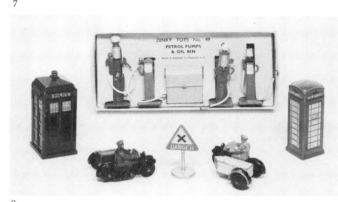

9

11

12

13

Britains Lead Soldiers and other figures

Britains lead soldiers still dominate the saleroom floor (see *Popular Antiques Yearbook*, vol. 1, pp. 174–5). Patrolling forward of the line are the rare cavalry sets, such as set No. 13, the 3rd King's Own Hussars (No. 1). Behind them are the rifle regiments such as the King's Royal Rifle Corps. In July '85 a boxed set of 7 riflemen carrying weapons at the trail with their officer carrying his sword reached £160. Centre of the line are the Guards regiments. The Grenadier Guards, at attention, with mounted officer, reached £190. This rare set dated from before the First World War. The figures were on oval bases with copyright labels stuck underneath (No. 2).

To the left of centre are the heavy infantry, such as the Devonshire Regiment, set No. 110. In Nov. '85 this set realized £110. To the right are Britains motorized units such as the Bren Gun Carriers, No. 1876. In Nov. '85 this reached £120. No. 1448, an Army Staff Car, reached £250 and No. 1335 made £160 in July '85 (Nos. 4 and 5). Covering enemy air attacks is the important set No. 1855 Mechanical Balloon Barrage Unit (No. 3).

In direct support is the Royal Artillery, set No. 1462, the covered lorry with caterpillar tracks, limber and gun (No. 7). In the same sale, a rare set No. 125, 'The Royal Horse Artillery' (dress uniform) in original box reached £220. To keep the Britains forces in the field, there is the Royal Engineer Pontoon Section (No. 8). To take the stores and ammunition up the line, there is the RASC, General Service Wagon, which made £360 in March '86. Highly sought after, too, is the RAMC Ambulance Wagon (No. 9) used to bring the wounded back to the field hospitals.

Holding the coast are the Royal Navy Units, set No. 79, 'The Royal Navy Landing Party', which reached £160 in March '86. Royal Navy Sailors, set No. 1510, in regulation dress, realized £55. To help maintain morale, military bands play their important part and the RAF Band, set No. 27, Band of the Line, reached £140 in the same sale (see also No. 10).

However, when the wars are over and the soldiers fade away back to their civilian lives, parades take place to honour the brave men. The Queen will be seen in her State Coach (No. 11). People from all over the world line the streets, many of these people are Country Folk (No. 12).

It is not just Britains that collectors seek. Flat soldiers by Heinrichsen and Heyde, made in Germany circa 1870, and circa 1840 respectively, realize high prices too (No. 13). Heyde 54mm scale soldiers, circa 1890, reached £420 in November '85. A rare Heyde circus reached £220 in March '86.

Composition soldiers maintain their high prices too. These soldiers were made in Germany before the Second World War, and a Lineol set No. 65, 'Parade of Scots' in original box, reached £850 in November '85. In the same sale German and British Infantry by Elastolin also gained high prices. The tinplate field guns, limbers and tractors made by Tipp and Hauser for the composition figures hold their own too – an Elastolin German Army Ambulance set reached £160 in March '86.

Two further points are worth making, one a word of caution, and the other of encouragement. *Popular Antiques Yearbook*, vol. 1, p. 174, mentioned the Britains Khaki RHA set which had sold for £6,000 in July '84 and £7,200 in January '85. This set was only produced between 1938 and 1940 and is rare. However, if a set is only rare, and not unique, the publicity produced by such prices is likely to flush more from the corners of forgotten toy cupboards. Thus in market terms, it becomes less rare, at least for a while. Because of this, comparable sets sold in London and New York since then have made slightly lower prices.

However, a positive encouragement to collectors and no doubt a boost to prices generally, will be given by the six month exhibition of the collector George Palmer's 'Delhi Durbar 1910' display at Bridlington during 1986. This shows that toy soldiers are much more than mere playthings. Two excellent books published in 1985 should also help: James Opie, *Britains Toy Soldiers, 1893–1932*, Gollancz (£29.95); Andrew Rose, *Toy Soldiers*, Salamander (£7.95). The second has full colour and actual size illustrations and is a bargain in itself.

Timothy Matthews

1. *Britains set No. 13, 3rd Hussars (Kings Own) at the trot, with carbines, officer on black charger, with sword, in original box. Mar. '86, £170.*

2. *Britains set No. 111, Grenadier Guards at attention, with officer on horse. Mar. '86, £190.*

3. *Britains set No. 1855, Balloon Barrage Unit, in original box. Nov. '85, £100.*

4. *Britains set No. 1335, 6-wheeled lorry, in original box. Nov. '85, £110.*

5. *Britains set No. 1448, Army Staff Car, in original box. July '85, £250.*

6. *Britains set No. 1203, Carden Lloyd type tank, in original box. Nov. '85, £90.*

7. *Britains set No. 1462, Royal Artillery covered limber, with caterpillar tracks, gun and limber in orignal box. Mar. '86, £180.*

8. *Britains set No. 1254, Royal Engineers Pontoon Section, in original box.* Mar. '86, £600.

9. *Britains set No. 145, RAMC Ambulance Wagon, in original box.* Mar. '86, £250.

10. *Britains set No. 1527, RAF Band in original box.* Mar. '86, £500.

11. *Britains set No. 9401, Her Majesty's State Coach, in original box.* Nov. '85, £160.

12. *A small collection of mint Britains farm items, including No. 4F tumbrel cart, people and animals, tree and hedges and the Village Idiot.* Jul. '85, £420.

13. *Heinrichsen, 30 mm scale, Napoleonic painted lead figures, including Prussian and French Infantry (5 Sets, approx. 100 figures) in original boxes, c.1880.* Mar. '86, £130.

9

11

13

Dolls

1

Introduction

by Olivia Bristol

The year 1985/6 has been a bumper one for toys, including dolls, their houses, and teddy bears. The world record price for a doll now stands at £24,200, reached by an extremely rare Kammer and Reinhardt character doll, mould 106, modelled as a rather fat-faced, double-chinned maid (Sotheby's May 1986). Another rare character doll, this time by the French S.F.B.J. factory, mould 252, was sold by Christie's South Kensington in April 1986 for £5,500 (No. 1). It was 27 in. high and was modelled as a pouting child, with strong flesh tones, and with a dirty, jointed toddler body.

Good automata still command high prices. Christie's South Kensington sold a Chinese standing smoking figure in January 1986 for £6,000 (No. 2); and a typical Vichy negro banjo player, the composition head with unusual white painted masquerade make-up, fetched £7,500 at the West Dean Sale in June when the Edward James collection was sold. Another collection, this time of mechanical music, also contained some automata. Interestingly, a Lambert figure with a German bisque head, although with no original clothes, had an unusual waist movement and so fetched a healthy £2,000 in March 1986 (No. 3).

It is interesting to see how original boxes and fine clothes make a difference to the price of a doll. A normal little Simon and Halbig girl, but with a coronet embroidered on the pinafore (the original owner had been given the doll by the Earl of Dudley) and the original Hamleys' box, fetched £340 in January 1986 against an estimate of £150–£180. Similarly, a large doll, 33 in. high, in elaborate silk smocked frock and in original box marked 'Genuine Walkure Doll', made £950, on an estimate of £350–£500.

Dolls' houses made up to the end of the last century, preferably furnished, are still very sought after. In November 1985 we sold for £3,500 an interesting painted wooden

2   3

house, that had a most unusual painted street-name in a white square on the corner. Called 'Seymour Place' it was probably made to represent the street of that name which is now part of Curzon Street in Mayfair.

1. *The sad-faced doll only reflects her unstrung condition, not her price.* Apr. '86, £5,500.
   Her companions were £160 for the lion by Steiff, £160 for a small Steiff of the 1950s, £1,700 for the large bear, also probably a Steiff, and £180 for the other 1950s Steiff bear.

2. *An amusing composition-headed smoking Chinaman.* Jan. '86, £6,000.

3. *A banjo player by Lambert, the head marked 'Simon and Halbig', with waist, hand and head movements.* Mar. '86, £2,000 – despite redressing.

Wax Dolls

2   3   4

Wax dolls are one of the few categories in the doll market that have not seen the spectacular price rises so evident in other types of material. Various reasons are put forward for this, the most important probably being their delicacy. Wax over composition dolls are notoriously difficult to store, and they can crack simply when taken into a different atmosphere or temperature. In fact it is rare to find a wax doll with composition reinforcement without some cracks, most commonly starting at the eye corners. Dipped wax dolls, that is to say papier mâché or composition heads that have been dipped into melted wax to give them a thin skin-like coating, often fare better, but because of their lightness and the fact that they were generally of poorer quality, and therefore less precious, they are often the worse for play.

The aristocrats of the wax dolls were those from England – and a few from France – made by the poured wax method. That is, wax poured directly into the mould and allowed to harden to the thickness of ⅛ inch before the residue is poured out. Delicately painted, with a finishing powder dusted over the cheeks, glass eyes and hair inserted with a hot needle into the scalp, sometimes individually, to my mind they re-create more realistically than other materials the cherished look of the Victorian child. Because of their fragility, well brought up children were made to treasure them.

This carefulness results in some dolls appearing on the market still in their original condition and elaborate layers of clothing. Some still have notes to the original owners from loving aunts and grandparents. If there is a stamped maker's mark on the body, especially those of Charles Marsh or Lucy Peck, this will add considerably to the price.

Poured wax, wax over composition and dipped wax dolls in good condition seem to me to be distinctly underpriced compared to their sisters and could prove a wise investment for the 1990s.

Olivia Bristol

1. *English poured wax doll.* May '86, £1,320. There were two unusual features: the eyes closed by means of a wire through the body, and the body was stamped with Lucy Peck's trade mark.
2. *Wax over composition doll, in contemporary sprigged muslin dress and cream satin bonnet, 1810–15.* 14 in. July '85, £240.
3. *Wax over composition headed doll with sleeping eyes wired from the waist, good condition.* July '85, £300.
4. *Early beeswax child doll in original clothes and good condition.* 17 in. Sept. '85, £450. A beautiful example.
5. *Centre: a good English poured wax baby doll with unusual small open-closed mouth, short hair inserted in slashes in the scalp, probably by Pierrotti.* 21 in. Sept. '85, £450. *On either side are typical and less good wax dolls of the mid-19th century in original dresses,* left, 30 in., right, 28 in. Sept. '85, £280 each.

5

Teddy Bears

As I pointed out in my Introduction in the *Popular Antiques Yearbook,* vol. 1 (p. 176), the teddy bear market really took off in the 1984/5 season, and by May '85 the record had reached £1,800 for a Steiff. A year or so later such a price seems to belong to a far-away age of innocence. By the beginning of June '86 the top auction price stood at £5,280, which was paid at a Sotheby's sale in Chester for a good, early Steiff in near mint condition. The buyer was an Englishwoman living in Germany who claimed that she was safeguarding 'the heritage of Europe' from transatlantic predators, and furthermore that the beast needed loving. One must hope that it will not now be loved until it is playworn to exhaustion!

Although the serious money seems only to be interested in early Steiffs (from 1903 to about 1910), recognized by their very long limbs, felt pads, boot-button eyes and humps, some of the bear enthusiasm has spilled over to lesser animals, and this was reflected in prices for unusual later bears throughout the year. As a result we decided to hold the first all teddy bear and soft toy sale in December '85.

The media picked up the story, and at 8.30 a.m. on the day of the sale the caretaker was disturbed by the television crews jockeying for position on the pavement. At 11 o'clock the auctioneer began the sale with nine international television cameras focused on him and a barrage of flashing bulbs from the world's press.

Condition is all important; although a little loving may add character, new pads, a worn tummy and embroidered eyes will inevitably detract from the price. Musical bears of the 1930s seem to have been very well made. One in pink plush and a nightcap, with a great deal of character, sold for £110. It still played a tune when pressed with the thumbs (No. 1). A probable Steiff with a clockwork key in the tummy and a metal rod at the back forming the tail and turning the head from side to side and up and down made £500, and another Steiff worked by clockwork fetched £220. Here the key was actually the arm, which when wound should have made him turn somersaults, but alas, it did not work (No. 1). A curiosity of the sale was

a little bear with a removable head which revealed a lipstick and with a powder compact in the tummy (No. 4).

It seems evident that the market in good quality bears is now firmly established, but lesser bears can still be bought at very reasonable prices.

Olivia Bristol

1. All Dec. '85. Left to right: *Nightcap bear,* £110; *standing unmarked but probably Steiff golden bear,* 10½ in., £550; *seated Steiff in good condition,* 12 in., £450; *unmarked Steiff dressing-gown bear,* £550; *large-eyed and pink padded bear in good condition,* cheap at £120; *somersaulting bear,* £220; *snooty musical bear,* £500; *early Steiff,* £450.

2. *Steiff hot water bottle bear.* 17 in. July '85, £1,100.

3. *Unmarked but probably Steiff bear, poor condition.* 21 in. May '85, £300.

4. All from Dec. '85. *Small toys from the 1930s,* left to right: *boy and girl bears in original clothes,* 7 in., £100; *Pip, Squeak and Wilfred, the 'Daily Mail' cartoon characters,* £100; *lipstick and compact bear,* 3½ in., £280; *bear in green bows,* £95; *pair of golden bears,* £50.

1

2

3

4

5. Another group from Dec. '85. Left: *portrait doll of the music hall artiste Lupino Lane, he of the 'Lambeth Walk', by Deans, £48; George Studdy's Bonzo in velvet, £55, mounted on a large Steiff cinnamon bear on wheels (growler not working), £170; bear in moth-eaten jersey, with embroidered claws and stiffened pads, £200; small bear, 'Bertie', c.1910, £190.*

5

Cloth Dolls

Although home-made cloth dolls have probably been made since children had leisure to play, few early ones remain because of the nature of textiles which rot easily, wear out or are eaten by mouse and moth. The dry Peruvian air preserved some 15th-century dolls, but apart from the fact that these are now faked extensively in South America, few doll collectors are interested in such ethnographica. 18th-century cloth dolls do exist but mainly in museums. 19th-century dolls on the other hand occasionally turn up at auction, mostly made at home, with well-embroidered features and usually in original clothes. Sometimes having been bought as souvenirs of foreign travels, they do not claim as much attention as their mass-produced sisters, although from a social history point of view they are often of far more interest. Some very fine black cloth dolls were made in the West Indies, with their skirts resting on layer upon layer of petticoats, with quantities of jewels – and they even have fingernails.

In 1910 a German artist named Käthe Krüse started making stuffed dolls with painted heads (No. 5). The bodies were well designed with joints at shoulder and hip, the original clothes often with parti-coloured knitted jackets and leg warmers. Her realistic baby, painted with eyes closed, was stuffed with sand so that it handled as the limp body of a newborn does. We sold a small Käthe Krüse baby for £1,400 in Jan. '86. Advertised in 1921 as 'Little Dangle Limbs', it was sold naked or in eight different outfits including that of a foundling. Unusually, it was modelled with an open mouth. Normally one would expect £400–£600 for a Käthe Krüse child in reasonable condition.

Another German doll maker whose products have shot up in price during the last year is Margaret Steiff. Known principally for her soft toys, especially teddy bears, she also made felt dolls, often caricatures of professions such as a sailor, or the policeman drawn by Beatrix Potter investigating the dolls' house after Hunka Munka and Tom Thumb had vandalized it in the *Tale of Two Bad Mice*. She also made child dolls, which have an enormous appeal despite the central seam down the face and the boot-button eyes. Like her other toys they have the Steiff metal button, sometimes removed for safety, but usually leaving two tiny holes in the left ear. We sold a girl doll in bad condition in September '85 for £200, while a good one made £700 at Sotheby's in February '86. Steiff's dolls do seem to be rarer than other makes, perhaps because they were made of felt rather than cotton cloth and are therefore susceptible to moth.

A later felt doll maker whose wares turn up far more frequently is Madame Scavini (Nos. 2 and 3). An Italian with great style, her dolls are characterized by their painted eyes glancing to the side, the mouths often with a slightly pouting, spoilt-child, expression, by the middle two fingers on each hand being joined and by highly elaborate, beautifully made, colourful felt clothes. Some of the lady dolls were also dressed in organdie, huge skirts with frills, but always with felt flowers, bows or other decoration, reminiscent of 1930s crinoline tea-cosy ladies. Christie's South Kensington have also sold a child doll of hers, dressed in a black skirt, and another as a boy from an alpine regiment with climbing ropes, boots and pitons. Her firm's name, Lenci, is found on the sole of the feet – irritating when you have to prize off tightly fitting socks and felt shoes to find it.

1

2

3

4

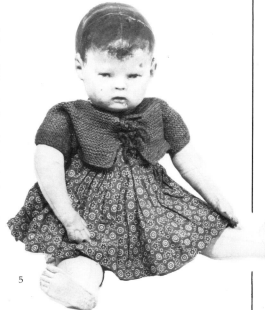

5

Perhaps the most prolific English cloth doll maker was Norah Wellings. Her sailor boys sold on board Cunard ships, and brown velvet Polynesians are the most common, but she also made girl dolls, two of which in original clothes, fetched £110 each in November '85. They were 21 and 22 in. high, and had elaborate felt clothes, one dressed for riding.

I feel that a new collector with modest means might do well to decide to specialize in cloth, starting with home-made dolls – invariably undervalued in my opinion – and seeking out good examples of the 1930s by Merrithought and other English makers (see No. 6).

Olivia Bristol

1. *A heavily oil-painted cloth doll by Martha Chase.* Apr. '86, £200. Chase was an American maker, and this doll was marked under the right arm.
2. *Three amusing painted felt dolls with Lenci-type eyes glancing to the side.* Jan. '86, £150, £130, £150.
3. *Three dolls probably by Lenci.* Jan. '86, £85, £85, £170. The smoker and the pierrot were in poor condition, and the young girl was marked on the feet, hence the price differential.
4. *A pair of dancing cloth dolls with floppy legs and feet and painted faces, in original clothes, by Deans Rag Book Co. Sold with a Japanese doll,* July '86, £12.
5. *Käthe Krüse cloth doll with painted hair and features, clothes not original.* July '85, £360. The typical rather sad look of Krüse.
6. *Four English cloth dolls.* Left: *Alpha Joy Dutch girl by J. K. Farnell & Co., with musical box in skirt.* July '85, £35. Standing behind: *Oxo advertising doll by Deans Rag Book Co.* July '85, £110. Sitting: *Deans composition doll in original Dutch clothes.* July '85, £40. Right: *Chad Valley Co. Ltd. felt-headed and velvet-bodied doll.* July '85, £70.

Lenci dolls turn up regularly on the market, and are in fact still in production. Easier to produce as they did not require the artistic talent of the totally oil-painted Käthe Krüse heads, they range in price from £85 to perhaps £400.

There were several firms making cloth dolls in England in the 1930s and before. Deans, known for their brightly printed rag books for babies, also made some amusing printed dolls. One of the First World War, produced for Boots and depicting a serviceman in convalescent blue uniform, with stick, sling and bandaged leg, sold in November '85 for £280. Another doll patented in 1917, of an 18 in. little girl with printed underclothes, fetched £55 in the same sale, and a later 'dancing' couple this time with 'real' clothes was sold together with a Japanese doll for £12 (No. 4).

Chad Valley, the huge toy conglomerate, engaged Mabel Lucie Attwell to design for them, and her bambina (influence of Lenci?) fetched £70 in April '86. The method of placing the eyes beneath the felt faces has worn badly over the years, as the felt has shrunk leaving the eyes below the surface of the face. Chad Valley also obtained permission from Walt Disney to produce Snow White and the Seven Dwarfs, a set of which fetched £260 in April '86.

6

14.   *Mechanical Music*

Introduction
by Christopher Proudfoot

1

The 1984–5 period covered by the first *Yearbook* saw a dramatic increase in the price of large disc musical boxes, especially the ever-popular Polyphon, playing 15¾ and 19⅝ in. discs. 1985–6 has had no comparable upsurge, but the Polyphons have stayed up there, and a 19⅝ in. upright model, without stand or pediment, reached £2,700 in June 1985. In September, a Polyphon mechanism, comprising motor, bedplate and combs, made £1,600. This seems expensive at first sight, but a case on its own is still around £100 (one sold for just that in December), so it may be cheaper to buy your Polyphon in bits. The equivalent Symphonion continues to trail behind the Polyphon, even though some collectors consider it musically superior and it is certainly less common. The only example sold at South Kensington in the year made £1,700 in September (No. 1), a whole £1,000 less than the June Polyphon.

The sale of a collection usually increases interest among buyers, even when that collection is unidentified or of mixed quality. There were two such collections in December 1985, while March 1986 was dominated by the collection of the late Roy Mickleburgh of Bristol. This was of very high quality, and included some considerable variety as well as a good cross-section of cylinder and disc musical boxes, with a notable shortage of the cheap, three-bell cylinder boxes which are so popular with the lay public (and hence with the dealers) and so despised by the serious collector. This is not to say that the Mickleburgh collection was for the serious collector only: its strength was in examples that were both interesting technically and appealing to the non-specialist. Impressive special effects such as Sublime Harmony, forte-piano and mandoline were to the fore.

These included the most valuable mandoline box seen at auction for many a year, for it had not one cylinder, but four, mounted on a rotating carriage so that any one could be brought into play by turning a large wheel at one end.

(No. 2). These 'revolver' boxes are very rare (they were expensive to make, and offered less scope for widening the choice of tunes than did boxes with interchangeable cylinders). It was difficult, therefore, to predict the final outcome, but the price of £9,000 indicates the level to which collectors will go for something that combines good quality with extreme rarity in a field where prices seldom exceed half that figure.

If the continuing trend with cylinder musical boxes has been for buyers to go for good examples needing no more than a routine overhaul, the year has seen one or two which made good money in spite of extensive (and expensive) repairs being required. In December, an interchangeable cylinder mandoline box by Nicole Frères brought £1,300, even though most of the treble teeth were missing. That someone was prepared to take on such a restoration project reflects the rarity of a mandoline box with 19½ in. interchangeable cylinders. Also, on a technical point, the treble teeth in a mandoline box are tuned in groups of the same note, so that tuning many adjacent new teeth is not as daunting as it might seem. In the same sale, £1,600 was found for a non-functioning overture box by Lecoultre & Falconnet, a rare make, and one of very fine quality (No. 3).

1. *Symphonion.* 19⅛ in. Sept. '85, £1,700.
   The diametrically opposed position of the two combs is characteristic of Symphonions, while on Polyphons the two combs are placed side-by-side. The 19⅝ in. Polyphon currently sells for around £2,500 in good condition, in spite of being more common.

2. *Rare mandoline harp Piccolo 'revolver' musical box with four cylinders.* Mar. '86, £9,000.

Although of good quality, this owed its high price to sheer mechanical rarity. The cylinders are 13 in. long, a very common size.

3. *Key-wind four-overture box by Lecoultre & Falconnet, No. 628.* Cylinder 10¾ in. long × 2½ in. diam. Dec. '85, £1,600.

This very plain looking example was not in working order, and the cylinder needed repinning, so why £1,600? The answer is that quality overture boxes are always good, and those by Falconnet, Reymond or either in partnership with another maker tend to be outstanding. The mahogany cross-banding on the case is a sign of quality—most cases of the period (1830–50) are even plainer.

4. *Mandoline Piccolo interchangeable cylinder musical box with four 13 in. cylinders.* Mar. '86, £1,500.

An interesting comparison with No. 2—musically very similar, but more conventional mechanically.

2

4

3

5. *Three-bell and drum musical box by B. H. Abrahams.* Mar. '86, £600.

With a cylinder only 6¼ in. long, playing eight tunes, this type of musical box was very down-market in its day, but its coloured butterfly bell strikers give it visual appeal and 'clean' examples like this always sell well.

6. *Sublime Harmony Piccolo musical box by G. Baker Troll & Co. with 17 in. cylinder.* Mar. '86, £1,600.

Another good quality 'special effect' musical box from the Mickleburgh collection. The Sublime Harmony is provided by the left-hand and centre combs, the Piccolo by that on the right.

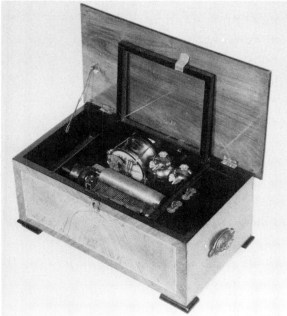

5

6

Gramophones — Visual Appeal beats Rarity

The past year has seen no remarkable developments in the gramophone and phonograph market, but a steady confirmation of existing trends. As in so many fields, it is not always the dedicated specialist collector who sets the price. Relatively common models with visual appeal can outpace rare versions, because there are more potential buyers with an eye for a 'lovely old antique' than there are rich collectors concerned about constructional niceties.

The most saleable gramophones include any open-horn model sold by the Gramophone Company (known as the Gramophone and Typewriter Ltd., 'G & T', 1900–7), later examples of which carry the famous HMV trade-mark. The remarkable fact about these is that they were at once the Rolls Royce and the Morris of the British market, outselling all their inferior contemporaries by a factor of perhaps six, judging by surviving examples. Quality usually tells, and these machines are consistently easier to sell today than other makes, with wooden horns particularly in demand. These are most often found on fairly late models of the 1910–14 period, although they were still available in the 1920s, and were also fitted to earlier models from 1908 onwards. Prices in the year have ranged from £480 to £850. Condition is the most important factor, rather than the individual model, of which there are several.

By contrast, one of the rarest G & T models of all appeared in the Mickleburgh Collection sale in March and made

1

2

only £450, reflecting the rather unattractive appearance of its long, plain brass horn and crude tone arm – the latter being the rare feature (No. 3). If rarity alone governed the price, the fact that a 1910 wood-horned version reached £800, might put this at about £3,000.

An even earlier rarity was an incomplete German Berliner toy gramophone of around 1890 (No. 5). At £480, this represented a satisfactory figure for its owner, who had found it in a rubbish skip – yes, it still happens. A slightly more common version of the same machine normally makes around £1,000 complete, and a particularly fine specimen topped the £2,000 mark some years back. Again, the commoner version happens to be visually better proportioned.

Another consistent seller is the HMV 'Lumiere Pleated Diaphragm' model of the mid 1920s. £400–£600 remains the price range, and brings a surprising number on to the market (No. 8). It was sold by HMV for only eighteen months or so, was an expensive addition to their range rather than a substitute for existing models, and again its handsome (and unusual) appearance is what appeals. Most of the contemporary HMV internal horn models can still be had for well under £100. Only the 're-entrant tone-chamber' cabinets of 1928–30 attract interest by their performance rather than their looks, and even the most common and smallest, the 163, this year topped £100. The 193/4 and 202/3 have long been

well into three figures on the rare occasions when they appear. Most other makes of cabinet gramophones will produce no more than a yawn from the seasoned collector, although always worth a few pounds to the constructor of bogus horn gramophones.

Christopher Proudfoot

1. *His Master's Voice 'Monarch' gramophone with oak horn, 1911 model.* Dec. '85, £850.
   This style of casework, with minimal carving and elaborately stepped plinth moulding, was introduced at the end of 1910 – it is found only in oak and commands similar prices to early more ornate Monarchs.

3

2. *Another example of the same model as No. 1.* Sept. '85, £480.

Also with the optional oak horn, which enhances the value. The soundbox is non-original, and the whole appearance is rather 'tired' – hence the lower price.

3. *'Monarch' Gramophone with rare 'sound arm' and brass horn, 1903.* Mar. '86, £450.

This untapered, not very strong form of tone arm was the first to carry the sound. Previous models, such as that in the HMV trademark had the horn connected directly to the soundbox. The sound arm was replaced after a matter of months by the tapered tone arm with 'goose-neck' and is very rarely found. That this ungainly rarity brought only £450 emphasizes the importance of visual appeal.

4. *'Victor' Gramophone, c.1905.* Mar. '86, £400.

The smallest and cheapest of all the tone-arm Gramophones. (Note the capital 'G' – it was still a trade name, and so displayed on the case of this model.) A consistent good seller in recent years, even with the plain black and brass horn as here. Visual appeal again.

5. *Berliner hand-driven gramophone by Kämmer & Rheinhardt, c.1890.* Sept. '85, £480. Lacking horn.

6. *Unnamed horn gramophone with brass flower horn, c.1912.* Sept. '85, £380.

Apart from its simpler tone arm, this machine bears a marked resemblance to the mahogany post-1910 Senior Monarch and is certainly of better quality than many anonymous gramophones. The price was still high, mainly because of the handsome brass horn.

7. *'Apollo' mahogany horn gramophone.* Mar. '86, £700.

A very high price for a non-HMV gramophone, but its crossbanded mahogany case was of exceptionally high quality, and was provided with a very unusual matching cover for the turntable. The petalled wood horn is often found on continental machines, and is distinct from the continuously laminated HMV variety.

8. *HMV model 460 table gramophone with Lumiere Pleated Diaphragm, 1924–5.* Mar. '86, £550.

One of the very few non-horn gramophones to make worthwhile money – consistently in the £400–£600 region, provided the diaphragm is not damaged.

9. *'Aeolian Vocalion' portable in hide case.* Dec. '85, £120.

This 'Aeolian Vocalion' is a rare model and a deluxe one, in its leather case. Most portables of this size in black cases are in the £10–£25 range.

10. Left to right: *'Bing Pigmyphone' tinplate toy gramophone,* £50; *unnamed German tinplate gramophone in tapered case,* £95; *'Bing Kiddyphone' in circular case,* £55. All Dec. '85.

11. *'Peter Pan' box camera portable.* Dec. '85, £85.

Strings, Pipes and Reeds

Self-playing pianos and organs form a small proportion of the mechanical musical instruments which appear at auction, but they do include a wide variety of different and often very collectable devices. Sizes range from the tiny 'singing bird' boxes (Nos. 1 and 2) to large orchestrion organs often exceeding 10 feet in height. The largest organ sold in the period under review was an Orchestrelle player reed organ, which brought £1,700 (No. 3).

Orchestrelles (the best-known make of reed organ operated by paper roll, and made at the same time as the Pianola piano) are very splendid instruments indeed in good playing order as this one was. They show how much better a reed organ can sound than the wheezy cottage and chapel organ which has given these instruments such a downmarket image. Different altogether is the authentic 18th-century sound of the chamber barrel organ (No. 6), while the sophisticated reproducing piano of the 1920s (ranging in price from about £50 for a basic upright in need of overhaul to £4,000 or so for a Steinway grand in working order) is a far cry from the street barrel piano of the early 19th century (No. 8).

The organette was a cheap and cheerful alternative to the musical box in the 1880s and 1890s, but a good one now is not so cheap (No. 5). Defective examples, however, are difficult to repair and often go for half the price (or less) of a good one.

1. *A gilt metal and enamel 'singing bird' box.* June '85, £750.
2. *A silver gilt 'singing bird' box, with hallmark for 1879.* June '85, £1,050.
   Nos. 1 and 2 were sold in the same sale; No. 2 obviously had the advantage of intrinsic value in its precious metal content, which also provided a firm date. No. 1 was probably rather later. Such singing bird boxes have continued to be made into modern times. Very early examples (mostly before about 1860) have fusee movements, detectable by a relatively thin winding arbor situated near one corner of the base. These do not need silver cases to reach four-figure prices.
3. *Aeolian Orchestrelle 58–note player-organ, 'Francis the First' model.* Dec. '85, £1,700.
   Like the 'Pianola' made by the same company, this is operated by perforated paper rolls and pedals. Non-working examples can often be bought for well under £1,000.

1

2

4. *Portable street barrel reed organ.* Sept. '85, £2,800.
   The true street organ, much louder-voiced than a chamber organ or an organette and often of continental origin. Pipe versions in similar cases are perhaps more common, but even more expensive.

5. *National Cabinetto 25-note organette.* Mar. '86, £400.
   Organettes represent the simplest form of automatic reed organ. The Cabinetto is one of the less common, and its 25-note compass is positively up-market compared with the 14 notes of many cheaper models. Like most American organettes, it has a walnut case decorated with gilt lettering and ornament.

6. *Sixteen-note chamber barrel organ by Muir, Wood & Co, Edinburgh, c.1800. 61 in.* Mar. '86, £2,400.
   The only form of mechanical music earlier than the musical box and still reasonably easy to obtain, English chamber (and church) barrel organs have at last moved up from a steady £800–£1,200 range to about twice that. This was a particularly good example, in good restored condition and complete with five barrels.

3

4

Price, however, does not always relate to size or sophistication. The portable street barrel piano is light and simple, and usually costs around £1,000. The player piano at £50 is heavy and large, but at least is a good piano which no musician need be ashamed of owning even if the player part is never used. True, one in really good working order (they seldom are) can go up to about £350, but even then they are not an attractive proposition for an auction house. The Steinway referred to earlier would be a 'reproducing' piano: more sophisticated still, operated by electricity, and able to play rolls 'recorded' by named, and often very famous pianists, reproducing their range of expression, touch and tempo. Even the most basic and common reproducing piano, in need of overhaul, a Steck upright Duo-Art for example, can bring £500–£700, and any Steinway is going to be in four figures. Piano rolls show a similar discrimination – ordinary ones around 20p each, Duo-Art around £4–£5 each, some other reproducing versions (e.g. Welte Mignon) even more.

Christopher Proudfoot

7. *Street barrel piano, late 19th century.* Mar. '86, £700.

Almost the size of a normal upright piano, and needing a cart to tour the streets, these are the street pianos often wrongly called 'barrel organs'. Their jangling sound is a standard film-maker's background noise for Victorian street scenes. Coin-operated versions, driven by a huge clockwork motor, were used in pubs, and bring similar prices.

8. *Another early (and indigenous) form of mechanical music, the Bristol portable street piano.* Mar. '86, £1,200.

Made in large numbers in the early 19th century by Hicks and others (this one was by W. Taylor), they are usually about 3 feet high and were carried strapped to the user's waist. The mechanism is exposed in this view, but is normally enclosed with a pleated silk panel in front of the strings.

6

7

8

Mechanical Music Miscellany

Shown on these pages is a selection of some of the more interesting items to come under the hammer in this field during the 1985–6 season.

Christopher Proudfoot

1. *Regency penwork sycamore tea caddy with musical movement in the base.* 12 in. wide. Mar. '86, £2,000.

Tea caddies have long been collected, and this was a particularly attractive one, but the musical movement itself (pictured right), very early and rare, made this quite exceptional.

2. *Amorette 16-note organette with dancing dolls in mirrored glazed compartments.* Mar. '86, £550.

Although not an immaculate example, this still managed a very respectable price for a 16-note organette, on account of the dancing dolls, which move on a wire stem as the handle is turned.

3. *'Improved Celestina' 20-note organette.* Mar. '86, £600.

The Celestina was one of the more sophisticated organettes (20 notes are always better than 14, of course), and £600 is at the top end of the auction price bracket for organettes.

4. *Fine automaton doll magician with Jumeau bisque head.* 24 in. Mar. '86, £3,000.

A particularly attractive automaton, with well-preserved clothes and unusual subject: the large nutshell in his left hand opens to reveal a small rodent (it isn't entirely clear whether it is a mouse or a rat!) chewing a turnip.

5

6

7

5. *Rocking ship, automaton in glass dome.*
   Mar. '86, £600.
   One of the most popular forms of late 19th century automaton, these all have a small musical movement concealed under the 'sea' (made of crumpled paper or cloth), which also makes the ship rock up and down and the sentry patrol the top of his tower. Water-wheels and windmills are also often included. £600 was an above average price: by contrast, the succeeding lot was almost identical, but with the painted glass dome broken, and it made only £140.

6. *Symphonion 'Eroica' musical longcase clock.*
   103 in. Mar. '86, £9,500.
   The Eroica is a triple disc musical box – three discs playing three sets of combs (in unison or harmony), driven by two motors. These superb-sounding instruments have long been highly regarded (with or without the added bonus of a clock), and £9,500 represented an increase that was perhaps overdue on the long established £5,000–£7,000 price range.

7. *Single comb Regina.* Dec. '85, £1,700.
   This uses the same discs as the Polyphon (see No. 9), but the Regina (an American-made version of the Polyphon) is highly regarded for its superior tone.

8. *Rare 24¾-inch table Polyphon.* Mar. '86, £6,500.
   The price here reflects both the rarity and the magnificent sound of this enormous table Polyphon. The casework is surprisingly utilitarian, compared to most smaller models (and the upright versions).

9. *19⅝-inch table Polyphon, double comb model.* Dec. '85, £1,800.
   Much prettier than No. 8, and also much more common – £1,800 is now a typical figure for examples in good condition. Single comb models, usually in much plainer walnut cases, are around a thousand pounds less.

10. *Rare Type N Graphophone.* Dec. '85, £200.
    One of the earliest home entertainment Graphophones, introduced in 1895, this is a classic example of rarity not necessarily relating to high value. An Edison model of the same era would certainly arouse more interest.

9

10

15.   Cameras and Photographic Equipment

Introduction
by David Allison

Well, what's happened since our last look at photographic equipment? Leicas stayed level, Rollei equipment is moving fast owing to a very active Society. Optical toys are selling briskly – a comprehensive Danish collection at South Kensington in December '85 attracting a lot of interest. Wood and brass maintain an even keel, and again stereo apparatus shines through. The backbone items remain static: Kodak folders, folding plate cameras, 35 mm single-lens reflex, range-finders, non-rangefinders, etc. The regular three-figure named cameras – such as Luzo; tropical: Soho, Tenax and Deck Rullo; Contax, Robot, Linhof, and a number of other technical type manufacturers – have taken a little dip in price, mainly because of the over-subscription of such items to the available collectors. The general mood, however, is as strong as ever, if not always totally evident in the saleroom. Club activity in the United Kingdom is strong – so again, if interested in the field, telephone the Photographic Collectors Club of Great Britain – or, better still, come and see us at our regular sales.

1. *'The Photographer's Studio', large oil on canvas study of the interior of an 1860s photographic studio. Dec. '85, £1,000.*
2. *A fine 3 × 4 cm. Nagel Rolloroy reflex camera, c.1932. Apr. '86, £380.*

2

Stereoscopes

1

2

3

As in most fields, we would have to look way back into the annals to explain the collector's excitement over 3-D viewers. Possibly the most exotic of all was seen at auction here in 1977 and at Sotheby's in 1986. The Hirst and Wood's 'Naturalist' had such refinements as interocular spacing, polarizing filters, superimposition facility, the possibility of viewing both cards and transparencies and, to boot, all contained in the most over-the-top Victorian design you are ever likely to come across (No. 2).

However, back to less heady levels – the most popular stereoscopes were those designed by Brewster, a truncated box-type viewer; and by Oliver Wendell Holmes, which has a viewing hood, folding handle and simple card holder, focusing up and down a central flat stick. Brewsters generally sell today around the £40–£50 mark for plain examples – look out for solid-back models made for viewing daguerreotypes and hence early (£100–£200). Any in a boxed set with cards and maker's labels, or those made from papier mâché, sell for £150–£300. Others mounted on pedestals sell anywhere from £100 to £1,000. The more elaborate the base, the higher the price. Holmes-patterns are still to be found around the £15 mark. In each case, however, any deviation from the norm will increase price.

Another fairly commonly seen stereoscope is the upright box-form table stereoscope, generally French, in plain mahogany, ebonized and veneered casings, and with a chain magazine for loading a multiple of cards or glass transparencies (No. 3). Good working examples should make £100–£150, more complicated designs with, say, double viewing facility, or tall floor-standing models £200 plus. Again, the more outrageous the design as a piece of furniture, the higher the price, as shown by a $1,500 bid for a floor-standing 1880s coin-in-slot model, sold at Christie's East, New York, in 1984.

The stereographoscope is often seen, consisting of a platter holding a magnifying lens and a pair of stereo lenses, normally folding on to a matching base when not in use. Prices range from £50–£100 for the common French ebonized models, to £100–£200 for the better quality mahogany English equivalents. Look out for brass strapping, card drawers in the base, candlelight illuminants for diapositives, etc. – all will up the estimate.

There are many specials around – too many to specify here. However, any stereoscope that differs from the standard should be of interest. Ones to note are the Ives' Kromscop colour stereoscope, which looks like a flight of stairs in profile – £700–£1,000, depending on the amount of accessories and slides (No. 1); Negretti & Zambra's 'Magic' pedestal viewer £600–£800, if complete with all its supplementary lenses; and the pièce de résistance, an original Wheatstone Stereoscope, developed prephotography by the inventor of stereoscopy, Sir Charles Wheatstone, worth several thousands if complete. If you have anything you think is unusual, always pop down to your local library or The Patents Office and check it out.

David Allison

1. *Ives' Kromscop stereoscope for viewing 3-D slides in colour, c.1910.* Apr. '85, £700. A good complete example with original Kromograms, viewing hood and instructions. Special-purpose stereoscopes are always well received.

2. *Hurst and Woods 'Naturalist' stereoscope, c.1865.* Sotheby's, June '86, £7,000. One of the most sophisticated – and certainly the most elegant – of all Victorian stereoscopes. This represents a sevenfold increase on the 1977 price!

3. *London Stereoscopic Company's burr walnut table stereoscope, 1860s.* May '84, £230. Typical of good quality British chain magazine-load stereoscopes. They are popular not only with photographic collectors and dealers, but also with interior decorators and furnishers.

Detective Cameras

1

With the advent of George Eastman's roll-film in the late 19th century, miniaturization became possible. Cameras disguised as pocket or wrist-watches, concealed behind cravats or shirts, in top hats, as binoculars, walking stick handles, handbags, in heels of shoes, cigarette lighters, etc., were made in vast quantities – the imagination of inventors was boundless. True detective cameras, however, were very ordinary by comparison – simple, box-form construction, taking a useful-sized plate for the best results, an imperative if the cops from the *Boys Own Paper* were to solve the crime.

Today, there is considerable interest in the novelty-type detectives, with prices well into three figures for the rarest. The 'Ticka Watch Pocket Camera' by George Houghton (or Expo in the States) is arguably the most common, and a standard model with box and bits will sell around the £80–£100 mark (No. 1). Actual watch face Tickas, silver-cased variants or ones fitted with a simple focal-plane shutter can make much more – £200–£500. The first watch camera, The American 'Photoret' (No. 2), is much in demand, over £350 with box, and any of the Japanese 20th-century wrist-watch versions will at least equal this price.

Bizarre is best, and C.P. Stirn's waistcoat camera is one of the wackiest! A flat plate-form camera taking four or six exposures on a circular plate, the Stirn's was designed to tuck underneath your shirt (No. 4). The small button-hole lens replacing a shirt stud was the only visible sign. Look for maker's box, samples of pictures, original negatives, etc., as all will inflate the price. Six years ago, a Stirn's with box and instructions sold for £950. A similar cravat camera of oblong form is rarer – one recently being offered in the trade for a reported $3,000.

Another amusing model is the Watson's 'Detective Binocular', taking stereo pictures. To all intents the user would appear to be regarding some far-off sight, whereas in truth he is looking through a 90° viewfinder, and is more likely to be cuing up a shot of an adjacent bathing belle.

Certainly, the most sought after detectives are those designed as or hidden in items of clothing or personal apparel, such as hats, cravats, handbags, walking sticks, shoes or wherever else one might suitably conceal a camera! The Ben Akiba walking stick handle camera, for example, last sold at South Kensington for £3,400. Watch out for mock-ups and fakes – there are plenty about!

David Allison

2

1. *A Houghton's Ticka watch pocket camera,* c.1905. Sept. '85, £60.
   In the US 'The Expo'. Most popular of all the novelty-type watch cameras

2. *A rare Magic Introduction Co. Photoret magazine snap shot watch camera.* Feb. '85, £350.
   The first wholly American watch camera designed by W.K.L. Dickson and patented in 1893 by Herman Casler. If complete with maker's box, price can be higher.

3. *A quarter-plate Lancaster's Rover detective camera in leather 'luggage' style case, 1890s.* Apr. '86, £220.
   More typical of the true detective cameras, this model is more valuable than most of this type owing to its rarity.

4. *A Stirn's Waistcoat detective camera, c.1890s.* Sept. '85, £480.
   Designed to slip inside the waistcoat, a good example of an unusual concealed camera.

4

Cinematographic Equipment

A good proportion of it is of fairly small auction value as yet, but as a tip, get collecting! There is still a wealth of both apparatus and film to be found and as the dreaded video permeates our very being, I feel sure the rather antiquated film medium will become highly treasured for its true and yet abstract documentation of our world, and beyond.

On collecting film stock – be careful! The earliest, and therefore historically most important, can often be shot on highly inflammable cellulose–nitrate stock. In the early 1900s, Kodak introduced 35 mm Safety Film which saved many a projectionist from a trip to the local burns unit. Also copyright is an important thing to check as it doesn't pay to have Warner Bros. breathing down your neck because you've innocently found an original print of *'Gone with the Wind'*.

Pathéscope, the French firm, pioneered the home movie notion with their now defunct 9.5mm central sprocket system. A 1930s Pathé film catalogue will list many of the great feature films of the day, and today you can buy a few Chaplin classics on four reels, and a projector to screen them, for no more than the cost of seeing them at the local flea pit. Don't ignore some of the amateur stock as well; some of the best social documentary material of the interwar years is to be found on 9.5.

On the camera side, the highest prices are paid for the cumbersome wood and machined metal, hand-cranked pioneer monsters made in Britain and France by firms such as Prestwich, Newman & Sinclair, Williamsons, De Brie, Eclair and, of course, Pathé. A fine Prestwich Model 4, mahogany-cased, 35 mm cinematograph sold in February '86 for £850, and a Williamson's 'Kinematograph' made £240 in January. As developments happened almost weekly in the early days, many cameras of the period were modified; unless the reason for doing so is interesting, steer clear, as prices for lash-ups are generally low. Provenance can be very important – a Movietone News Wall Camera, known to have poked through the tent flap to record the signing of the German surrender at Lüneburg Heath in 1945, sold for £3,400 in 1980.

Projectors are generally less desirable owing to the unwieldy scale of the early Bioscope versions. They generally work out a £1-a-cwt., so unless you are contemplating the rebirth of the drive-in movie or you reside at the World Trade Centre, it is an area to avoid. There are a few exceptions among the pioneer models of the first ten years or so, especially the Lumière Bros. Cinématographe camera/projector, one of which sold for £3,000 in January '83; see also Nos. 1 and 3.

David Allison

1. *A 17.5 mm Biokam Cinematograph camera/ projector by Alfred Darling, Brighton, c.1910.* Apr. '86, £1,200.

    An extremely complete example with maker's box. The unusual film gauge also makes this a rare and desirable camera for collectors.

2. *'Monsieur Félicien Trewey', oil on canvas, portrait by Pierre Tossyn, c.1910.* Dec. '85, £900.

    Trewey was an important London-based pioneer in the early film world. The new Museum of the Moving Image in London bought this. Also early catalogues, books, illustrations and plans, etc. are much sought after.

3. *An early Cibis 35 mm cinematograph projector, c.1910.* Dec. '85, £750.

    Rare, more attractive and importantly less bulky than the standard Bioscope projectors of the period, hence the higher price.

Lantern Equipment

Certainly a field in the limelight at the moment! Indeed limelights themselves (gas-powered illuminants using the fluorescent properties of heated lime-stone, first used in magic lanterns) are attracting interest as a specific area of collecting.

Popularized during the last half of the 19th century with the aid of photo slides, the lantern lecture became a staple form of education and amusement during the Victorian era. The projected image, however, goes back to the 18th and 17th centuries, with itinerant lanternists giving shows using candle-illuminated projectors and hand-painted glass slides. Today any ephemera or actual items from this period are much sought after – a framed 18th-century engraving, *Korbenhaus Schilderie*, showing a lanternist at work, selling for £320 in December '85.

The lanterns themselves are of a graduated value depending on period and purpose. Early (late 18th-century) candle-powered lanterns with a handle and fluted chimney should sell for between £80 and £120. These are generally fairly small and of French manufacture, and some are elaborately enamelled and decorated, such as the Lapierre Lampascope sold in December '85 for £150. Towards the mid-19th century, the quality London instrument makers like Ross, Stewart and Newton started to supply the universities and schools with precision-made mahogany and metal projectors for use with the newly available glass photographic positive slides. Condition and level of sophistication are the key markers for value here. A standard mahogany, brass and iron lantern should make around £80–£120 if complete with illuminant and chimney.

However, prices soar for specials, especially for those developed for phantasmagorical effects such as superimposition, fading, microprojection – see No. 1. In February '86, a pair of dissolving view lanterns by toymaker George Carette & Co. made £600. Toy lanterns especially if complete with accessories and maker's box, are making good headway in terms of price. The later standard tinplate and brass lanterns, however, still seem fixed below the £30–£40 mark.

1   2   3

Well, I've got the lantern – what do I project? There are literally thousands of standard 3¼ × 3¼ inch monochrome and colour glass slides to be had, covering all aspects from the humorous to sombre war reportage. I can remember once selling a collection of some 10,000 with lecture notes and a lantern for £85, which gives some idea of the individual value of the common lantern slide. However, don't dismiss looking through a box here and there. Often things sell well because of subject – a set of 24 ballooning slides sold in an aeronautical sale for £150 in January '86.

In photographic sales, the wood-mounted slides seem most popular, especially hand-cranked mechanical versions; in February '86, a Wheel-of-Life-style Zoetrope cord and pulley slide sold for £400. Away from hand-cranked items, there are wood-mounted semi-rotaries at £5–£10 apiece, slipper slides at £5–£10, strip or panoramic slides showing a sequence of story events at £40–£50 for a good set of 10 or 12, and combination slides using devices from all separate types – a hand-cranked set with slipper action by Newton, of a mouse running into a moving man's mouth, sold with a cord and pulley in February '86 for £80.
David Allison

1. *A triple lantern with accessories, c.1870.* Feb. '85, £2,400.

   Nos. 1 and 2 were both made for special effects work including superimposing and colour anaglyph shows. The triple being more complicated and expensive in its day, is simply much more rare than its bi-unial counterpart today.

2. *A bi-unial magic lantern, c.1880.* Feb. '85, £400.

3. *A London Stereoscopic Company's 'Wheel of Life' lantern slide with spare disc, c.1870.* July '83, £480.

   Important because of its pre-cinema links, the idea based loosely on the Zoetrope optical toy with individually painted figures animated using a hand-cranked shutter mechanism.

4. *A Hughes patent automatic lantern slide changer/fader device, c.1880.* Jan. '85, £240.

   Special accessories for lanterns often sell beyond intrinsic value owing to their rarity and historical importance relative to later cinema developments.

Cameras

Here we show a selection of cameras and make comparisons between the prices.

1. *A 4.5 × 6 cm Thornton-Pickard F2 Ruby Speed camera, c.1935. Jul. '85, £2,000.*

2. *A 4.5 × 6 cm Ernemann Ermanox focal-plane camera, early 1930s. Aug. '83, £380.*
   Virtually identical cameras. Strangely, No. 2 is historically more important, being the first developed (i.e. No. 1 is a copy). However, No. 1, the British model, is much more rare than its German counterpart (No. 2).

3. *A Dandycam Automatic (daylight loading) ferrotype box camera, c.1900. Apr. '86, £140.*

4. *The Kodak factory-load box camera, c.1885. Apr. '86, £1,400.*

5. *A Kodak No. 1 factory-load box camera. Apr. '86, £200.*
   In their day, three relatively inexpensive box cameras. No. 3 is interesting as an unusual small box camera for taking tin-type metal photos. Nos. 4 & 5 were the first Kodak cameras, and although very similar, No. 4 is always more expensive as the very first, with rotating cylindrical shutter as opposed to sector-types (No. 5).

6. *An Ensign Tropical model focal-plane roll-film reflex camera, c.1915. Apr. '86, £280.*

7. *A 2¼ × 3¼ in. Marion's tropical Soho reflex camera, c.1920. Apr. '86, £1,300.*

8. *A 9 × 12 cm Goerz Tenax tropical folding-plate camera, c.1920. Apr. '86, £280.*
   If Nos. 6, 7 & 8 were the standard black leather versions instead of being made of metal-reinforced teak, the prices would be a fraction of those recorded above. The price variations are due to the availability of each particular model.

9. *A 45 × 107 mm Houghton's Royal Mail Stereolette camera, c.1910. Jul. '85, £550.*

10. *A 45 × 107 mm Ernemann Reflex Jumelle-style stereoscopic camera, c.1925. Jul. '85, £190.*
    Similar format cameras. No. 9 is a rare derivative of the popular Royal Mail multiple lens postage stamp cameras, and No. 10 had an added reflex facility, hence the prices are higher as they appeal to more than once collecting brief.

1

2

3

4

5

7

8

9

10

16. *Scientific Instruments*

Introduction
by Jeremy P. Collins

It is true to say that collecting scientific instruments is still in its infancy. As is well known, there have been major collections in the past, many of which have been passed on to our museums and other institutions, but these collections were formed by scientific men whose primary interest lay in the development of instruments for the furtherance of scientific research.

The 20th-century collector, however, is altogether a different breed of animal. At last the history and development of science has new champions who collect instruments not only for their functional purpose but also for the beauty of design and construction and meticulous craftsmanship. These collectors now seek out in the auction rooms and dealers' shops those craftsman-made instruments which fit in with the other art disciplines of their age, and whose construction in many cases follows the design and decoration of their contemporaneous buildings, furniture and fashion.

One only needs to look closely at many instruments to recognize many period features. For instance, a microscope may have a stand featuring Ionic or Corinthian columns; a sundial might have as its border 'wheat-ear' decoration; the flowering of rococo decoration is copied on fine German instruments, making them not only functional but also works of art; and last but not least, the instrument cases often follow the cabinet-making practices of the country of origin.

The last twelve months have seen a steady growth in the new, or perhaps revived, interest in scientific instruments. The large Arthur Frank collection has now been sold and thus dispersed, but more remarkable has been the discovery and subsequent sale of the remnants of a true collector's cabinet of 18th-century origins, which, perhaps for the first time in half a century, released a splendid array of rare instruments by the great Augsburg maker, Georg Friedrich

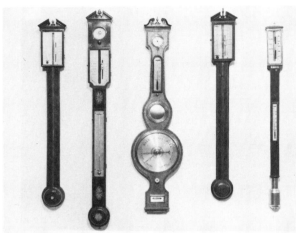

Brander, on to the market. This collection, now known as the 'Zallinger Cabinet', is discussed on pages 184 and 185.

Trends over the last twelve months have indicated, as in other collectors' fields, a healthy demand for quality, originality and condition. As one would expect, some areas have suffered as a result, with generally falling prices. Medical instruments are an example, but in other areas, such as barometers, prices have jumped by as much as 50% and sometimes more. Other groups of instruments—for example philosophical, electrical and those concerned with geophysics and geomagnetism—have remained most unpredictable.

The field is thus wide open: there are plenty of good instruments available, and the person of modest means can easily build up a good collection. The primary requirements are time and patience. Bonne chance!

Left to right: *19th-century stick barometer by P. Orteli; unusual 19th-century stick barometer by John Hilliard; fine bird's-eye maple banjo barometer by John Chatta; 19th-century mahogany stick barometer by N. Orteli; unsigned late 19th-century ship's barometer, restored, but with accessories.* Apr. '86, £300; £1,600; £480; £480; £800.

The Hilliard is in a boxwood and ebony strung case and includes a long thermometer and a hygrometer. Although bird's-eye maple was much used for picture frames and tea caddies, it is unusual on barometers. The Ortelis, like Chatta, were British makers, despite their names.

The market in barometers has shown a slow but steady increase over the last year, with renewed interest from both dealers and collectors.

Trade Labels and their Importance

Collectors of scientific instruments can be fortunate, as a surprising number of instruments survive in their original cases complete with the maker's or supplier's trade label or card. The presence of a label without doubt makes an instrument more interesting, and a premium of perhaps up to 20% over and above the normal market price will be paid by keen collectors. These labels are significant as they provide information about the manufacturer's range of goods supplied (No. 1) as well as his terms of trade, and, not least, they give the modern collector some idea of the date which can be applied to the instrument in question (No. 2). Many labels are aesthetically pleasing works of art in their own right, with written and pictorial content finely engraved and often within an elaborate rococo border.

Until about 1760, business addresses in London and elsewhere were normally given by reference to the sign which hung over the premises, with further reference perhaps to a street or an inn. The street numbering system was then introduced but it took many years to complete, and labels and cards can often be found incorporating mixed addresses or alternatively a pictorial representation of the shop sign as well as the new address (No. 3).

Trade labels were 'portable advertisements' and were sometimes used as bills or even contained instructions for the use of an instrument. Styles of printing and changes in artwork assist in dating a label and its attendant instrument. Most manufacturers were loath to fall behind in fashion, and labels tended to keep pace with current trends, much as modern packing and advertising ephemera do.

Not all labels gave a true representation of the instrument, the artist being given, it seems, plenty of licence to distort the image so that the prospective purchaser would be able to see quite plainly the range of goods offered (No. 4). In more modern times it became fashionable to proclaim one's success by the use of labels or cards to advertise awards and to depict extensive manufacturing premises.

Care of trade labels is most important, as they make the history of the instrument more complete. They should not

1

be removed from the cases, unless, due to the ravages of time, they can be better preserved elsewhere. In any event, a record must be made and kept with the instrument. Incidentally, everything said here applies equally to all the other antiques that may carry labels — from fans to violins and even the frames of paintings.

Jeremy P. Collins

1. Fine label for John B. Dancer, showing the extensive range of instruments retailed by this provincial instrument maker—note terms of sale— 'Cash on delivery'!

2. A dated label (1856) of the eminent makers W. & S. Jones—note the address giving street number as well as location, 'Furnivals Inn'.

3. Young & Son's label, which as well as giving the address, has a pictorial representation of the maker's street sign of the 'Hand & Scales', which pre-dated the street numbering system.

4. Isaac Bradford—a fine maker. Note the text '. . . most Accurate Manner . . . Best & Latest Improvements & Inventions . . . Most Moderate Terms . . .'

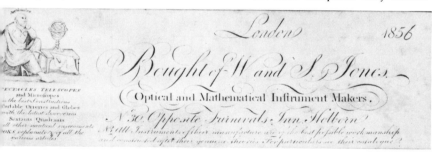

Fakes, Forgeries and Marriages

It is a fact that certainly since the middle of the 18th century scientific instruments, like many other art subjects, have suffered at the hands of the faker, forger, copyist and lately the commercial manufacturer of reproductions (Nos. 1 & 2). By the latter half of the 18th century there was a sufficient market for craftsmen to fake earlier instruments, such as astrolabes or complex sundials, so as to capitalize on the growing fashion for collecting early scientific apparatus. Even today, many scholars and museum curators are concerned that earlier, or even near-contemporary, attributions are false. The current wave of interest in the history of science, allied to the latest developments in metallic research, has led many museums and collectors to examine closely and reappraise the instruments in their care.

All is not necessarily, therefore, what it seems. A few years ago, a number of magnificiently made and mathematically correct instruments – astrolabes, dials and surveying items – appeared on the market. As instruments in their own right, they were quite excellent, but their maker made one mistake and that was to counterfeit signatures. This error was to cost him dearly and land him in gaol. Only three or four years ago a number of fake Adams and Dollond library telescopes began appearing at country auctions. The less experienced eye missed the false ageing of the brass, the plastic lenses and incorrect screws, and many were sold before the faker was apprehended.

Over the years many instruments have lost various component parts, and have at a later date acquired replacement parts, often from other genuine instruments. These replacements are generally easy to recognize. Look for different colouring of brass, the use of a variety of 'knurling' on adjustment wheels, different screw threads and crude soldered or brazed joints. Marriages become fairly easy to identify. Not necessarily evil, they should, if possible, be avoided – the purist collector will always reject them.

Of marriages, surely none is more obvious than the gilt-brass polyhedral sun dial table lamp (No. 4). Fate shone unkindly on this superbly engraved instrument, as at some time in its life an uncaring infidel cut off the silver pin gnomons, gouged out the compass, drilled through the dial and mounted it on a late 19th-century fake Louis XVI ormolu column with calcite base, before adapting it for electricity and fitting a plastic wave-form lampshade with lace decoration. Surely the final indignity! This fine dial was fully restorable and sold for £22,000 at auction.

Jeremy P. Collins

1. *An amusing mid-1930s cube dial after an antique original.* Apr. '86, £140.
2. *A good reproduction Wimshurst electrostatic friction machine.* Apr. '86, £250.
3. *Front and back of a 19th-century copy of a 17th-century calendar dial.* Jul. '85, £221. This is not a fake, more a tourist trifle.
4. *Gilt brass polyhedral sundial by Michael Coignet, Antwerp, c.1590. Lampshade and alterations by a 20th-century barbarian!*

1

2

3

4

Laboratory Apparatus

As interest in the more popular areas of scientific instrument collecting grows, and as fine examples of certain types of microscopes or surveying items become more difficult to obtain, collectors have begun to look at the largely neglected area of laboratory apparatus. Most scientific instrument sales contain sections under the more general title of 'miscellaneous and philosophical instruments', and it is in these sections that many weird and truly fascinating items can be found.

Thinking back to our school days and lessons in the 'lab' reminds us of all the wonderful demonstration and analysis apparatus with names such as Dr Haldane, Berzelius, Bunsen, Lewkowitsch, Geissler and Wimshurst attached to it. Sadly, owing to lack of space, general ignorance and little interest, many fine instruments from laboratories all over Great Britain have been consigned to the scrapman. Those that remain are often in poor condition, but some remarkable survivors exist and are eagerly competed for when they appear in the auction rooms.

The scope for the collector in this area is almost limitless, and many items are still to be had for the proverbial song. Items such as polarimeters (for reading sugar percentages and designed for breweries and general chemical laboratory work), flash-point apparatus (for 'close test' determinations), hydrometers, gas analysis apparatus and spectroscopes remain inexpensive. However, more decorative instruments and those more easily understood such as electrostatic induction machines (No. 1), gyroscopes (No. 2) and dip-circles (No. 3), remain popular and can be expensive.

Among the more fascinating objects are the Geissler tubes: vacuum tubes in a variety of shapes and sizes for showing the brilliant effects produced by electric current in vacuo. With the use of an induction coil (No. 5) and battery, these tubes can be made to illuminate and will provide endless entertainment for the family! Other tubes, used for light experiments, can be similarly used to demonstrate shadows, mechanical action (No. 4), conductivity of heat and the properties of phosphorescence.

Pneumatics is another area where the collector can at the same time entertain and instruct his family, by using the air pump to demonstrate that air is essential to sound, and to perform innumerable other experiments. It is perhaps in this area of science that most fun can be had – the instruments may be used and will not lie dormant, lifeless and just gathering dust!   *Jeremy P. Collins.*

1. *Wimshurst electrostatic induction machine, on mahogany stand.* 21½ in. wide. Apr. '86, £250.
2. *Lacquered brass gyroscope by Newton & Co., Opticians and Globe Makers to the Queen, London, 19th century.* 9½ in. wide. Oct. '85, £420.
   This handsome object came with two weights and other accessories in the original pine case.
3. *Lacquered brass dip-circle, unsigned.* 3¾ in. diam. Apr. '86, £340.
4. *'Railway Tube', on oak base,* 10⅞ in. Oct. '85, £110.
   This rare instrument was devised to demonstrate the strong action of radiant matter.
5. *An 18½ in. induction coil by Philip Harris Ltd., on mahogany base.* Oct. '85, £130.

1

2

4

5

Medical Apparatus

Science and medicine are natural partners, and many disciplines of the former develop with the latter. Thus it is that medical items are so often included in the sales of scientific instruments.

The choppy seas of collecting and fashion have been cruel to the collector of medical items over the past year. Cruel, that is, if the collector is an 'investment' type, but a joy for the serious collector. Why so? Prices have dropped in the sale rooms and also in dealers' premises. It is just this movement of value that makes a nonsense of certain types of price guide for antiques. To illustrate the point, phrenology heads by L.N. Fowler (No. 1) have dipped from a mighty £900–£1,200 in 1984/5 to a lowly £350–£500 in early 1986. Domestic medicine chests have also dipped, except, that is, for the finest quality examples (No. 2) which continue to do well.

It seems that interest in homeopathy is also on the wane, in sharp contrast to items of more esoteric interest such as the amusing ivory cuff-links (No. 3), which sold for a rousing £400 in October 1985.

Like many areas of collecting interest, medical items offer an incredible variety, from surgical, optical and dental through obstetrics to the more decorative world of specie jars, leech pots and other porcelain and glass items. Currently there is a great interest in ophthalmic items. Spectacles particularly have caught the imagination of collectors and dealers, with auction prices reaching dizzy heights. To reach these prices and beyond, the spectacles must be in fine condition and complete with original cases.

Other interesting areas for collecting include razors. Many 18th-century cut-throat examples are shielded by exquisitely carved tortoiseshell guards, while the 'Monday-Sunday' sets in fitted cases are ever popular but remain cheap at say £30–£50 a set.

Small silver items of medical interest offer wide scope for collecting, but prices can be erratic, so be cautious when buying and remember to view all sales if you can. The major auction houses all now produce worthwhile catalogues, some with learned notes, and most of these catalogues are profusely illustrated to support the descriptions of each lot.

Teaching aids have always had their loyal following, and most sales include the odd rather gruesome reminder of medical school! Illustrated here (No. 4) is one of a pair of plaster relief anatomical models of the head, which realized £460 in December 1985. Models of this type can also be found in wax or even carved wood, and will, of course, make an interesting if rather macabre diplay!

Jeremy P. Collins

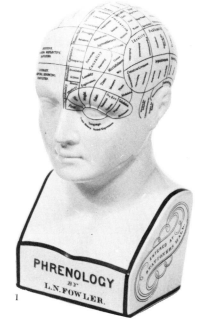

1

1. *Phrenology head by L.N. Fowler.* Oct. '85, £450.
   Two years ago this might have made £1,000.
2. *Early 19th-century domestic medical chest.* Oct. '85, £850.
   Here the fine original labels made the difference, boosting the price from around £500.
3. *A pair of 19th-century ivory cuff-links showing one of the less comfortable aspects of domestic bliss.* Jul. '85, £400.
4. *Two plaster relief anatomical models of the head, 19th century.* Dec. '85, £460.

2

3

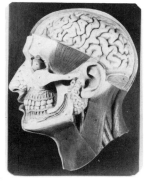

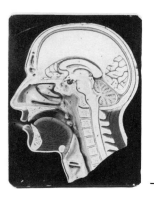

4

A Diversity of Creations

1

2

3

The diversity of items that appear under the label of Scientific Instruments is truly remarkable. The history of science has in itself led to this diversity. Some, indeed most, of the items that are included in saleroom catalogues are familiar to collectors and dealers. However, over the last year a few 'oddballs' – curiosities and rarities to many people – have appeared in these catalogues, as well as some other items which are not only unusual but perhaps not previously considered or understood. *Jeremy P. Collins*

1. *Second World War German prismatic binocular periscope by Carl Zeiss. Oct. '85, £900.*

2. *An ivory seal top carved in the form of a skull with serpents; and porcelain seal top in the form of a phrenological head. Apr. '86, £290 and £320.*

3. *A late-19th-century German astronomical planisphere. Dec. '85, £420.*

4. *A good bronze figure of a scientist with his electro-magnetic induction machine. Dec. '85, £1,100.*

5. *Gentleman's steel razor by W. Hides, with carved and pressed horn guards, with original case. Apr. '86, £75.*

4

5

The Zallinger Cabinet

As mentioned in the Introduction to this section, a most remarkable collection of instruments and their associated books came to light during the closing weeks of 1985, and was dispersed in a sale at Christie's South Kensington on 17 April 1986.

Little is known of the collector Josef Peter von Zallinger (1730–1805). All records of his considerable contribution to surveying and science seem to have passed into oblivion, with the exception of a small, privately printed part-biography, which gives us part of the following:

The Zallinger family were first recorded in Augsburg in the 13th century. Josef Peter studied philosophy at the University of Innsbruck, where he concentrated on mathematics and physics. He later became renowned as an architect and engineer in the Tyrol, being responsible for the building of bridges and for various drainage schemes which transformed high-lying valleys and bogs into valuable agricultural land. He was reputedly the first to fit lightning conductors to the church towers of the Tyrol.

The majority of Zallinger's instruments were ordered directly from the eminent Augsburg maker, Georg Friedrich Brander (1713–83), while others came from the illustrious workshops of English makers such as Dollond, Glynne and Ramsden. Zallinger was also prolific in the construction of instruments to his own design (Nos. 1 & 2), using component parts and material from other instruments which were either surplus to requirements of just plain out-of-date. He had a particular fascination with electricity, and proof of this can be found by reference to the many books on this subject that he left at his death. He is known to have made use of electrophors to aid his experiments with lightning conductors. Like his contemporary, Martinus van Marum from Haarlem, he often gave demonstrations of his experiments and willingly lent his instruments to doctors in the pursuit of medical science. He is noted as having a valuable concave mirror with which magical views could be projected. A surviving gold leaf parabolic reflector (No. 3) was included in the Christie's sale.

Brander was a curious maker. His instruments were often to be found wanting in sophistication and have been described as being perhaps fifty years behind the products of the English and Dutch makers of the time. However, no one can doubt their excellence, and the high prices paid for surviving examples illustrate the point. Superbly engraved and ingenious in design and construction, Brander's instruments obviously found favour with Zallinger, whose collection certainly numbered more than 135 items—his highest recorded inventory number. Fortune smiled on the history of science in that Zallinger was keen to record his possessions, and attached neat little labels to many instruments.

It is fruitless to speculate what the Zallinger Cabinet must have contained at its zenith. It is known, however, that many valuable and possibly unique instruments were consigned to scrap after the Second World War, in the same way that hundreds of fine vehicles and aircraft, which would now cost a king's ransom, were scrapped. One must remember that there was scant interest in such items at the time, and they were considered of little value.

The Zallinger Cabinet as it survived

caused a stir in the world of scientific instrument collectors. Brander instruments are scarce at the best of times; the largest extant group is at the Deutsches Museum, Munich, and the majority of instruments held there came from the Bayrische Akademie der Wissenschaften, which received them from the scientific cabinets of various monasteries following their secularization in 1803. That was two years before Zallinger's death, when his collection was valued at 5,000 fl., a large sum of money by any account. The Cabinet was much admired at the time, and was said to be comparable with those of the various monasteries and leading universities of the time.

In some ways, the most exciting part of the collection was the individual leather etuis, or cases, lined with chamois leather and superbly tooled in gilt. Other instrument cases made of Augsburg marbled paper, brilliantly coloured caused abnormal interest. The Cabinet with its associated books represented a valuable insight into scientific endeavour in the second half of the 18th century, nothing equal is likely to be seen again. Despite depletion, the collection offered for auction in seventy-four lots realized a total of £114,000.   *Jeremy P. Collins*

1. *Brass heliochronometer on wood box base,* c. 1700. Apr. '86, £2,400.

2. *(opposite below) Brass sundial, on walnut block base, mid-18th-century.* Apr. '86, £700.

3. *(opposite below) Parabolic reflector, attributed to the Brander workshop.* Apr. '86, £2,400.

1

The Man and His Instruments

The portrait of Zallinger was not included in the sale of his collection on 17 April 1986. All the following, with the exception of 11, 12, 14 and 16 are by Brander or his workshop.

1. *The chamois lined and gold tooled leather case for No. 7.*
2. *Lacquered brass distance measuring instrument with fruitwood case, £1,700.*
3. *Satin birch and brass trigonometer with fruitwood case, £6,000.*
4. *Brass reflecting telescope with walnut case, £2,600.*
5. *Mahogany distance meter incorporating a micrometer, £8,000.*
6. *Boxwood sector with varnished paper scales (sold with boxwood scale rule) £1,700.*
7. *Part theodolite in mahogany and brass, with the case shown as No. 1, £7,000.*
8. *Hydrostatic float and wooden case, £380.*
9. *Triple leaf steel horseshoe magnet – similar to the one used by Zallinger to remove a large nail from the nose of a child, £550.*
10. *Conical glass prism with card box (sold with two brass optical toys) £360.*
11. *Early 18th-century lacquered brass compound monocular and simple microscope compendium, £5,500.*
12. *Brass universal equinoctial ring dial by R. Glynne, London with leather covered case, £2,600.*
13. *Brass hygrometer, £240.*
14. *Late 18th-century lacquered brass miniature refracting telescope by Dollond, London, on folding stand, with fishskin covered case, £1,400.*
15. *Surveyor's lacquered brass level with green gilt tooled leather case, £1,400.*
16. *Planispheric astrolabe, probably German, c.1600, £13,000.*
17. *Set of five walnut and lacquered brass scale rules with gilt tooled leather case, £1,000.*
18. *Small brass sextant with leather case, £2,000.*

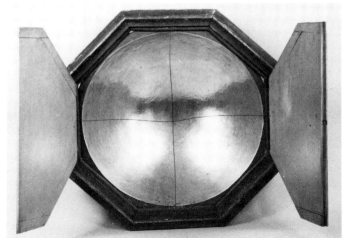

2

3

17. Tools and Machines

Introduction
by Christopher Proudfoot

'Tools, Scientific and other Apparatus' is a title seen four times a year now at South Kensington, and it may seem tantalizingly vague. Tools are obvious enough, and so are scientific instruments, although they cover a wide range of applications, but almost anything could (and often does) come under the third category.

Most obviously it covers 'Domestic and Office Machines' (see opposite page), a long-established, if commercially somewhat minor, collecting subject, which consists mainly of sewing-machines and typewriters. These are both products of 19th-century inventiveness, particularly of American origin; both are commonplace objects, of which only the rarer types are of any interest to collectors; and many collectors of one are also interested in the other. The Grover & Baker machine illustrated opposite indicates by its price that interest in sewing-machines is still growing, and the tendency seems to be for their prices to catch up with those of typewriters. Many typewriters have been static in price for some time (the Lambert, for example, has long been around £300 in good condition), and average examples of common collectable models like the Hammond and the Blickensderfer have tended actually to go down in price of late.

This is a familiar pattern in the development of price levels: a new subject comes into vogue, competing collectors push the value of a given item up until they all possess an example, and the price sticks there and moves no further for a time. The increasing number of collectors often seems not to match the increase in the number of available examples. (Incidentally, there is a common misconception that antiques are getting rarer all the time; they are not, in fact as more come out of captivity in attics and cellars, the number in circulation among collectors and dealers specializing in a given subject can only increase.)

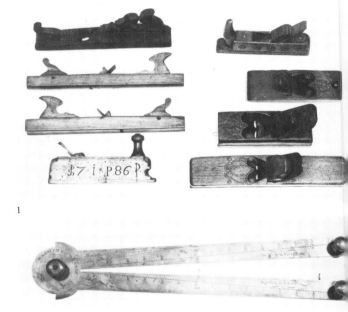

1

2

Tools have certainly been subject to this cycle of fashion in the six years or so since they became established as a separate auction category; braces had their day, English metal planes had theirs, moulding planes are now beginning to be taken more seriously than they were, and who knows, perhaps there will be an upsurge of interest in the simpler tools – axes, adzes, billhooks and the like.

1. All sold Feb. '86. Left, top to bottom: *round-sole plane, undated, probably 18th century, lacking cutter and wedge*, £180; *pair of hollow and round sole planes, 19th century*, £150; *smoothing plane, dated 1786, with initials I.P.*, £180. Right, top to bottom: *typical Dutch/German 19th-century plane, with simple geometric carving*, £65; *Bossingschaaf, or panel-raising plane, carved and dated 1734, but in poor condition and lacking wedge and cutter*, £60; *a similar plane with hollow sole, dated 1736, in good condition*, £500; *a panel plane, dated 1789*, £320.

    The practice of carving and dating planes was common on the continent, especially in Holland, until well into the 19th century, but it is very seldom found on English planes. An English plane carved with a 1730s date in a cartouche would probably fetch well over £1,000.

2. *A tool? A scientific instrument? Or just 'Other Apparatus'? Rare and beautiful 18th-century engineer's sector rule, with scales for calculating sizes of machine wheels and mill gear wheels, and engraved W. Wright, Glossop; complete with a fitted mahogany case.* Oct. '85, £1,300.

Machines for Office and Home

It is often difficult to explain what makes a typewriter or sewing machine collectable, but the watchword for both is 'unconventional'. A conventional typewriter is the sort still in universal use until electrics took over a few years ago, and type bars gave way to daisy wheels. It has the type on the end of bars which hinge up and strike the front of the platen through a ribbon, activated by keys in three or four straight rows. To interest a collector, a typewriter has to depart radically from this pattern, and in the early days (from 1870s up to 1914) many did. The golf-ball principle of ten years or so ago was not new: the first really successful portable, the Blickensderfer, used it, and a Blickensderfer is the most likely 'unconventional' typewriter to come your way. So successful was it, that it exists in vast numbers (portables have a high survival rate because they do not receive the daily nine-to-five bashing of an office machine). It still sells in the £30–£60 bracket. Technically very similar, but much rarer, is the Munson, for which £200+ could be expected. Some of the most desirable typewriters are absurdly simple in design, little more than toys in fact, but prices up to nearly £2,000 have been recorded for rare models. Perhaps the best illustration of the difference between the rare and commonplace occurred a year or two back, when a Mignon was sold for £1,300. The Mignon is one of the most unconventional of all successful typewriters, and this price would certainly be expected if it were rare. It isn't, and it normally makes £30–£60. So why £1,300? Well, it was finished in red, and very few are known in this cheerful attire, black being the normal garb.

A conventional sewing machine is a Singer, or one of the many Singer look-alikes, mostly made in Germany. It measures about 12 inches from the needle to the flywheel, and, in hand models, is mounted on a wood base approximately 1¼ inches thick, which is hollowed out in the centre to accommodate the shuttle mechanism. £5 is about the norm for such machines, and don't be impressed by inlaid mother-of-pearl, or elaborate marquetry cases – they don't help. Most interesting machines are small, and wood bases, if there at all, are merely flat boards, invariably of mahogany. As with typewriters, there is no simple way to tell a rare one from a common one, but a common unconventional sewing machine, of which the Willcox & Gibbs is the prime example, is saleable *in good condition*. This means no rust, and with 90% of the gilt decoration intact. Anything described as 'in working order' is likely to be scruffy in appearance, and while this is acceptable in a rare model, it is not for a Willcox. *Christopher Proudfoot*

1. *Mignon Model 2 typewriter, finished in the usual black, with gold lettering.* Feb. '86, £45. The later No. 4 is similar in value and appearance with the name in silver rather than gold and no lining on the central block.

2. *Salter Standard No. 7.* Feb. '86, £250. Almost 'conventional', the Salter none the less attracts collectors, and earlier models with a curved keyboard make even more. The No. 7 is 'unconventional' only in so far as it has three rows of keys instead of four, and the type bars swing down on to the top of the platen instead of hitting it in front.

3. *Hall typewriter.* Jul. '85, £220. The fine workmanship and highly unconventional design of this machine, fitted in an attractive mahogany carrying case, make it seem surprisingly cheap. Even the best examples seldom go over £300 or so. The actual type is moulded in a sheet of rubber, usually found (as in this example) in an advanced state of decay.

4. *Grover & Baker sewing machine.* Jul. '85, £1,100. Not the rarest of sewing machines, but the Grover & Baker has always been a favourite among collectors. This example was not in very good condition, and in the light of this its price, double the pre-sale estimate, was a surprise.

5. *Taylor's Patent Friction hand sewing machine.* Oct. '85, £160. In many ways typical of the small iron-based machines produced by various English makers in the 1860–80 period, this was distinguished by its drive system. Power is conveyed from the handwheel to the countershaft by an adjustable metal-to-metal friction contact. It seemed to work surprisingly well.

1

2

4

5

Metal Planes

Most woodworkers today use planes made of metal, but old planes are usually thought of as being made of wood. In fact, metal planes go back to Roman times, and they became popular with cabinet-makers in the 19th century. Two distinct types emerged, one in Great Britain and the other in America. The latter type is still used on both sides of the Atlantic, but early examples and rare models are avidly collected, particularly in the States, and all the so-called 'English' metal planes (many were actually made in Scotland) are of interest. It is not only collectors who are after them: many are bought by cabinet-makers, for there is no modern equivalent for working hardwoods to a fine finish. Because of this, some of the most common and recent models command healthier prices than older versions.

The best-known maker was Norris, and many Norris planes that come up for sale date from after the last war. Although they do not have the weight and overall quality of earlier models, these late planes all have a screw adjustment to the cutter, which makes them attractive to the user market. The adjustment first appeared in 1913, but was not immediately fitted to all the huge range of models available. By the 1930s it was available on most, including some special purpose planes like shoulder and mitre planes. However, relatively few of these were sold in adjustable form and even a shoulder plane can make over four times as much with the adjustment as without (No. 1).

Another variation that has a dramatic effect on price is the use of bronze (gunmetal) for the body of the plane, particularly if it is a bench plane (smoother, panel or jointer). In February 1986, a rather battered 50G (the '50' series was a range of budget-priced planes made from 1913 onwards) made £280, against perhaps £60–80 for a similar iron one. A near mint one brought £480 in October 1985 (No. 2). It should be emphasized that we are talking about Norris planes. Many metal planes were 'user-made'. Perhaps an apprentice set out to make himself a plane from scratch, using the services of a friendly foundry worker, or he could buy a rough casting from a tool dealer and finish it off, fitting his own wood handles and infill. Such planes are very seldom adjustable, and when made of bronze they often lack the essential steel sole found on Norris and other commercially made planes. At their best, user-made planes, particularly shoulder planes, achieve a standard of finish and ornamental shaping that leaves commercial models standing, and they can command very good prices in spite of their anonymity.   *Christopher Proudfoot*

1. *A Norris A7 dovetailed steel shoulder plane, with patent adjustments.* Dec. '85, £420.
    This example is in excellent condition, but a slightly less clean plane brought only £300 in Feb. '86, reflecting a loss of rarity value as more examples have come to light in the last three years.

2. *Norris 50G smoothing plane.* Oct. '85, £480.

3. *Two user-made 'chariot' planes of unusually large size for their pattern.* 5 in. and 6¾ in. (measured at sole). Oct. '85, £100, £95.

4. *Chaplin's patent adjustable smoothing plane.* May '86, £95.
    One of the less well-known American iron planes of the late 19th century, this failed to rival the stanley in popularity.

5. *Norris A51 iron smoothing plane.* May '86, £85.
    See the very similar A50G, made of bronze (gunmetal) in No. 2.

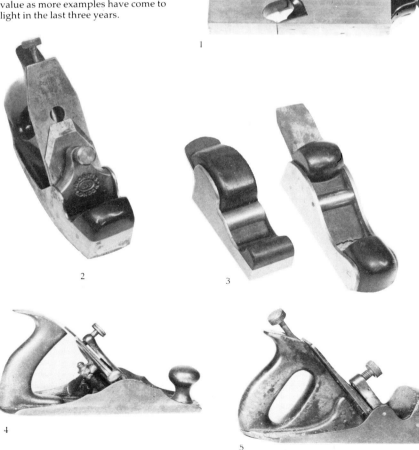

6. *Iron brace.* Feb. '86, £85.

7. *Gouging machine for wind instrument reeds.* Feb. '86, £240.

8. *Dutch smoothing plane, dated 1824.* Feb. '86, £60 (with another).

9. *Iron mitre plane by Gabriel.* Feb. '86, £380.

10. *Miller's plow No. 141 by Stanley Rule & Level Co.* Feb. '86, £220.

11. *Mitre plane by John Moseley & Son, Bloomsbury.* Feb. '86, £140.

12. *Late Norris adjustable panel plane.* 14½ in. Feb. '86, £220.

13. *Dutch fruitwood plane, dated 1769.* Feb. '86, £70.

14. *Group of three bronze thumb planes.* Feb. '86, £170.
    The Miller's Plow was a precursor of the Stanley 45 and 55 planes, and its ornamented surface has a part to play in its value. The two mitre planes date from the early and late 19th century (Nos. 9 and 11 respectively) and this explains the difference in price, all the more notable as the Gabriel plane was very badly corroded. The price of the Norris (No. 12), a post-World War II example, represented a hardening of prices for these late models, which had been edging even higher.

15. *An unusual user-made side-rebate plane with shaped brass stock.* May '86, £260.
    A good example of an unconventional and decorative user-made plane bringing a high price.

16. *An iron rebate plane by Buck, Tottenham Court Road, with skew mouth and rosewood infill.* ⅝ in. wide. May '86, £65.
    Bearing in mind its condition, with several patches of corrosion, this was also quite a high price, accounted for by the skew mouth (i.e. the cutting edge is not at right angles across the sole).

17. *A late Norris plane.* 17¼ in. Feb. '86, £190.

18. *A very unusual user-made bronze shoulder plane with steel sole, skew mouth, screw adjustment and bronze 'wedge'.* Feb. '86, £220.
    This example is not as well finished as the other user-made planes illustrated on this page, but its interesting design took the bidding to this price.

19. *Stanley 55 combination plane with all accessories and cutters, in virtually as new condition.* Feb. '86, £160.
    Average examples of the Stanley 55 combination plane, complete, are usually around £100–120. Another plane in similar condition but with the added attraction of an unusual maker's wood case, brought £190 in the same sale.

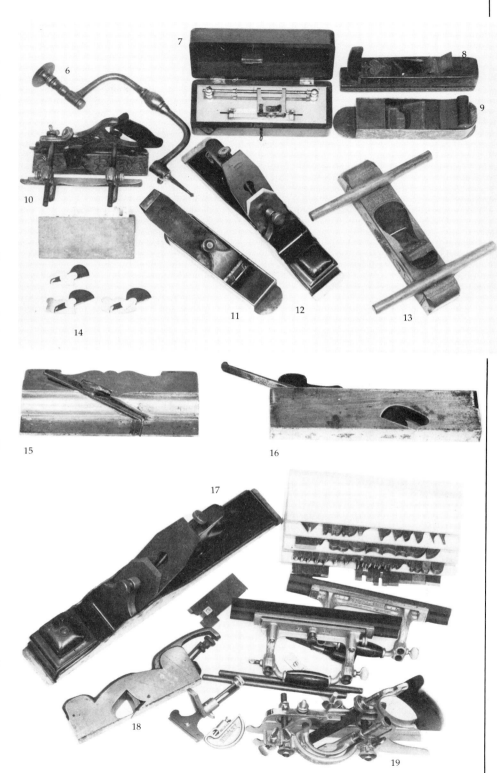

18.   *Transport Memorabilia*

Introduction
by James Knight

From as early as 1972 Christie's have been part of this relatively small but competitive market, with regular sales of Motoring, Aeronautical, Nautical and Railway Art and Literature at South Kensington since 1976.

The four fields are vast and all have their strong facets, and their weak ones for that matter. Each sale may include books, magazines, photographs, postcards, prints, posters, paintings and miscellanea relating to any of the specific fields.

These markets have all changed or developed. The motoring market, after a shaky start to the decade, has now picked up, and prices over the past few years have reflected this. The aeronautical and nautical fields are exhibiting an extremely healthy growth, and I still believe that there is much more potential. For example, in August 1984 we sold a complete diving suit (helmet, suit, weighted boots and air pump) for £900. Now a helmet alone will make between £700 and £900.

Unfortunately the same cannot be said for the railway field. This is possibly the smallest market, it is not expanding at present, and there is no sign of it doing so in the immediate future. Collectors are still looking for the interesting items, a locomotive nameplate for instance, but there is a distinct lack of turnover. So it might be a good time to move in.

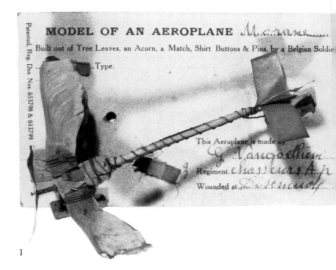

1

1. *An unusual model of an aeroplane constructed from leaves, matches and other items by a Belgian soldier injured during the First World War.* Jan. '86, £30.

2. *Stanley Orton Bradshaw, Gipsy Moth G-AADS, signed and dated 29, watercolour.* 9¼ × 13 in. Jan. '86, £450.

2

Motoring Art and Literature

First of all: good, clean, high-quality items will always fetch their expected prices or more. General items that appear in most sales and shops are a more difficult matter to gauge.

Early literature (pre 1920) has always sold well. Recently, however, there has been a steady growth in 1950s art and literature, recapturing the heady days of Fangio, Moss and Clark. Mascots and badges along with the other areas suffered a shaky period during the very early '80s. Motoring artists have always been fairly strong in numbers. If buying, it is recommended to stick to established artists such as Frederick Gordon Crosby, Bryan de Grineau, Frederick Nevin, George Lane, Terence Cuneo, Roy Nockolds, Nicholas Watts, Alan Fearnly and David Shepherd.

Crosby was the official illustrator for *The Autocar* from about 1900 to 1940, and his motor racing scenes now make from £1,000 upwards. De Grineau was Crosby's opposition and illustrated for the rival magazine *The Motor*. He did not quite have the Crosby touch. Cuneo, who is renowned for his railway scenes, also painted motor subjects which can be £1,500 or more, with a good racing scene at £3,000 upwards. Nevin and Lane (still the old school) extensively used the medium of charcoal, pencil, chalk and washes, and their drawings make anywhere from £50 to £500 – depending as ever on quality.

Contemporary artists such as Shepherd – the wildlife painter – at from £1,000 to £3,000; Fearnly and Watts at from £300 to £1,000 still have the technical expertise of their predecessors. The final part of a Motoring Art and Literature catalogue is referred to as miscellanea. The views before sales sometimes resemble a senior motorway pileup with the trunks, motoring clothes, wheels, exhausts, picnic hampers and headlamps heaped and scattered everywhere. But sometimes there are fine Rolls-Royce silver desk sets (see illustration), trophies, bronzes, various compendiums and penny farthings. A few

items in this field have been faked: Rolls-Royce (Spirit of Ecstasy), Bugatti, Bentley and Hispano Suiza car mascots among them, and inevitably Gordon Crosby has been copied.   *James Knight*

1. *A Rolls-Royce catalogue for the 40–50 h.p. Phantom III.* Apr. '86, £85.

2. *George Lane:* Memory and Prospect, *signed and inscribed, grisaille.* 13 × 20½ in. Nov. '85, £350.

3. *A Rolls-Royce silver timepiece modelled as a radiator.* 5½ in. This is one part of a desk set which sold for £900 in Nov. '85. This piece alone would fetch £300–£400.

4. *An unusual De Soto umbrella, 1931.* 34½ in. Nov. '85, £170.

1

2

3

4

Mascots and Badges

The first recorded use of a mascot was in 1896 when Lord Montagu of Beaulieu adopted a St Christopher for his Daimler. To date there are reputedly more than 5,000 different types. France probably had the most prolific designers and the most numerous mascots. However, the infamous 1941 December 14th law enforced by Hitler ordered that all pre-1925 automobiles in France were to be destroyed, and inevitably many mascots shared their fate. Mascots can be divided into three categories.

FACTORY MASCOTS

Perhaps the most familiar factory mascot is the Rolls-Royce 'Spirit of Ecstasy' (No. 1). This one made a good price because it was genuine, and not one of the many copies around. It is early, probably from a Silver Ghost – earlier models were about 6½ in. high. Look for all the correct markings under the wings and around the base. No. 2 shows a Rolls Royce master model; basically, the later the 'Spirit of Ecstasy' the smaller and cheaper.

Although the Rolls-Royce could claim to be one of the most expensive cars, the same cannot be said of its mascot. No. 3 will fetch more than the early 'Spirit of Ecstasy'. No. 4 shows a popular subject, the stork. This is the Lorraine-Dietrich stork and not to be confused with the Hispano-Suiza stork, which was always depicted in flight.

GLASS MASCOTS

You might be excused for assuming that René Lalique was the only glass mascot designer. But there are also Red Ashay, Corning Glass, Sabino, Warren-Kessler and Luciene-Bloch. The most popular is René Lalique's 'Victoire – Spirit of the Wind' (No. 5). This made a good price, but it would have been much more if it had been amethyst tinted and, more importantly still, not chipped. No. 6 shows Red Ashay's equivalent – do not be confused. The gentleman who owned this one told me on the telephone it was a Lalique 'Spirit of the Wind'. You can imagine how he felt when I unwrapped the package in front of him and broke the news – nevertheless, it made a very healthy price. It was not tinted but in perfect condition. Other glass mascot makers are less expensive on average

1

3

2

4

than Lalique and Red Ashay, but you can expect prices of over £100 if of a reasonable size and high quality.

FANTASY MASCOTS

Fantasy mascots were introduced to make the owner's mass-produced vehicle unique, to differ from Joe Bloggs's at No. 23. These were mascots that could be bought from jewellery and accessory shops. Not surprisingly policemen are subjects of satirical humour. No. 7 shows John Hassall's caricature of a policeman with moveable helmet and porcelain head. Hassall's 'Aviator' (No. 8) is worth £500 if it still has its revolving propeller.   *James Knight*

1. *A Rolls-Royce 'Spirit of Ecstasy', the underside of the wings indistinctly marked Reg. U.S. Pat. Off. Trade Mark Reg., the base inscribed Charles Sykes, R.R. Ltd. 6.2.11. 6½ in. Nov. '85, £220.*

2. *A Rolls-Royce 'Spirit of Ecstasy' master model, the base inscribed Charles Sykes, Rolls-Royce Limited, Feb. 6, 1911. 7 in. Nov. '85, £450.*

3. *A Farman figure of Icarus inscribed Colin George, made in France, syndicat des Fabrt. bronzes 1818 unis France, Finnigans, c. 1922. 6 in. Nov. '85, £400.*

4. *A Lorraine-Dietrich stylized stork, inscribed 'ARTUS', c. 1924. 6½ in. Nov. '85, £200.*

5. 'Victoire – Spirit of the Wind', a Lalique glass female head with stylized flowing hair, moulded 'R. Lalique', small chip to hair. 10¼ in. long. Nov. '85, £1,900. A second version with an almost identical chip made £3,400 in Apr. '86, which would certainly indicate a boom in the market.

6. A Red Ashay glass female head. 9½ in. long. Nov. '85, £350.

7. A brass caricature of a policeman with painted porcelain head and moveable helmet, inscribed Hassall. 4¾ in. Mar. '85, £140.

8. A brass caricature of an airman with painted porcelain head and moveable helmet, inscribed Hassall (lacking propeller). 4½ in. Apr. '86, £360. A similar figure with propeller made £500 in Mar. '85.

9. 'Sir Kreemy Knut'. 5½ in. Nov. '85, £180. This was Sharp's promotional figure from the 1920s to the 1950s. A chromium-plated version in perfect condition made £250 in Apr. '86.

10. A bronze bulldog, the oval base depicting an enamelled Union Jack (chipped). 4 in. long. Nov. '85, £130.

11. A full member's Automobile Association badge, the red enamelled heart inscribed 'Available to 1/5/16, No. 94096'. 5 in. Nov. '85, £90.

19. *Arms and Militaria*

Introduction
by *Melvyn Gallagher*

As usual, quality, condition and rarity have been the key factors in the prices for Arms and Militaria during the past year, and trends carried over from last season include the growing interest for quality Indian, Islamic and Japanese weapons, and anything considered unusual or odd such as combination and miniature items.

Medals, Orders and Decorations, especially interesting groups awarded to known recipients, have been strong sellers, the story behind the medals having a great bearing on the price. It is particularly pleasing when the right home is found for items such as the group of RNLI lifesaving awards to the coxswain of the Clacton lifeboat, bought by the Colchester and Essex Museum in October 1985 for £950.

Demand for English sporting guns continues apace, with prices shooting up. With fewer and fewer English gunsmiths still in production (most guns are now imported from Spain, Italy and even Russia), guns in original condition are at a premium. Even examples which require some repair or have been rebarrelled are selling well, such is the desirability of an English 'named' gun. British firearms legislation has without question restricted any significant price increases for many vintage and modern sporting rifles and handguns. However, there is increasing demand for good vintage handguns in original condition.

Militaria is marching into its own. Items of major importance are now coming to light from years of neglect in cellars and attics, and their prices certainly do justice to the often quite superb, painstaking workmanship employed in their production. Apart from the established collectors' favourites, such as military head dress, sabretaches and crossbelts, court dress too has proved popular. Another new collector's field with many possibilities for the future is that of police uniform and memorabilia; a large collection including some 200 items of headgear from around the world was sold in January 1986.

1

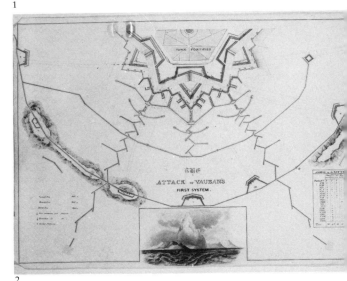

2

1. *Four items of police headgear. From left to right: A Berlin shako, £120; a Russian cap, £60; a Belgian shako, sold with two Belgian police caps, £60; a Bremen police shako, £50. Jan. '86.*

2. *One of a collection of 32 unframed annotated pen, ink and wash drawings of fortifications by Gentleman Cadet W. E. Warrand, 1847–8. Oct. '85, £450. Drawings, watercolours and plans with military associations are attracting increasing interest.*

Medals and Decorations

There are many categories of medals and decorations, firstly those awarded to servicemen for campaigns from Waterloo to the Falklands, together with awards for bravery and long service. Then there are medals to non-combatants such as nurses, usually with related Red Cross or St John's awards. Lifesaving medals presented by the Royal Humane Society, the RNLI and even the Scout Association are all collected.

Awards to civilians either for bravery or service are not, however, so desirable unless part of larger group or if the recipient was a famous personality, and minor foreign medals of this type are not popular in this country.

Groups should never be split up as they often are by families, this lessens their value to others considerably. The story behind awards and the service details of the recipient are almost as important as the medals themselves. Old bestowal documents, pay books, discharge papers, photographs of the medals being worn, diaries or flying logbooks should be kept with the medals. Collectors can establish through records (at the Public Record Office and Services museums) the full service details. Postings, wounds, punishments received for being drunk or AWOL are all recorded. These, with 'Medal Rolls' which list who in different regiments took part in battles, confirming a soldier's entitlement to a 'clasp' or bar or medal, help make the story live.

With today's rising prices, it is not unknown for the unscrupulous to add rare clasps to medals, or repair broken suspensions and add them to medals that have been mounted as brooches, leaving telltale marks where the pin was soldered.

Most medals bear a name, service number and regiment stamped or engraved around the rim. Some are found renamed, that is the original inscription removed, usually by filing, and another added. Sometimes a few letters in a name or a rank were officially altered when an error was made, and someone who lost a medal might obtain another, remove the name and have his added. But others have been altered recently in order to make a medal more desirable to collectors. The correct style of lettering should be checked, and other signs of alteration looked for, including file marks and a thin rim where metal has been removed.

Awards for famous actions are in most demand, such as those for the Charge of the Light Brigade, Rorke's Drift, the defence of the Legations at Peking, or more recently, the Yangtze Incident. So too are awards to airmen, especially the RFC and RNAS, submariners and polar expedition members. A notable tale of bravery in the citation published in the London Gazette can add to the value.

During the Great War, some 115,000 Military Medals and 37,000 Military Crosses were awarded. Today they sell for between £40 and £100. Issues of World War Two and after are rarer, and as most recipients are still alive have not come on to the market in large numbers.

Condition affects prices, although not so much as with coins. Where they have been worn as a group, medals often show contact marks and may have been polished. However, the best possible condition helps, and original boxes of issue and ribbons are also desirable, especially for 19th-century awards.

Orders of chivalry are very desirable, especially the higher grades of the principal orders, some of which rarely appear on the market. The most common are the lower grades of The Order of the British Empire, founded in 1917. The BEM, MBE, OBE and CBE insignia awarded to civilians do not normally excite collectors, and a Commander's neck badge (CBE) only realizes £50 – £60.

Foreign orders and decorations continue to rise in price, as many have previously been undervalued despite often being superb examples of the jeweller's and goldsmith's craft.

Melvyn Gallagher

1. *A miniature of the French Legion of Honour in gold and diamonds.* Apr. '86, £210. Good quality miniatures are much sought after.

2. *A Naval General Service Medal, 1793–1840, with three clasps.* Apr. '86, £130. The top two clasps are unofficial, and the medal has been renamed to Stephen Horn. Official records show that he was, in fact, entitled to the top two clasps: Peterel March 1800 and Anholt 27 March 1811, he being an Ordinary Seaman on HMS *Peterel*. The thinned lower half of the rim indicates where the original naming has been filed away.

   five clasps including the Defence of Ladysmith and Relief of Mafeking, two of the famous Boer War sieges. To Serg W. McGregor Imp. Lt. Horse (& Scots Horse), the latter added officially. Apr. '86, £110.

4. *The New Zealand Medal, 1845–7 and 1860–6, renamed to David FitzPatrick 1st Bn. 12 Regt. The crude re-lettering and faint file marks can be seen. Worth about £30.*

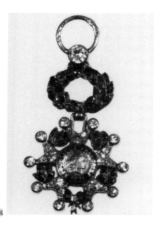   

2   3   4

Militaria

Few fields of collecting give people such good opportunities to buy themselves 'a little slice of history' as militaria does: items connected with a famous person or event arouse very keen interest (generally reflected in the price) and several such pieces have emerged at auction during the last year (Nos. 1, 2). No. 3 is associated not with a famous person but with the Peninsular Campaign, an event that was in historical terms very glamorous, although 'glamorous' is doubtless the very last description that the participants would have chosen. For the purpose of valuing militaria the term glamorous can be stretched to include the whole of the Napoleonic Wars or the entire American War of Independence.

No. 3 however, had pure rarity as well as association to give it strength, the simple cotton trousers being virtually unique. Other examples of rarity appealing to specialist collectors are an officer's silver-laced coatee of the 6th Dragoons of *c.* 1831 which fetched £1,100 (Feb. '86) and a Victorian Colonel's uniform of the South Australia Militia Cavalry (Adelaide Lancers) which realized £3,800 (Sept. '85). None of these was highly spectacular in appearance, so clearly rarity can count for more than aesthetic appeal. So too does the regiment involved, the 11th Hussars being one of the best-loved regiments with collectors as a whole (No. 4).

Indeed one can almost discern an order of regimental popularity which in the regular army is led by Hussars and Household Cavalry, followed by Lancers (No. 7), Heavy Cavalry and Horse Artillery, then Foot Guards and Highlanders: the latter come before most other line infantry, who in turn are well ahead of Field Artillery, after whom come the supporting services whose material is not generally in great demand. Similarly there is a pecking order among nations: other than Britain and the Empire, the most desired is probably Imperial Russia (No. 5) of any period, followed by Germany (Nos. 8 and 9). Then come France and America, but almost only if earlier than about 1880.

Obviously these rules of thumb yield to numerous other factors, and a perfect and complete Line Infantry uniform might well be more desired than an incomplete Foot Guards equivalent. Recently collectors have been putting greater emphasis on the completeness of a uniform, which can partly compensate for it being otherwise slightly mundane.

Unfortunately uniform clothing has drawbacks for collectors (No. 6), and the sheer practical convenience of objects that can easily be stored and displayed clearly counts enormously. Thus headdress and certain accoutrements (pouches, pouch-belts and sabretaches in particular) and the more important forms of badge (notably shoulder-belt plates) are convenient to collect and at the same time are frequently very attractive objects. It is natural that these are normally the most keenly collected categories within the whole militaria field, and one could reasonably claim that an 18th-century British regular officer's embroidered mitre cap meets every requirement and represents the collector's ideal; very rare, richly ornate in itself and decorative in any setting, historically evocative and also convenient in size. It could perhaps command something of the order of £8,000. Lower down the scale, more modest mitres are of considerable interest (No. 10).

Because headdress, pouches etc. are regularly collected they have a well-established market and thus relatively predictable prices: for example, a late British Lancers officer's full dress headdress (chapka) with plume, generally fetches £1,100–£1,300, whereas an officer's blue cloth spiked helmet normally makes between £175 and £250, although No. 11 did better because of the corps.

On the other hand, one of the most unpredictable sectors of the field seems to be colours, standards, banners and similar material. In price terms these are almost perverse: finely wrought, decorative, frequently of great historical interest and often easy to display in frames like a picture, even in quite good condition, they by no means always fetch the price they deserve. By contrast, painted drums which, although decorative, are rather bulky and awkward to display, consistently achieve good prices.

One of the great charms of militaria for both experienced and novice collectors is its immense variety. It encompasses almost everything connected with all aspects of the life of soldiers in many parts of the world in the last 300 years at least and it continues to grow. First and Second World War material is already well-established, and now Falklands and Vietnam material is following. Then naval, diplomatic, court and police uniforms tend to be grouped with militaria.

Some items overlap from other fields; modest watercolours (No. 13), prints, documents, books, oil paintings and photograph albums of military interest and occasional items of camp furniture, military silver, mess ornaments and musical instruments appear in our Militaria sales.

Perhaps, however, the most obscure item we have offered (as part of a World War II officer's kit) was a container of moustache-wax, which must surely mark the outermost limit of this huge field.

Aubrey Bowden

1. *The Order of the Bath banner of Queen Victoria's 'wicked uncle', the Duke of Cumberland.* Feb. '86, £1,500 (with two other banners).

2. *The Inniskilling Dragoons helmet of Captain Oates of Antarctic fame.* Sept. '85, £2,200.

1

2

4

5

6

3. *One of two short coatees.* Sept. '85, £5,000. Sold with a saddle cloth, trousers and minor sundries, all of which belonged to a Connaught Rangers officer who fought in the Peninsular War.

4. *A shabraque (saddle cloth) of the 11th Hussars with overalls and tunic.* Feb. '86, £800, despite only moderate condition.

5. *An Imperial Russian Ambassador's uniform.* Sept. '85, £1,700.

6. *A Norfolk Imperial Yeomanry officer's uniform,* Sept. '85, £2,200.

7. *A 17th Lancers officer's headdress.* Feb. '86, £1,100.

8. *A helmet of Prussian Regiment of Gardes du Corps.* Sept. '85, £1,600.

9. *A German Cuirassier's helmet and cuirass.* Feb. '86, £2,000.

10. *A Grenadier's fur mitre cap, 1768 pattern,* Feb. '86, £1,800.

11. *A Royal Marine Light Infantry officer's blue cloth helmet.* Feb. '86, £380

12. *Three side drums.* Feb. '86, £480, £650, £500. The central example is a Coldstream Guards' drum.

13. *Richard Simkin watercolour of 1st Life Guards uniforms.* Feb. '86, £350.

9

11

12

13

Pocket Pistols

The mugger of today is descended from the 18th-century footpad and highwayman who molested unwary travellers before the days of the police. By then, the flintlock pistol had developed into a simple and reliable arm, and types of a size suitable for carrying in a pocket were an effective short-range deterrent.

The earliest common type is called a 'Queen Anne' pistol, although this style continued to be produced until the end of the 18th century. Its characteristics were a multi-stage cannon barrel, usually in brass, with a slab-sided wooden butt, generally inlaid with patterns of silver wire. Such weapons formed the bread and butter trade of most 18th-century gunsmiths, and the quality varied considerably.

They were also made in pairs (the barrels engraved 1 and 2), and there are double-barrelled examples with a 'tap-action'. The main disadvantage with many was the exposed lock and trigger which could easily catch in clothing. So evolved the folding trigger which lay flush with the frame until the pistol was cocked. Some even smaller pistols were produced, known today as 'muff pistols' as they were supposed to have been carried by ladies in their fur muffs when travelling. These are sometimes so diminutive that their effectiveness must have been tiny too. This was a general problem with pocket pistols, so many were made with heavy barrels to take a stronger charge of powder, and heavy bore barrels to give more stopping power. Other attempts to improve performance included using 'blunderbuss' barrels with flared muzzles, and fitting spring bayonets as a secondary line of defence.

With the change to the percussion system of ignition in the 1820s, production of small pistols boomed. The cheap and simple boxlock became usual. Birmingham fast became Britain's biggest manufacturing centre, with a gun barrel proof house from 1813. Their crossed sceptre mark is found on many pistols. Hundreds of small provincial gunsmiths bought Birmingham parts and barrels, engraving their own names on the pistols made up from them. Top makers' names were engraved on many cheaply made pocket pistols, the London gunsmiths D. Egg and H. Nock being the most common. Liège in Belgium, another major arms-producing area, exported thousands to Britain, some of quite appalling quality.

With the self-contained cartridge, or 'bullet', American inventors and manufacturers took the lead with names such as Colt, Remington, and Smith & Wesson to the fore. Early rimfire cartridge pistols of .23 calibre or above (excluding 9 mm) are now treated as antiques by many police forces and can be purchased without a licence, but if in doubt, check with your local firearms officer. The Colt .41 rimfire Deringer is typical of such pistols produced in the 1860–90 period. The late 19th century saw a vogue for pistols concealed in cigar cases and purses as well as 'squeezer' pistols held in the palm of the hand, including the 'Gaulois' and the 'Protector'. Combination weapons included the single-shot knife pistols made by Unwin & Rogers of Sheffield.

From America came the mass-produced 'Saturday Night Special' pocket pistols by Harrington & Richardson, Hopkins & Allen and countless others. Models had names like the 'Bang Up', 'Bluejacket', 'Protector' and 'Bulldog', the latter being a copy of the popular 'British Bulldog' revolvers by Webleys of Birmingham.

The final development was the automatic, loaded by means of a magazine, which rendered the small cylinder revolvers obsolete. Many were scaled down versions of larger designs in reduced calibres, both Colt and Webley & Scott producing .25 versions of their larger models. Others are of even smaller calibres, the 4.25 mm 'Lilliput' and the 3 mm 'Kolibri' for example – both of which could give a nasty wound at close quarters.   *Melvyn Gallagher*

1. *A .41 rimfire 'Thuer' Deringer by Colt (the 'No. 3' model); May '86, £100. Over 45,000 of this model were produced between 1871 and 1912. This example has lost most of the nickel plating from its barrel and is generally worn. In better condition it would realize £150.*

2. *A German 6.35 × 21 mm 'Velo-Dog' pocket revolver which features a folding trigger and covered hammer. Worth about £30. Made from the 1890s to 1920s, they were intended for cyclists to protect themselves from dogs. The RSPCA would certainly object to their use today!*

3. *A fine pair of early 19th-century flintlock pocket pistols with 2½ in. barrels by McLaughlan of Edinburgh. Apr. '86, £750. Pretty well-proportioned pair, although refinished.*

1

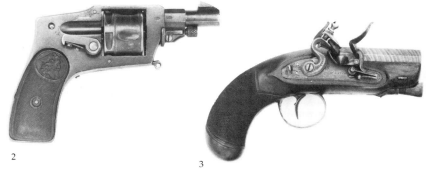

2

3

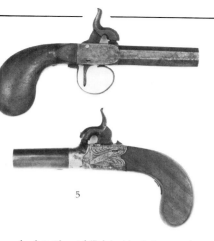

5

6

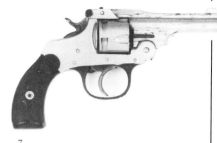

7

4. *A continental (Belgian) boxlock percussion pocket pistol. One of thousands of cheap pistols made in the second half of the 19th century, worth about £30.*

5. *A Birmingham-made boxlock percussion pistol with folding trigger, engraved D. Egg. Apr. '86, £75. Durs Egg (1770–1834) was a leading London gunsmith with a shop at 1 Pall Mall, and many contemporary copies of his guns are still seen.*

6. *A cased pair of Belgian percussion boxlock pocket pistols with 1½ in. barrels in their wooden case. Apr. '86, £280. Of average quality, but overcleaned.*

7. *An American .32 revolver by Hopkins & Allen, worth about £10. One of many pocket revolvers known as 'Saturday Night Specials'.*

8. *An American .30 rimfire pocket revolver with stud trigger. Apr. '86, £65. Late 19th-century predecessor of the Hopkins & Allen revolvers. This example is engraved 'Hard pan'.*

9. *A pair of cheap Birmingham-made percussion pocket pistols, engraved H. Nock, London. May '86, £150. Like D. Egg, Henry Nock was another often imitated top London gunsmith. The lower pistol is 'fully cocked', with the trigger lowered ready for use.*

10. *A 19th-century continental flintlock blunderbuss pistol with brass 3¾ in. barrel. Apr. '86, £130.*

11. *A Queen Anne pistol with typical wire-inlaid butt and cannon barrel by Chadwick, London, average condition. May '86, £320.*

12. *A .22 single shot knife pistol by Unwin & Rodgers. Apr. '86, £230. A popular combination weapon with collectors.*

13. *A 6.35 self-loading pocket pistol by P. Beretta, with gilt full scroll and floral engraving and gilt finish with tortoiseshell grips (dated 1953) in its silk-lined case. Sept. '85, £380.*

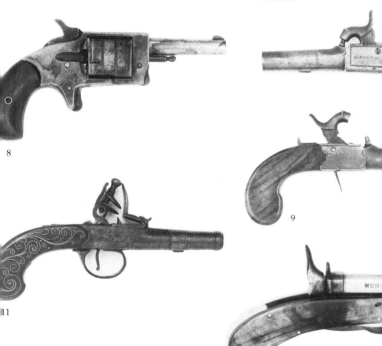

8

11

9

10

12

13

20. *Tribal Art*

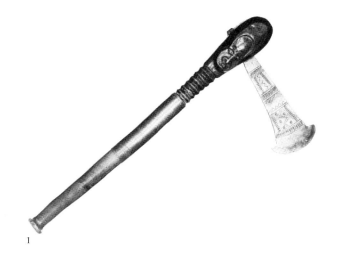

1

Introduction

by Tim Teuten

When one considers the term 'popular antiques', tribal art may not seem applicable but early and rare pieces do, from time to time, appear amongst the old clocks and china at car boot fairs and jumble sales. Usually brought back as mere souvenirs from foreign travels by earlier generations, tribal artefacts have rarely been regarded as valuable family heirlooms and in time might easily be confined to the attic if not the dustbin; they therefore tend to appear at the lower end of the antique market (No. 1). A few pounds is usually all one is expected to pay for such amusing bits of nonsense and there is therefore little to lose by taking a chance.

The enormous variety of objects sold in tribal art sales and their geographical diversity makes a comprehensive survey of the field impossible, but as collectors tend to specialize in specific areas a few trends are worth highlighting.

The market for North American Indian art continues to grow. A scarcity of early pieces and the large number of collectors in Europe as well as in America has led to some fierce competition in the saleroom (No. 2). England seems to be one of the few places where discoveries are still to be made, the general awareness of such pieces being far greater in America.

Amazonian art has also proved popular during the past year, the novelty aspect no doubt contributing to the price realized for the drug kit (No. 3). By contrast, ancient pottery from Central and South America has been more difficult to sell. Recently unearthed pieces have been flooding the market and this, added to the number of fakes in circulation, many with a good deal of age, has led to collectors concentrating on only the finest examples, damaged and repaired pieces or those of lesser quality frequently being ignored.

2

African art is the most likely of the tribal categories to be encountered and also the most likely to prove a disappointing investment. Modern Makonde art, the ebonized, sometimes quite abstract wooden sculpture from Tanzania, has yet to have its day (No. 4) and so-called 'airport art', once it has been stripped of its romantic associations with a safari holiday, has little to offer even the least discerning collector. However, it would be wrong to suggest that all 'westernized art' should be avoided, as one can see from the popular figures of Europeans made by the Yoruba carver Thomas Ona early this century (No. 6). The Yoruba of Nigeria were the most prolific wood carvers in West Africa, producing a large variety of staffs, bowls, trays and masks for use in the many cults which they practised. These fine pieces, often by recorded carvers, are widely collected and have recently made some exceptional prices (No. 5).

1. *Mangebetu axe, found in a box of 'kitchenalia'. 15½ in. Dec. '85, £400.*
2. *Chinook mountain-sheep horn bowl. 7½ in. wide. Dec. '85, £3,800.*

African textiles and sculptures tend to be bought by different buyers. The very decorative and colourful cloths from West Africa, such as the *kente* cloths of the Ashanti of Ghana, have attracted interior designers as well as textile specialists and their wide appeal has ensured a healthy market.

Clubs and paddles of Oceania are also collected by those interested in arms, and so they continue to fetch good prices. Rarity, good form and a glossy dark patina are the main requirements for a high price. Pacific jewellery is equally popular, whaletooth necklaces usually fetching several hundred pounds. A good creamy or golden brown patina is the most desirable, and no attempt should be made to clean this jewellery. A proud owner recently brought in a brilliant white example, having removed all the patina with Steradent and with it a couple of hundred pounds of the value. The sculpture of Polynesia is very rare and thus sought after. That of New Guinea is more common, and an early provenance and fine detail are essential for a high price.

Australian Aborigine items have fared less well due, in part, to the restrictions imposed by the Australian government on the sale of Aborigine religious artefacts. Indonesian textiles are also out of favour on the market at present, with many pieces of relatively recent manufacture fetching considerably less than five years ago.

An interesting development is the increase in demand for early photographs for their ethnographic rather than aesthetic interest. Early books and albums are bought by both collectors and museums. (See also Photographic Sales, pp. 136–7.)

3

Provenance has been playing an increasingly important role in auction prices, with so many later pieces appearing in the salerooms, and this trend is likely to increase as techniques for artificial 'ageing' become more sophisticated. Any information concerning when, where and by whom a piece was collected can greatly enhance its value.

In a field such as tribal art, where almost every piece is in some way unique, it is exceptionally difficult to assess the value of outstanding and rare items, and it is an indication of the strength of the market that expectations have often been exceeded for the finest pieces.

3. *Amazonian Indian four piece* yoppo-*taking kit.* The dish 6¼ in. wide. Dec. '85, £1,500.

4. *Modern Makonde carving.* 36¾ in. Estimated price, £10–£20.

5. *Yoruba wood bowl, by Olowe of Ise.* 25 in. Christie's King Street, Jun. '85. £162,000.

6. *Group of figures in a boat, by Thomas Ona.* 12½ in. long. Christie's King Street, Nov. '83, £1,404.

5

6

Stools

Every sale of tribal art includes several examples of stools from around the world and, being useful as well as attractive, their appeal is wider than that of other tribal items. The majority of those seen in the saleroom come from West Africa, due to their popularity with expatriates working in the old colonies.

The most familiar type is the classic stool from the Akan, including the Ashanti of Ghana (No. 1); this type has been carved in the same form for well over 300 years. Such stools can fetch as little as £25 but well patinated examples in good condition frequently make over £100. They have a curved rectangular seat and a rectangular, sometimes stepped base, on five column supports. There are also a variety of other supports that were used by the Akan chiefs. Rattray in the 1920s compiled a list of more than 30. Most supports are geometric, but figurative ones are not uncommon, illustrating popular Akan proverbs. Those with elephant or leopard supports, symbolizing kingly virtues of greatness and a fierce nature, were formerly for the exclusive use of the Ashantehene (or king), their sale to others being forbidden on pain of death.

As elsewhere in Africa, stools were not regarded by the Akan solely as items of general use, but were closely connected with the spirit of the owner. When not in use they were tipped on their sides to prevent any bad spiritual power entering them. Stools belonging to certain people of high rank were sometimes blackened on their death with an application of soot, raw egg and the blood and fat of a sheep, which in time gave them a glossy black patina. Hair and nail parings were inserted into a cavity often found in the central support of old Ashanti stools. These ancestral stools were stored in a windowless room of the palace at Kumasi, and sacrifices were periodically offered to them.

The Lobi stool of unusual form (No. 2) was carved by Sikire Kambire of Gaoua, Upper Volta. This stool dates from the beginning of this century and shows a marked influence from contact with Europeans. It does not, however, suffer from this fusion of styles; rather the artist has created a new, original and pleasing form. Similarly a Yoruba artist

1

2

4

from the Igbuke carving house at Oyo developed, again purely for expatriates, the little stool with monkey support (No. 3) carved in about 1925/30.

The 'title' stools made by the Ibo at Awka in Nigeria (No. 4) were originally for use by those who paid to join the Ozo society. Their unusual form appealed to expatriates and many found their way back to Europe. Prices depend on quality and patination and vary between £200 and £800.

Stools from the Cameroon are more numerous and varied. Almost invariably circular with a pierced base, the supports are carved with a variety of figures or animals, certain features often being highlighted with scorching. One of the most original types has tiers of flying fox heads. No. 5 was exceptionally large; prices normally range from £50 to £300.

5

1. *Ashanti wood stool.* 11 in. Dec. '85, £140.
2. *Lobi wood stool.* 24¾ in. long. Christie's King Street, July '82, £160.
3. *Oyo wood stool.* 15 in. Christie's King Street, July '82, £220.
4. *Ibo wood 'title' stool.* 25¼ in. Christie's King Street, June '84, £1,080.
   The exceptional price of this stool was due to its being of double form, i.e. carved as a stool superimposed on another.
5. *Cameroon wood stool.* 23 in. Dec. '84, £1,700.

7

8

The stools which have realized the highest prices at auction are from the Luba of the Katanga area of Zaire (No. 6). They reflect the status of chiefs and are usually carved with a caryatid. The legs of the seated or kneeling figure are often carved in relief on the circular base, and great attention to detail is sometimes given to the face, torso and elaborate coiffures which are a feature of this area. Prices may vary from a few hundred pounds for a late or poor carving, to £300,000 for a work from the village of Buli.

The Jokwe also carved fine stools with figure supports, but are better known for their chairs and stools which followed European forms and were decorated with numerous figures and animals. A fine example can fetch £5,000 but the modest example here (No. 7) made £400. The tribes of north-west Zaire, such as the Poto, use simple forms, sometimes covered in upholstery nails; a fine example can fetch £2,500 but a small one as little as £30.

Stools from the Pacific are less common, being confined almost exclusively to eastern Polynesia. Though often of considerable size, they are always carved from a single piece of wood. The Tahitian stool (No. 9) is the largest of only four to have survived the 300 years of European contact. William Ellis in the early nineteenth century gives the best account of these stools: 'The rank of the host was often indicated by the size of the seat, which was used on public occasions, or for the accommodation of a distinguished guest . . . .'

9

More numerous, but by no means common, are the smaller Cook Islands stools (No. 8) on four short curved legs with drop-shaped feet. Well patinated examples frequently fetch more than £1,000 at auction. Equally elegant in shape, though of a more mundane purpose, are the coconut-grater stools of the Caroline Islands (No. 10). Carved as stylized quadrupeds these would originally have a shell-grater attached to the 'head' and in time would develop a fine patina through use. The scarcity of fine old specimens ensures high prices, which have exceeded £2,000.   *Tim Teuten*

6. *Luba Hemba wood stool.* 23 in. Dec. '84, £7,500.

7. *Jokwe wood stool.* 17 in. Christie's King Street, Nov. '81, £400.

8. *Cook Islands wood stool.* 16¼ in. wide. Christie's King Street, Dec. '82, £3,024.

9. *Tahiti wood stool.* 39 in. wide. Christie's King Street, July '82, £21,600.

10. *Caroline Islands wood coconut-grater stool.* 25½ in. long. Dec. '82, £1,620.

10

World Figures

In the limited space of two pages it would be impossible to illustrate the full range of materials and objects to be found in Tribal Art sales, but these photographs give an idea of the range of quality, and the comparisons illustrate a few of the factors which can affect auction prices. *Timothy Teuten*

1

1. *Yoruba wood ayo board.* 22½ in. long. Dec. '85, £1,000.

   The game of *ayo* (or *mankala* as it is more generally known) is played throughout the Islamic world as well as in Africa. As is to be expected from a genuine gameboard, No. 1 has a fine glossy patina from years of use. The fine carving can be recognized as the work of Oniyide Adugbologe of Abeokuta from the early years of this century.

2. By stark contrast to No. 1, this shows no sign of use – not surprising when one considers the very inferior quality of the carving. It would fetch only a few pounds at auction.

3. *Eskimo walrus-tooth bear.* 4 in. long. Christie's King Street, June '85, £648.

   The bear is pierced twice for suspension and would have been used as a toggle, perhaps for pulling the carcases of dead seals after a hunt. It has a fine, smooth surface and creamy to golden colour and probably dates from the 18th century or earlier.

2

3

4. *Ashanti wood doll.* 11½ in. June '85, £250.

   These fertility dolls or *akua'mma* (singular *akua'ba*) were kept by Ashanti women who feared they were infertile. They were carried on the back like real children and were given to young girls to play with, as gazing on their idealized features was thought to produce beautiful children in later life. As they were carefully looked after many survived. Good examples usually fetch between £200 and £300 at auction.

5. Over 16 inches high, this was clearly made for sale and it would be difficult to imagine an Ashanti mother wishing her daughter to gaze on it, so remote is it from the idealized image of a genuine *akua'ba*. The shape of the head and the naturalistically carved body clearly indicate that this is a tourist piece. Large numbers were made for sale, one English dealer in 1968 buying over 7,000 in a single lot from an African dealer in Kumase.

4   5

6

6. *Owo ivory divination tapper*. 17¼ in.
Dec. '85, £9,500.

This divination tapper or iroke from
Owo in Nigeria, carved as a bird, was
used in the widely practised cult of *Ifa* and
has the marvellous array of symbolic
ornament for which these carvings are
famous. It has a fine dark reddish-brown
patina and probably dates from the 19th
century.

After years of handling, ivory develops
a fine smooth surface and frequently a
discolouration, which can vary from
cream to dark brown. Though it is
unfortunately possible to fake the
patination on ivory, it can be a good sign
of age, and being attractive to collectors, it
can also favourably affect the price.
Though elephant tusks are the most
familiar ivory, the teeth of walruses,
whales and hippos have also been used in
different parts of the world.

7. *A pair of Yoruba wood twin figures*. 13¾ in.
Christie's King Street, June '85, £11,340.

There is an exceptionally high incidence
of twins among the Yoruba and they are
believed to have strange powers. In the
event of one dying, it was thought
necessary to carve an image of the same
sex as the dead child to appease its spirit.
These figures or *ere ibeji* were then cared
for by the mother by frequent washing
and sometimes anointing with palm oil
and camwood powder, which gives them
their characteristic smooth, glossy patina.
The coiffures, scarification and style of
carving frequently make it possible to
attribute figures to a particular carver or
village. The above pair was carved at Ila-
Orangun in North-East Yorubaland in
about 1900.

8. *A pair of Yoruba wood twin figures*. 10½ in.
Christie's King Street, June '85, £8,100.

Twin figures were often dressed in
coats covered in cowrie-shells or beads.
The former symbolized the dedication of
wealth to the cult of twins. Beaded coats
are less common, their use being mostly
confined to figures of royal twins. This
pair is from Oshogbo, about 50 miles
south-west of Ila-Orangun.

9. *Maori figure neck pendant*. 4 in. Christie's
King Street, June '83, £23,760.

These pendants or *hei tiki* were worn
about the neck suspended on a fibre cord
and bird-bone toggle, both of which
survive in this example. One eye retains
the shell inlay which was superseded by
red sealing-wax in post-European contact
times. The nephrite from which tikis were
made is very hard stone, and without

metal tools they probably took several
weeks or months to complete. The superb
carving of this example accounts for its
exceptional price. To the Maoris,
however, it was was not the quality of
carving or the size which was considered
important but the *mana*, or life-force, the
tikis acquired from contact with the great
people who had worn them, the features
often being worn smooth with years of
handling.

10. *Maori-style bone tiki*. 2¾ in. Dec. '85, £160.

Although it is believed bone may have
been used at one time to make tikis, no
bone examples survive. Though clearly in
a Maori style, this is unlike any stone tiki
still extant and is now thought to be the
work of James Edward Little (1876–1953).
Little's hand was recognized towards the
end of the 1900s by the more astute
dealers and collectors, but not before
many of his works had found their way
into museums and important collections.

Pictures

Introduction
by Nicholas Lambourn

In last year's *Popular Antiques Yearbook* this Introduction noted developments in the market for pictures – more buyers in the salerooms, a big increase in prices for good paintings as their availability decreases, a related interest in hitherto overlooked painters and their rapid commercial appreciation, and the growth and consolidation of the market for watercolours, and, to a lesser extent, prints.

During 1985–6 these developments have continued and become more clearly defined. The auction houses have positively sought out new buyers. Aggressive marketing has created demand and encouraged new price levels. New categories of sales have responded to new buying tendencies and have targeted other areas for development. Good pictures have continued to sell well in spite of a varied economic year. Political and economic instability in 1986 has, however, had an effect on certain areas. Demand for pictures of Arab interest has fallen away owing to the conflict in the Gulf, and the American buyers have been less in evidence following the lowering of oil prices (see also pp. 220–1).

High prices for works by minor artists in all categories continue. Still lifes by unattributed Old Masters (Nos. 1, 2 & 3), sporting pictures by late 19th-century English painters and sunny beach scenes by early 20th-century British painters (pp. 216–217) – all pictures which can be described as derivative and which appeal solely on a decorative level – have on occasion secured five-figure prices and are in danger of threatening the ascendancy of 'important' pictures in the saleroom.

As oil paintings by lesser mortals soar in price, more attention has inevitably focused on watercolours. Watercolours have traditionally been cheaper than oils, a prejudice which probably derives from their original subservient role to the High Art of oil painting. Early sheets in pencil and watercolour which were cartoons for oil paintings and not

1

2

valued in their own right by artist or collector in their day, have ironically become the first works in this medium to challenge the supremacy of oils. Old Master 'working drawings' now fetch as much and often more than finished Old Master pictures. 18th and 19th-century watercolours have been the subject of belated promotion by the trade. The first International Watercolour Fair held in London in January '86 brought international attention to this peculiarly English art form and secured prices quite inconceivable a couple of years ago. A similar new annual international print fair in London has sought to inject life into this unfashionable market, which still remains an acquired taste to the picture buying public.

1. *Circle of Jean-Baptiste Monnoyer, 'Flowers in an Urn on a Stone Ledge', oil on canvas.* 22 × 28 in. Dec. '85, £6,000. Though not fully attributed to this prolific 18th-century French flower painter, a work of the artist's period of fair quality treating this most popular subject will manage to approach the price of an autographed work. A fully attributed still life of the same subject by Monnoyer may be expected to fetch £10,000 – £15,000.

2. *Follower of Michele Pace, Il Campidoglio, 'A Still Life of Melons, Pomegranates, Figs, Peaches, Grapes and other Fruit on a Sculpted Plinth', oil on canvas.* 34 × 46 in. Dec. '85, £6,000. Still lifes of fruit approach prices for still lifes of flowers. Again a big price for a decorative work which is neither by the artist nor even, in this case, contemporary.

3

3. *Manner of Margarita Caffi, 'Flowers in an Urn on a Stone Ledge', oil on canvas.* 28 × 39 in. (one of a pair). Dec. '85, £5,500. Even late 18th-century and 19th-century copies and pastiches of Old Masters are redeemed by the decorative appeal of their subject. While prices are still regulated by the level of skill, date is less important to price than before.

4. *Julliard, 'Parisian Flower Seller', signed and dated 1879, oil on canvas.* 34½ × 45 in. (one of a pair). May '86, £4,400. Flowers again push up the price of a picture which has few other obvious recommendations. The painter is unrecorded and shows little sophistication in his treatment of figures and architecture.

5. *William Henry Davis, 'A Short Horn Cow', signed and dated 1849, oil on canvas.* 27 × 27 in. Apr. '86, £1,800. While less obviously appealing than flowers, cow portraits sell as 'decorative' pictures. Sporting pictures are perhaps our national equivalent to the still life on the Continent.

6. *William Sidney Cooper, 'The Bridge House', signed and dated '89, pencil and watercolour.* 8¼ × 13½ in. (one of a pair). Apr. '86, £250. While watercolours are particularly popular in England where the tradition has flourished, they remain much cheaper than oil paintings. A comparable subject in oil by a lesser artist will still prove more expensive in the saleroom.

7. *R. B., 'A Reclining Beauty', signed with monogram and dated 1889, watercolour.* 20 × 29½ in. Apr. '86, £550. Watercolour and oil painting as yet unattributed to artists often encourage speculation – which can push prices up to and beyond those attained by fully attributed works of similar quality.

4

6

5

7

Bad Pictures

From time to time you may come across a painting which you like or at least feel should be worth money, and when you go to have it valued you are met by remarks such as: 'it's not really all that *good*', or 'the intrinsic quality of the work is not what it might be', or any one of a variety of diplomatic evasions which serve to dilute the pithy aesthetic judgement that the valuer has in mind. 'However', he may continue, 'it could still make £200 or £300'.

Why, if something is actually bad, should it make money?

To be frank, there are an awful lot of people around who have the money and the desire to buy paintings, but who are incapable of recognizing good and bad workmanship. To them it does not matter if a Victorian cow has both eyes on the same side of its nose – even though they would never buy a Cubist painting. Bad but pretty is good enough for them.

The herd in No. 1 has at least got the eyes on the right sides of the heads, but it is still a poor painting. This subject was done to death at the end of the 19th century, most notably by one Louis Bosworth Hurt, who was a jobbing painter, but obviously a shrewd judge of his market. Hurt hardly ever painted the hooves of his Highland cattle, since they are difficult, and his imitator here has used the same trick. He has also made a

1

very poor fist of the matted pelts of the beasts.

No. 2 is familiar enough, but she is not even one of the many early versions, or one of the six forgeries which are supposed to have been made when the original was stolen from the Louvre in 1912. This is a rather inept student copy. The fingers (in a phrase of the late David Carritt's) 'resemble some form of medieval pasta'. It is also in poor condition, but it could still make as much as £400 as decoration and as a humorous talking point.

Even a copy which is trying to be a fake can be worth money. Whatever one's taste may be as to the confections of Sir Lawrence Alma-Tadema, there is

no doubt that he was a masterly technician. The copyist who put Tadema's signature and Roman opus number to No. 4 was not. The bare feet of the patrician lady are painted as if enclosed in woollen socks, and she undoubtedly suffers from hay fever. Even so, perhaps £300 to £400.

1. *'Highland Cattle'.* 20 in. × 30 in., one of a pair.
   A pair such as this could sell for between £200 and £300.

2. *After Leonardo da Vinci: a 'Mona Lisa'.*
   Not Gioconda but jocose, and, remarkably, worth £200 to £400.

3. *Another 'Mona Lisa'.*
   A better quality copy on an early panel, this raised £20,000 in February 1986.

2

3

4

5

6

No.5 is a more impressive object at first sight. Canaletto, or perhaps an early 19th-century imitator, might one say? Well, unfortunately no. It was apparently painted – indeed in Italy – in the very recent past. It has, however, got quality, and even if offered as a modern copy it should make about £300.

In other cases bad paintings sell well not because of decorative appeal, but because of interesting subject-matter. A primitive or amateur portrait of a well-known but rarely painted figure would fall into this category, as do many early views of America, Australia and the more exotic parts of the world.

However, please, please, regard this article as a caution, rather than an encouragement to buy bad paintings. If you buy such things because you like them, there is no more to be said, but if

you have thoughts of speculation, remember that these paintings must end up on somebody's wall – and they could remain on yours as a dreadful memento. *Jonathan Horwich*

4. *After Sir Lawrence Alma-Tadema, R.A.*
The artist was immensely popular in his day and commanded high prices. He numbered each picture, and when opus CCCXXXVIII was rumoured to have been destroyed, imitators produced fake Alma-Tademas bearing a false signature and this number, hoping to pass for the 'lost' original. The original, a portrait of Miss Onslow Ford in fact still exists, as do hundreds of 'substitutes', of varying quality. The present picture, though among the least accomplished and in poor condition, may still make up to £400.

5. *After Canaletto: 'The Grand Canal', c.1986.*
Even when accepted as a fake, this has quality enough to sell for £300.

6. *After Raphael: 'Madonna della Sedia', tondo.* 18 in. diam. Worth approximately £200–£300.
For some reason, or none, this is one of the most copied of all Old Masters. Perhaps it was used as an exercise in late 19th-century art schools. This is a very poor copy, but as so often it came in an elaborate frame which deserved better.

7. *English School: 'The Prisoner'.* 53 in. × 67 in. Worth approximately £200–£300.
This was actually a jobbing copy of *The Last Sleep of Argyll* in the Commons corridor of the Houses of Parliament. The original, which is about four times the size, is by E. M. Ward, and in terms of history painting, which is unfashionable, it is a fine thing.

8. Post-war souvenirs of Paris from the Place du Tertre make no impression at auction. This picture would be expected to sell for under £100.

8

Scottish Paintings

It would have been natural to assume that after the considerable publicity given in the Scottish and national press during the second half of 1985 to the activities of Mr Conduct and to his forgeries of some of the best known names of 20th-century Scottish painting—Samuel John Peploe, John Duncan Fergusson, Robert Gemmell Hutchison, Sir William Gillies and others—that a subsequent fall in auction prices for the real things would have been inevitable.

Surprisingly, quite the opposite has occurred. The publicity actually had a beneficial effect in alerting new buyers around the world to the fact that if such artists were worth faking, they were worth collecting. This was particularly evident in April 1986, when Christie's Scotland put together the first sale of Scottish pictures ever to produce more than £1m. Over the previous two or three years the market had seen a dramatic rise in the prices of the four artists known as the 'Scottish Colourists', Peploe, Fergusson, George Leslie Hunter and Francis Campbell Boileau Cadell. In the April sale this rise continued still more strongly.

There were six works by Peploe on offer, including still lifes and landscapes, and they sold for prices running from £18,000 to £34,500 (Nos. 1 & 2). Despite this surge of popularity, he did not overshadow his friends and contemporaries entirely. In particular Fergusson (No. 3) and Cadell were in great demand.

Dr T. J. Honeyman, a much admired collector and author and a former director of the Glasgow Art Gallery, was of the firm opinion that Hunter was by far the most exciting of the Colourists. In the past the market has not demonstrated a perfect accord with his judgement. However, in this same sale a fine still life (No. 4) did much to confirm it. Unfortunately, here we are only able to show the Colourists in black and white, thus losing much of their power.

John Maxwell left even these favourites far behind with No. 8. He can be seen as a Scottish cross between Chagall and Dame Laura Knight.

With all this, the Scottish artists of the 19th century have taken something of a back seat this year. However, there have been exceptions. The advantage of selling Scottish works in a Scottish saleroom was demonstrated by two pictures which came from Brighton to Glasgow. One was a splendid painting (No. 6) of the great engineer James Watt in mid-experiment, by the lesser known of the Lauder brothers, James Eckford. This went to the Edinburgh National Portrait Gallery—although it was painted long after Watt's death and was a reconstruction rather than an actual portrait. The second was a distant view of Edinburgh by Alexander Nasmyth which sold for £25,920.

Continuing the topographical theme, a view of Port Glasgow in the heyday of the Clyde by Samuel Bough—although born in Carlisle he is claimed by the

1

Scots as one of their own—also did remarkably well (No. 5).

Strong prices were also obtained for Wilkie's charming little *Domestic Life*, perhaps representing Mary, Queen of Scots, and the infant James I (No. 7); and for the scene at Kellie Castle (No. 9) by John Henry Lorimer – brother of the famous architect Sir Robert.

Alexander Meaddowes

All the paintings shown here were sold at Christie's Scotland.

1. *Samuel John Peploe 'Roses in a Japanese Vase',* c.1923, signed, oil on artist's board. 20 × 16 in. Apr. '86, £34,560.
2. *Samuel John Peploe 'Kirkcudbright',* c.1916, signed, oil on canvas. 21 × 25 in. Apr. '86, £23,760.
3. *J. D. Fergusson, 'Boulevard Montparnasse',* signed and dated 1907, oil on board. 10¾ × 13¾ in. Apr. 86, £16,200.

2

3

4. *Leslie Hunter, 'The Ginger Jar', signed, oil on artist's board. 17 × 22 in. Apr. '86, £14,580.*

5. *Samuel Bough, 'Port Glasgow, Evening', signed and dated 1854, oil on canvas. 26 × 42 in. Apr. '86, £21,600.*

6. *James Eckford Lauder, 'James Watt and the Steam Engine', signed twice with monogram, oil on canvas. 58 × 94 in. Apr. '86, £41,040.*

7. *Sir David Wilkie, 'Domestic Life', signed and dated 1836, oil on panel. 12¾ × 9¼ in. Apr. '86, £18,360.*

8. *John Maxwell, 'The Circus Pony', signed and dated 1941, oil on board. 36 × 30 in. Apr. '86, £45,360.*

9. *John Henry Lorimer, 'The Garden, Kellie Castle', signed and dated 1892. 50 × 40 in. Dec. '85, £23,760.*

Victorian Pictures

1

2

If we leave aside the peaks of Victorian painting—Landseer, the P.R.B., Whistler, Tadema and the rest—and ignore the troughs of 'furnishing painting', the middle ground falls into several loose categories, some of which inevitably overlap.

A good deal of 19th-century landscape painting can be said to derive from Constable, both directly in the work of disciples (No. 1) and imitators like F. W. Watts and B. W. Leader, and more generally in an approach to light and composition. No. 2 is an example of this; it shows a painting in tempera (an egg-based opaque paint) by William Davis, a mid-19th-century artist very much in the Constable mould. His strong use of shading in the clouds and mill roof are typical signs of this. The composition, although at first sight a little sombre, does have a very powerful atmosphere. The dark mill and clouds, and the small boy scurrying away with a sack of newly milled flour, give one very much the feel of an impending storm.

History painting in the grand manner of Italy never became naturalized in England, the efforts of B. West found no school and those of Haydon ended in frustration and suicide. With the exception of murals in the new Houses of Parliament and similar lucrative commissions, Victorian figure painters and their clients preferred the compromise of literary and costume genre. The Stuart period, the 18th century and even the Regency were cleaned up and romanticized for the staid homes of the middle

classes. As often as not, the results need a very sweet tooth to be appreciated, although several Scottish painters in the second half of the century managed to produce strong work in this line without over-much sentiment.

The British peasantry was disappearing, and so it too was idealized as in No. 4, which shows a faintly sentimental scene of a faithful ghillie presenting his true love with a book. It presents a both touching and pleasing scene.

The new rich of the post-Napoleonic period distrusted Old Masters. They were felt to be the preserve of the old aristocratic collectors and many were suspected of being fakes. The middle classes wanted contemporary works even if they were overt exercises in the Dutch 17th-century manner, such as No. 3, a typical Dutch interior by Christoffel Neurdenburg, a German painter. Inevitably, the picture was entitled *The Letter*. Painted in 1841, it captures the feel of two centuries before and does illustrate perfectly this rather peculiar Victorian fashion.

Along with the disappearance of the peasants, much of the British countryside was being changed beyond recognition by the railways and the consequent development of commuting and dormitory towns. The most obvious example of the attempt by artists to preserve something of the vanishing Home Counties, and Surrey in particular, is in the watercolours of Helen Allingham, Birket Foster and their school. A similar nostalgic feeling is perhaps evident in the

many paintings of old fashioned farmyards by the followers of the Herrings, as in No. 7, a painting entitled meritably *Milking Time*. The scene is a rural delight, sheep obediently emerging from the gate, farmer leaning on a cow, chatting to the milkmaid, the whole feeling one of peace and tranquillity.

Today there are many painters who can make a living by painting portraits of

1. *Frederick Whitehead, 'The River Frome', signed and inscribed on a label on the reverse.* 24 × 36 in. June '85, £1,700.

2. *William Davis, 'Ditton Mill', signed and inscribed on reverse.* 11½ × 15½ in. Mar. '86, £6,500.

3. *Christoffel Neurdenburg, 'The Letter', signed and dated 1841.* 18¾ × 15½ in. July '85, £550.

3

4

pets. In the 19th century, when many people kept horses, horse portraiture was lucrative business. A standard formula, which was popular with the artists because so little work was needed for the background, was the horse standing sideways in a loose box. In the hands of a painter such as the elder J. F. Herring (No. 6) this could be very effective, but as used by lesser artists like James Pawley (No. 5) or J. A. Wheeler, the formula becomes repetitive, although the horses are well painted.

The new middle class also began to take seaside holidays, and there arose a demand for coastal landscape paintings as well as pictures of the resorts. Earlier marine paintings had tended to use coasts as backdrops for boats and battles. Now the painter was looking out from the land or along the shore and did not need to include incidents or even figures (cf. W.P. Frith's great *Ramsgate Sands,* in the Royal Collection).

By contrast with the broad sweep of coastal landscape for its own sake, there was also a great demand for finely detailed still lifes of wild flowers, fruit, birds' nests and the like. They too were an attempt to preserve something of nature in an increasingly urban way of life. They appear in both watercolour and oil, although they stick to a basic formula, and quality and condition vary enormously. Some of the better versions in oil were painted by the Clare family of Birmingham, of whom George is probably the best and the most well known (No. 8). A few years ago he was occasionally making four figures, but now prices seem to have settled down to the £350–£500 range. *Jonathan Horwich*

4. *William Henry Midwood, 'The Ghillie's Gift', signed and dated 1866. 14½ × 11½ in. Mar. '86, £1,700.*

5. *James Pawley, 'A Black Hunter in a Stable', signed and inscribed 'Bath'. 20 × 26 in. June '85, £600.*
   Bath was the centre of operations of the Wheeler family which produced large numbers of horse portraits of this type.

6. *John Frederick Herring, Sen., 'A Harnessed Bay in a Stable', signed and dated 1838. Sold by Bonham's, June '86.*

7. *S. J. Clark, 'Milking Time', signed and dated 1879. 49½ in × 29½ in. June '85, £1,700.*

8. *George Clare, 'Bird's Nest on a Mossy Bank', one of a pair, one signed. 6 × 8 in. July '85, £650.*

5

6

8

Australian Paintings

1

Australian paintings have leapt dramatically in value over the last few years with major examples by the early colonial artists, the Impressionists and the Moderns securing six-figure sums. Most notably, Arthur Streeton's 'Golden Summer', perhaps the quintessential picture from the Impressionist school in the late 1880s, changed hands for over a million Australian dollars in 1985.

At the risk of simplification, pictures of Australian interest can be divided into four general categories: early topography of New South Wales (c.1800–35), mostly the work of barely trained soldiers and convicts (No.1); the more sophisticated, picturesque views of colonial painters (c.1835–75) such as

Martens, Glover, Von Guerard and Chevalier (Nos. 2 and 6); Impressionism, dating from the mid 1880s in the work of Roberts, Streeton, Davies and Conder (No. 5) and generations of followers extending well into the twentieth century (No. 7); and finally, the Moderns, such as Dobell, Drysdale, Nolan, Williams, Boyd and Blackman, a variety of painters practising original styles of painting which attempt to break from European traditions.

In the saleroom, Australian museums and institutions have shown increasing interest in works of historic and artistic importance and have had to compete with a new breed of rich collectors who are rewriting the value of their nation's

art. Vigorous buying at the top end of the market and a temporarily booming economy fuelled an almost reckless pursuit of Australian pictures by the trade in early 1985. Since those heady days the market has steadied and become much more discriminating. While buyers continue to pay enormous prices for good examples by the major artists, the love affair with names appears to be over. Martens, Streeton and Boyd no longer guarantee sparkling prices.

Young markets can be strongly influenced for good or ill by political events as well as economic factors. The constitutional crisis over the dismissal of the Whitlam government in 1975 killed the Australian picture market for about a year. In June 1986 an austere budget has again depressed immediate prospects. While fears of the economy weakening have tempered enthusiasm, the major touring exhibition of Australian Impressionist pictures in 1986 in Australia and preparations for the bicentennial celebrations should counter pessimism and contribute to the consolidation of this relatively young market over the next two years.   *Nicholas Lambourn*

1. *John Eyre, 'View of the Town and Cove of Sydney, New South Wales, in Sept. 1806, as seen from the East', tinted lithograph with handcolouring. 8½ × 16⅓ in. Jun. '86, £4,800.*

    John Eyre was a convict, transported for theft, whose views in New South Wales are amongst the earliest pictorial records of the New Colony. Some of the convict artists had been transported for forgery and put their skills in draughtsmanship to more social use. Two such convicts, Lycett and Watling, produced enough 'good work' to earn reductions in their sentences.

2

3

4

5

2. *Conrad Martens, 'A view of Sydney Harbour looking East, with Shipping Anchored off Fort Denison', signed and dated 1850, watercolour and bodycolour with gum arabic.* 18 × 26 in. Oct. '83, £42,000.

   Martens arrived in Sydney in 1835 and settled there for the rest of his life. His watercolours concentrate on the harbour and surrounding New South Wales countryside.

3. *George Edward Peacock, 'Government House and MacQuarie Fort, from the Botanical Gardens', oil on board.* 4¼ × 5⅞ in., one of a pair. Nov. '85, £6,500.

   Peacock worked in Sydney in the 1840s and normally produced small-scale views. Though not highly skilled, his pictures have a passable charm and the popularity of his subject attracts good prices.

4. *Joseph Fowles, 'A Three Masted Barque off South Head', signed and inscribed Sydney, oil on canvas.* 15 × 21 in. Jun. '86, £16,000.

   A good price for this artist, reflecting the twin appeal of marine painting and a relatively early Sydney view.

5. *David Davies, 'Moonrise', oil on canvas.* 16 × 20 in. Jun. '86, £25,000.

   A painting from Davies's most sought after Australian period in the early 1890s. Davies worked in the footsteps of the founders of Australian Impressionism, Tom Roberts, Arthur Streeton and Charles Conder, whose brightly painted panels of the hot and dusty Australian landscape shocked critics and public at their first exhibition in Melbourne in 1889.

6. *Nicholas Chevalier, 'The Yarra River, Victoria, Australia', signed with monogram, pencil and watercolour.* 8½ × 8¼ in. Jun. '85, £1,400.

   Chevalier was a Russian-born artist who worked in Australia and New Zealand in the 1860s. He continued to produce views of Antipodean scenery, based on his original sketches, when he returned to London. Prices range from around £1,000 for small picturesque vignettes to £42,000 (Jun. '86) for a large finished watercolour of New Zealand scenery.

7. *Lloyd Frederic Rees, 'The Hills of Bathurst', signed, oil on canvas, c.1950.* 18 × 30 in. Jun. '85, £30,000.

   Rees works in the tradition of his Impressionist predecessors. He has recently enjoyed renewed interest, borne out by this high price for the work of a living painter.

6

7

Modern British Pictures

The most notable trend in the modern British market over the past year has been the growing enthusiasm for pretty pictures by popular British artists, from the Newlyn school onwards. The craze for Newlyn painters (Nos. 1 and 2) now extends to an unashamedly philistine love affair with pictures of the seaside. Minor painters' variations on the theme of sirens in the idyll of sun, sea and sand have proved irresistible and have attracted enormous prices. Five years ago few artists other than household names (Alfred Munnings, Walter Sickert, John Lavery, L.S. Lowry and Russell Flint) could hope for consistent prices over £5,000. In 1986, pot-boilers by Ernest Higgins Rigg, Edwin Harris, Dorothea Sharp, Wilfred Gabriel de Glehn and Algernon Talmage (No. 3) all passed £10,000. Unheard-of prices (£85,000 for Arthur Spooner's *The Nottingham Boat Club*) for pleasant pictures by unheard-of artists have made the headlines and emphasized the strength of the market.

The 'modern British' tag does however cover a broad range of very different schools, and the commercial progress of each is distinct. The British Surrealists, a 'group' at odds with popular notions of art and taste in the 1930s, have yet to muster widespread support in the saleroom. Other than a glimpse in the 'Dada And Surrealism Reviewed' exhibition in 1978, they have not had much of a showing since the 'International Surrealist Exhibition' in 1936. Recent provincial exhibitions and London 'sideshows' have lacked major exhibits and have not stirred the trade. Nevertheless, works by the group have been appearing more regularly in the salerooms (among the names to look out for: Roland Penrose, John Melville, Conroy Maddox, John Banting, John Tunnard, Humphrey Jennings, John Armstrong, Eileen Agar, F. C. McWilliam), and good early examples have attracted modest attention.

Edward Burra (No. 5) alone, an artist on the fringe of Surrealism, has made significant impact in the saleroom. The major Burra exhibition in London last year, coinciding with the appearance of good examples of his work in the saleroom, encouraged prices above the norm.

Major exhibitions and monographs invariably boost prices for the artists concerned. Recently the Omega Workshop exhibition roused Bloomsbury prices, and the Gwen John retrospective and new literature are pushing her past the revered Augustus—as he predicted! In the footsteps of the earlier Newlyn exhibitions, the St. Ives show at the Tate directed attention to later 'Cornish' pictures.

As the market in general concentrates heavily on the pretty pictures of the traditionalist painters, the Surrealists will be seen to represent excellent value for money by comparison: in 1986 a rude original drawing by John Banting may be acquired for less than the price of a rude picture after Sir William Russell Flint (Nos. 6 and 8).

The Bloomsbury school (Roger Fry, Duncan Grant and Vanessa Bell), the Camden Town and London Group painters (Walter Sickert, Spencer Gore, Robert Bevan, Harold Gilman) and the Vorticists (Wyndham Lewis, William Roberts, David Bomberg) have progressed steadily, much as expected. An exceptional portrait by Bell, a filmic interior by Gore (No. 7) or a major picture by Lewis will fetch over £15,000, with lesser examples now comfortably settled in the low thousands.

New candidates for promotion to this price level might now be sought in the ranks of the post-war abstract painters. In the meantime, it is to be expected that the traditional painters will continue their glamorous progress, with Munnings (No. 4) once again awarded the glittering prices.   *Nicholas Lambourn*

1. *Albert Chevallier Tayler, 'The Yellow Ribbon', signed and dated 88, oil on canvas. 18⅛ × 14 in. Sept. '85, £24,000.*   All the beauty and romance of Newlyn in this intimate study. Tayler is not always this good. Prices at auction range from £61,000 (Nov. '83) for a major large exhibition picture of comparable quality, to a couple of hundred pounds for sloppy late work.

2. *Harold Harvey, 'Morning Sunshine', signed and dated 1911, oil on canvas. 35½ × 27½ in.* Christie's King Street, Mar. '86, £22,000. More familiar Newlyn ingredients. Of all the Newlyn painters, Harvey has made the most dramatic leaps in price in 1986. This picture sold well in March after failing to find a buyer in 1985 at Phillips.

1

2

3

4

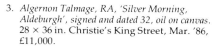

3. *Algernon Talmage, RA, 'Silver Morning, Aldeburgh', signed and dated 32, oil on canvas.* 28 × 36 in. Christie's King Street, Mar. '86, £11,000.

4. *Sir Alfred J. Munnings, PRA, 'Gypsy Tales', signed oil on canvas.* 24 × 30 in. Mar. '86, £25,000.

5. *Edward Burra, 'Room with a View', pencil.* 24 × 19¼ in. Mar. '86, £1,000.

6. *John Banting, 'Bureaucrats', signed and dated 1943, pen and ink and red crayon.* 6¼ × 9½ in. Mar. '86, £320.

7. *Spencer Frederick Gore, 'Behind the Blind', with studio stamp, oil on canvas.* 19½ × 15⅜ in. Christie's King Street, Mar. '86, £26,000.

8. *Sir William Russell Flint, RA, 'Models for Goddesses', reproduction, signed in pencil.* 18 × 25 in. June '86, £340.

6

8

Nineteenth- and Twentieth-Century Illustrators

Often it seems that with the work of illustrators the most obvious is the most expensive. It is not surprising that Aldin's smug looking bullpup (No. 1) or his *Approbation* (No. 2) should have made their money, and indeed they are good examples of his range from the near-winsome to direct if simple portraiture.

More surprising to a general collector, perhaps, might be the price realized by the collection of pen and ink drawings and watercolours by Mervyn Peake (Nos. 3 and 4), who is best known as the author of the weird *Gormenghast* trilogy. But then Peake has a growing reputation as one of the better British artists of the recent past, and there were 28 of them, which works out at little more than £100 each.

Obviously the prices for the work of some illustrators are largely dictated by their reputations in a wider artistic world. Charles Ricketts is a good example. No. 9 is a little laboured and confused in the drawing, and the subject – Phaedra hanging herself – may not entice, but his work is comparatively rare and he is highly thought of.

In a general way anything coloured, or even washed, is likely to be more expensive than a pen and ink drawing, however good. Hence the much greater prices for Nos. 7 and 8 than for Nos. 10 and 11. Incidentally, Ardizzone has a number of strong champions among the dealers, and they have done much to raise prices since his death in 1979. He often included a rotund self-portrait such as the top right-hand figure in No. 8.

The distrust of the uncoloured means that it can still be possible to acquire drawings by some of the best Victorian illustrators and cartoonists such as du Maurier, Frank Reynolds, Starr Wood, Bernard Partridge and even – with great good fortune – Charles Keene, for between £80 and £150. Whistler called Keene 'the greatest English artist since Hogarth', and as a draughtsman he has been compared to Rembrandt without too great an exaggeration. Although you could not get a good example at this price, such a level even for secondary works is ludicrous, and it only obtains because he and the others are still dismissed by some as mere cartoonists.

This blind spot in market appreciation seems all the stranger when you consider the prices for the Bonzo the Dog watercolours by George Ernest Studdy, which are charming, but hardly great works of art. Four or five years ago they too could have been bought for £50 or £80 (Nos. 5 and 6).   *Trixie Millar*

1. *Cecil Aldin*, A Bullpup, *signed, water and bodycolour*, 17 × 13 in. Dec. '85, £2,600.
2. *Cecil Aldin*, Approbation, *signed, coloured chalks*, 12 × 17½ in. Mar. '86, £2,800.
3. & 4. *Two of 28 drawings and watercolours by Mervyn Peake, many signed and annotated.* Sep. '85, £3,000. These drawings were made as illustrations to *Witchcraft in England* by Christina Hoyle.

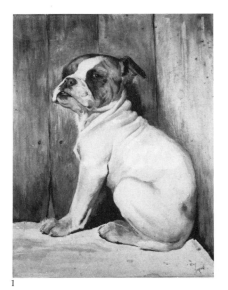

1

2

3

4

5. *George Ernest Studdy*, Wake up Lazybones, Breakfast Time!, *signed and inscribed, pen and black ink and watercolour*, 15× 10¼. Mar. '86, £1,100.

6. *George Ernest Studdy*, What about a Beer in Berlin?, *signed and inscribed, pencil, pen and watercolour*, 15 × 10¾ in. Mar. '86, £1,200.

7. *Edward Ardizzone, R.A.*, At the Beach Hut, *signed with initials, brown and grey washes*, 7½ × 11 in. Mar. '86, £650.

8. *Edward Ardizzone, R.A.*, The Life Class, *signed with initials, pencil and watercolour*, 11 × 15¼ in. Dec. '85, £420. This was quite a favourite subject with Ardizzone. The only problem about his charming drawings and watercolours is that rather too many of them have been put on the market in recent years.

9. *Charles de Sousy Ricketts, R.A.*, Phaedra and Ariadne, *signed with initials, pen and brown ink*, 5¾ × 3½ in. Sep. '85, £7,800.

10. *Edward Ardizzone, R.A.*, The Milldale Riot, Chapter XIII, *pencil, pen and black ink*, 7¼ × 10½ in. Mar. '86, £220.

11. *Edward Ardizzone, R.A.*, A Clumsy Young Devil, *inscribed, pencil, pen and black ink*, 7¼ × 10¾ in. Mar. '86, £200. This drawing and No. 7 are illustrations for *Milldale Riot* by Freda Nichol (1965).

5

6

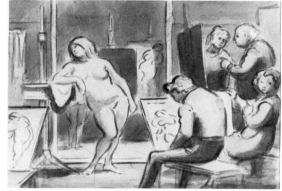
8

9

11

Nineteenth- and Early Twentieth-Century Watercolours

Over the last decade English watercolours have been one of the great successes of the fine art market. In particular, works produced by late Victorian and Edwardian artists have seen dramatic price increases. Certain artists of this period have become almost household names: Helen Allingham (No. 1), Myles Birket Foster, Sylvester Stannard (No. 2), Kate Greenaway and W. H. Robinson, to name but a few. It is unfortunate to note, however, that as these artists have reached such heights of popularity, their prices have also increased so that they are beyond the scope of the small collector.

The market is seeing strong competition for 'The Cottage Scene', that is to say pretty landscapes and watercolours that are picturesque and highly decorative. This is amply demonstrated by the work of Allingham. However, one can buy a similar subject by the equally competent but less popular artist E. A. Chadwick for much less (No. 3). It is easily understandable that there are not many people who are able to pay £5,000 plus for a decorative watercolour, but there are a considerably greater number of buyers in the purchasing range of £800–£1,200. It is therefore worth taking into account that while the leaders become more and more expensive, the mass of their followers are often to be picked up at a fraction of the price, for instance E. A. Chadwick, Wilmot Pilsbury, Samuel Elgood, E. A. Rowe (No. 4). In any case, fashion has boosted the school so rapidly that there may well be a revaluation and a slowing, or even falling, of prices before long. If that happens there may be opportunities to secure the best before a new rise occurs.

The Orientalist market, however, has already experienced a downturn in prices and has been a victim of fashion and politics. Until the beginning of summer 1985, works by the latest leader in this field, A. O. Lamplough, and artists such as H. Lynton and H. Hansen — and indeed any watercolour that depicted scenes of 'Desert Riders', 'Eastern Bazaars', 'Harem Girls' and even 'Aged Gentlemen Haggling over the Price of a Rug' — resulted in strong bidding in sales (No. 5). At the time certain people ventured to say that the prices realized for some of the minor works were far in excess of their real merit. The words of those individuals have come true, as more and more buyers will only continue to pay high prices for watercolours of quality. Works by Lamplough that once fetched £4,000–£5,000 are now struggling in the £1,000–£1,500 region. Lyntons that sold for £400–£500 are hard pushed to find a buyer; at best he would realize perhaps £50–£70.

To diversify, the work of the illustrator (see pp. 220, 221) would appear to be one of the watercolour markets of the future, for as this market gains in strength, so it does in depth. Artists such as Dudley Hardy, Frank Reynolds, E. H. Shepard, Lawson Wood and many others are emerging as promising investments. For as prices for works by Rackham and Co. steadily increase, so does the demand for quality illustrations by other artists at a lower price. *Julian Jones*

1. *Helen Allingham, 'The Kitchen Garden, Farringford', signed, with inscription on reverse, heightened in white.* 14¾ × 11¼ in. Mar. '86, £4,200.

2. *Henry John Sylvester Stannard, 'A Country Cottage'.* 10 × 13½ in. Dec. '85, £1,700.

3. *Ernest Albert Chadwick, 'A May Morning', signed, inscribed and dated 1927 on the reverse.* 14¼ × 10½ in. Apr. '86, £1,600.
   This is nearly half the price of a very similar painting sold in Feb. '85, and indicates the start of a slump for this type of picture.

4. *E. A. Rowe, 'View of a Country House', signed, pencil and watercolour.*
7¾ × 10¼ in. Nov. '85, £650.

3

John Harrington Bird, 'Tribesman Riding a White Stallion', signed,
heightened with white. 12 × 17¾ in. July '85, £3,400.

6. *T. C. L. Rowbottom, 'Extensive Landscape View', signed and dated 1856,*
heightened with white. 7½ × 13 in. Nov. '85, £250.

George Samuel Elgood, 'Avenue of Trees, the
Sea Beyond', signed and dated 1898, pencil
and watercolour heightened with white. 7¾ ×
14¾ in. Sept. '85, £260.

8. *Will Anderson, 'Donkey Cart and Figure on a*
Roadway', signed. 10 × 14 in. Jan. '86, £420.

Posters

The whole point of a poster is impact. It is created to demand attention for a specific product, a theatre or film show, an actor, a political movement or whatever. The lithographic process was an ideal medium which enabled the art of the poster to develop quickly and imaginatively, and collectors have not been slow to spot the artistic and monetary potential. Over the years this has not only been defined by the product which was being advertised, but also by rarity, condition, artist, school/movement and, to a certain extent, investment. All play important parts in determining prices for individual examples.

First of all, to illustrate the exceptional, and perhaps explain why people can pay vast sums for a mere poster. In Apr. '85 a poster by Kolomon Moser (No. 1) was sold to an American collector for £62,000. This was naturally a world auction record, and several of the factors mentioned above went into its making. The artist belonged to an important movement, the Secessionists, who were highly influential and have a strong following. Their original work is rare and very expensive, but this poster typified the style. It dated from 1902 and was in excellent condition. So here you had a rare example – the only one ever known to have come on the market – by an important artist of an important school. Everything combined to make it the most expensive poster in the world.

Other examples of the same sort of thing are Nos. 2 and 3. Andri was another Secessionist, although not as rare or as important as Moser. However, the school, period, condition and impact were all important. The Mucha (No. 3) was one of a well-known set of the four seasons. It is sensuous and sought after, not exactly rare, but also not common. It is typical of Mucha in his role as high priest of the Art Nouveau, which is as popular as ever. It was also in excellent condition, and it was entirely new to most serious dealers and collectors.

These are exceptions, either by price or by quality, and obviously they appealed particularly to serious and moneyed specialists. However, the points that they illustrate are relevant to any poster one may look at. Prices will be dictated by them even at much lower levels. The poster was made to attract: the strength of attraction is obviously a prime factor in pricing.

The purpose of a poster, whether political (No. 4), ideological, artistic (No. 5) or commercial, can be important. Among the various artistic movements one might look out for Art Nouveau, Art Deco, Secessionist, Futurist, De Stijl, Bauhaus and Constructivism. Examples from some countries, such as Russia, are rare. Some schools can be equated to national tastes: Art Nouveau, France and Belgium; Constructivism, America; Secessionist, Austria. Some products, such as food, drink (No. 7), clothes, the theatre, cars (No. 8), politics – and even advertising space (No. 9) may appeal to the taste of one country or all.

The artists, of course, matter enormously, and the big names from a wider artistic field make the big money here too. Names such Kokoska, Dudovichi, Cassandre (Nos. 10 and 12), Steinlen, Toulouse-Lautrec, Picasso, Laurencin (No. 11), Andri, Moser, Mangold and many others carry a premium, even though, for the most part, we are not dealing with their original work.

The poster is a commonplace article in the street, but as yet not in the home. In studying all these points and following auctions, one will quickly ascertain what is most desirable from a purely pecuniary point of view, and more slowly which posters are most agreeable to one's own taste (No. 12 for my own). Finally though, the sheer size of some posters may be important – depending on where you live.   *Richard Barclay*

1. *Koloman Moser, 'Ver Sacrum', lithograph in colours, 1902. 68⅜ × 23¼ in. Apr. '85, £62,000.*

2. *Ferdinand Andri, exhibition poster, 'XXVI Ausstellung Secession', lithograph in colours. 36¼ × 23¾ in. May '86, £8,700.*

3. *Alphonse Mucha, 'Spring, Summer, Autumn, Winter', lithographs in colours, 1896. Each 41 × 20⅞ in. May '86, £6,800.*

1

2

3

4

5

6

4. *K. Polliarkova and R. Mozchaeva, 'Lenin's Push into the Business Generation', lithograph in colours. 38 × 25⅝. May '86, £85.*

5. *Adolphe Crespin and Edouard Duych, 'Alcazar Royal', lithograph in colours. 39¾ × 30½ in. May '86, £280.*

6. *Paul Colin, 'G. Marconi', lithograph in colours. 62⅛ × 44½ in. May '86, £220.*

7. *'Sem' (Von Serge Goursat), 'D.O.M. Benedictine', lithograph in colours. 50⅜ × 77¼ in. May '86, £85.*

8. *Henry Monnier, 'Automobiles Unic', lithograph in colours, 1925. 59½ × 44½ in. May '86, £700.*

9. *Alan Cracknell, 'A Company Needs You', offset lithograph. One from a folio of designs by various artists for 'The Sunday Times' classified columns, 1960s. 60 × 40 in. May '86, £190.*

10. *Adolphe Mouron Cassandre, 'Nord Express', lithograph in colours, 1927. 41⅜ × 29⅝ in. May '86, £1,300.*

11. *Marie Laurencin, 'Bal des Petits Lits Blancs', lithograph in colours, 1931. 31⅜ × 22¾ in. May '86, £1,000.*

12. *Adolf Mouron Cassandre, 'Bonal ouvre l'Appétit', lithograph in colours, 1935. 61⅝ × 47⅛ in. May '86, £320.*

7

8

9

10

11

12

Sporting Prints

In *The Popular Antiques Yearbook*, Vol. 1 (p. 232), I described how one set of Henry Alken hunting aquatints (No. 1) could be worth several thousand pounds and another, very similar at first glance, only £100 or so. Is it a crisp, early impression or a later reprint? Is the colouring contemporary? Is the hunt socially, and thus financially, desirable? Good reference books are almost as rare as good impressions, and the salerooms and the galleries of specialist dealers are almost the only places where one can make comparisons and learn the differences.

The different sports, like the hunts, have their hierarchy. Horses are still the kings, whether indulging in racing, hunting or coaching (Nos. 1–5). Sir Alfred James Munnings has proved immensely popular in Britain and America, with prices for major oil paintings rising from about £40,000 four or five years ago to as much as £300,000 now, and even coloured reproductions of his racing subjects are now selling for between £800 and £1,200 (No. 5).

Fishing is one of the most popular British pastimes and it is classless. There are surprisingly few fishing prints and naturally the best tend to be expensive, although as No. 6 was one from a large set of different sports the price was very reasonable. However, the allied activity of salmon spearing or 'leistering' (No. 7) is less popular, given today's sensitivity to bloodiness in sports. It is interesting to note that when the original painting for this mezzotint was offered by a dealer in London and Edinburgh three years

ago, it proved difficult to sell, although ultimately it found a Scottish home. There are similar problems with such 'sports' as bull-baiting and cock-fighting, although some of the coursing prints still have a ready market.

Golf, cricket, and real and lawn tennis, have their enthusiastic followers, and as the market grows already-rare prints become still rarer and more expensive. Obviously, too, certain prints can command something of a premium because they have a ready-made special interest audience. This applies to such subjects as sporting events at particular schools, or yachting subjects (No. 9), which appeal not just to the British sea-dog tradition, but also to particular clubs.

In one case the influence of television can be seen. Only four years ago, the few 19th-century prints of snooker that exist might have made about £100 in good condition. After all, snooker and billiards were regarded as ways to fill an idle hour rather than serious sport. Now even a worn and damaged impression will command between £400 and £600.

Richard Barclay

1. *After Henry Alken, by C. Bentley, 'The Grand Leicestershire Steeplechase', one of a set of 8 coloured aquatints.* Aug. '85, £1,200.

2. *After James Pollard, by G. Hunt, 'Approach to Christmas', coloured aquatint.* Mar. '83, £2,200.
   A very good price for the time, which should be bettered now. The sale of this fine impression was no doubt helped by the Dickensian 'Dingley Dell' subject-matter.

5

3. *After John Frederick Herring sen., by T. Sutherland, 'Barefoot and Memnon', coloured lithographs, a pair (only one illustrated). Feb. '86, £360.*

4. *After Henry George Laporte, by R. G. and A. W. Reeve, 'Liverpool Grand National Steeplechase', one of a set of 4 coloured aquatints. 20 × 40 in. May '85, £450.*

   These were rather tired impressions, thus the unremarkable price.

5. *After Sir Alfred James Munnings, 'October Meeting', signed, coloured reproduction. 16 × 28½ in. Jul. '85. £850.*

   Such is the popularity of Munnings at present that these reproductions can make much more than many original prints.

6. *After Henry Alken, by J. Clark, coloured aquatint, one from the set of fifty 'National Sports of Great Britain'. Nov. '85, £6,500 (the set).*

7. *William Simpson, 'Salmon Spearing by Torch Light', mezzotint. July '85, £410.*

8. *After Fown, by R. Earlom, 'Dogs and Badger', coloured aquatint. Aug. '85, £160.*

   Earlom was one of the greatest 18th-century printmakers, usually working in mezzotint. Here the subject perhaps worked against the print's popularity.

9. *C. Taylor, 'Surprise', coloured lithograph. Christie's King Street, Mar. '85, £918.*

7

9

22. Books and Maps

Introduction
by Adam Langlands and Tom Lamb

With individual books and maps, the only certainty when looking for short-term trends in prices is that there won't be any. However, over the last year a general trend is discernible. 1985 saw a marked increase in the price of books, while maps (following the trend of the last three years) have been static in price, and have even occasionally shown a decrease.

The general increase in book prices has various causes. Firstly, the dearth of good quality works available to the book-buying public has brought about the sort of fierce competitive bidding that all auctioneers hope for. This has resulted in sharp increases in the prices of good quality books, and less dramatic, but still appreciable increases in those of a lesser standard.

Another factor is the increasing number of collectors buying at auction. Fifteen or even five years ago, auctions were attended exclusively by trade buyers, but this is no longer so true, on account of extensive publicity campaigns and also an increasing awareness amongst private collectors of the possibilities of bargains.

Fashion also plays her part in short-term price increases. This is most evident with modern first editions. For instance, 1984 was a good year to sell a first edition of Orwell's book of the same name, particularly in the rarer maroon dust jacket. The highest recorded auction price was £220 in July. In 1985, the highest UK price for the same title was £100. This was surpassed by a copy in Australia which made 280 Australian dollars. The more common green dust-jacketed edition showed similar fluctuations, and to a lesser extent Orwell's other works were also affected.

On a slightly macabre note, the death of a well-known author can also have an effect on the prices of his books. Sir John Betjeman's death in 1984 is already producing slight upward movements in the prices of his works, and over the

1. *A.S.G. Butler, 'The Architecture of Sir Edwin Lutyens', 4 vols., 1950.* Jan. '86, £950.
   The set sold was similar to the one shown in this photograph.
2. *E. Adveno Brooke, 'The Garden of England', folio, 1857, title and 24 plates on India paper.* Nov. '85, £3,000.
3. *W.H. Pyne, 'History of the Royal Residences', 2 vols., 4to, 1819, 100 hand-coloured aquatints, later half-morocco.* Feb. '86, £3,200.

next year or so, one can reasonably expect the same to apply to Philip Larkin, Robert Graves and Christopher Isherwood, among others.

The final area where fashion plays a part involves the 'Bunker Hunt syndrome'. Over the last year, it was rumoured that a particular collector (through the agency of a firm of booksellers) was interested in books by or designed by the Victorian architect and Gothic revivalist Owen Jones. This produced quite dramatic price rises in his *Grammar of Ornament* (first published in 1854): *circa* £450 in 1983–4 to £1,200 and £1,800 for two copies in 1985. So, a warning note to collectors: book prices do vary with demand and fashion. The demand will, one suspects, always be a factor, but fashion changes—remember bell-bottom trousers?

While the book market has been buoyant over the past year, it is sad to report the continued stagnation of prices for maps. Many decorative maps have fallen from the high prices achieved in the late 1970s and early 1980s, firstly as a result of an oversupply of material, and secondly as a result of changes in fashion. In terms of established British collecting there has been a move away from some of the popular 17th-century mapping such as Morden county maps, Ogilby road maps and Braun and Hogenberg town plans, and even county maps by Blaeu, Jansson and Speed have not significantly increased in value over the past year. As some of the 17th-century cartographers have been less in demand, so there has been a greater interest in 18th-century mapmakers, particularly the work of Emmanuel Bowen, Thomas Kitchen and Herman Moll. Similarly 18th-

3

4

and 19th-century large-scale county surveys, such as Rocque's maps of Berkshire and Middlesex, or André and Chapman's Essex, have sold well during the past year (see pp. 232–3).

Maps which have shown significant gains over the past few years have been closely allied to the interests of overseas collectors. Maps of North America, world maps, Australia and Asia have been eagerly purchased, the high prices often aided by currency fluctuations and the purchasing power of institutions keen to complete their collections.

One trend to emerge among 'New World' material is a re-evaluation of late 19th-century maps, particularly those published separately in slipcases, rather than atlas form. For example, in February 1986 a folding map of 'The Seat of War in Mexico', published by Disturnell in 1847, brought £350, while a late Crutchley edition of Wyld's map of Australia, circa 1850, sold for £170. For Asian mapping, despite the decline in interest from Hong Kong, Japanese and Chinese maps (pre-1800) are still sought after, and again a re-evaluation of 19th-century material has brought an increased interest in British Surveys of Malaya, Burma and India. While maps of these continents, together with world maps, have become increasingly popular, European and African mapping has been static in value.

Although many individual sheet maps have not appreciably risen in price, there has been an increasing market for complete atlases in good condition. This increase has been seen throughout the range, from volumes of Blaeu's *Atlas Major* to the mid 19th-century atlases by Black, Johnston or Gall and Inglis. This trend, together with the move to collect specialized 19th-century mapping such as geological surveys and Ordnance Surveys, bodes well for the future, and I hope more people will begin to appreciate the cartographic and scientific skills of mapmaking in addition to their decorative appeal. In January 1986 a map of Kent published by a local paper in 1945, showing the sites of 'doodlebug' landings, sold for £35, so perhaps a new era of map collecting has already arrived!

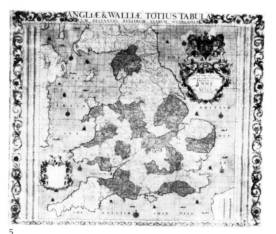

5

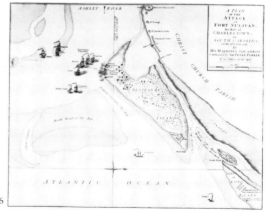

6

4. *Tate Wilkinson, 'My Own Life', memoirs, 4 vols., 12mo, York, 1790, fine morocco binding, bookplate of Frances Currer. Jan. '84, £750.*

5. *Robert Morden and Joseph Pask, engraved wallmap of England and Wales, c.1702. 57 × 65 in. July '85, £2,000.*

6. *Robert Sayer and John Bennett, 'Plan of the Attack on Fort Sullivan', engraving, 1776. 20 × 16 in. May '85, £600.*

What Makes A Book Valuable?

'What makes a book valuable?' is a question that is easily answered: supply and demand. The difficult question following on from this is 'What is in demand?'

With the proviso that the exceptions are almost as numerous as the inclusions, it is possible to point out broad bands where books on a particular subject, in good condition, are likely to be sought after, and of value.

Subject	Valuable if	Examples
Medicine	Pre-1850	Quain (Richard), *The Anatomy of the Arteries of the Human Body*, folio, 1844, poor condition. Oct.'83, £140.
		Boyle (Robert), *Medicinal Experiments or a Collection of Choice and Safe Remedies*, 12mo, 1692, poor condition. Apr. '85, £100.
Science	Pre-1850	Boyle (Robert), *Tracts ... containing New Experiments Touching the Relation betwixt Flame and Air*, 8vo, 1673, modern calf binding. Aug. '85, £140.
Gastronomy	Pre-1850	Smith (Robert), *Court Cookery*, Second Edition, 1725. May '80, £200 (No. 4).
		Glasse (Hannah), *The Art of Cookery made Plain and Easy*, new edition, 1788, average condition. Nov. '85, £100.
Law	Pre-1770	Blackstone (Sir William), *Commentaries on the Laws of England*, 4 vols, 4to, Oxford, 1765–9, good condition. Aug. '83, £2,700.
Philosophy	First editions of seminal works	Marx (Karl), *Das Kapital*, Hamburg, 1867, good condition. Apr. '82, £3,200.
		Comte (Auguste) *Cours de Philosophie Positive*, 6 vols, Paris, 1830–52, modern binding. Feb. '84, £200.
Religion	The earlier the better, preferably pre-1700	Bunyan (John), *Pilgrims Progress*, third edition, 12mo, 1679, poor condition. Jul. '85, £1,900.
History	A few selected works, leather-bound sets in good condition, pre-1850 social and economic history	Gibbon (Edward), *The History of the Decline and Fall of the Roman Empire*, 6 vols (second state of Vol 1), 4to, 1776–88, poor condition. Jul. '85, £450.
		Hume (David), *The History of England*, new edition, 13 vols, 1812, contemporary Russia binding. Sept. '82, £140.
Travel	Contemporary accounts of early exploration; America 17th-18th century	Smith (Capt. John) *The General Historie of Virginia, New England, and the Summer Isles ...*, 3rd issue, folio, 1627, Lord Baltimore's copy. Jun. '85 £10,500.
	Australia, 18th-19th century; Central Asia/ Himalayas, 19th-20th century	Cook (Capt. James), *A Voyage towards the South Pole and round the World*, 2 Vols, 4to, 1777, good condition. Mar. '85, £1,600.
		Stein (M. Auriel) *Serindia*, 5 vols, folio, 1921, cloth. May '85, £2,275.
	18th and 19th-century works incl. plates (some areas more collectable, e.g. Switzerland, Germany, America)	Beattie (William), *Switzerland Illustrated*, 2 vols, 4to, 1836, average condition. Mar '85, £300.
		Beattie (William), *The Danube*, 4to, (nd), good condition. Oct. '84, £200.
		Willis (N.P.), *American Scenery*, 2 vols, 1840, average condition. May '85, £300.

1. *Tissot (J.J.),* The Life of Christ, *2 vols, folio, 1897–8, fine vellucent binding by Cedric Chivers.* Jul. '85, £800. Copies in ordinary bindings make no more than £100.

2. *Huxley (Aldous),* Brave New World, *first edition, 1932, pristine condition.* Aug. '84, £220. Copies in average condition make no more than £100.

3. *Grosz (George),* Ecce Homo, *Ausgabe D, folio, Berlin, 1923, good condition.* A copy of the same work with a worn binding made £155 in November 1980. This work is one of the classic works from the early 20th-century German school of artist/illustrators.

4. *Smith (Robert),* Court Cookery, *second edition, 1725.* May 1980, £200. This work has survived the rigours of greasy smoke-filled 18th/19th-century kitchens remarkably well.

1

2

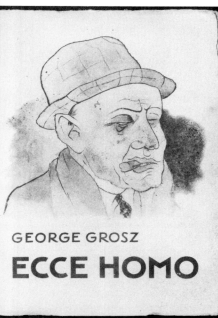

GEORGE GROSZ
ECCE HOMO

Fiction	18th and 19th century first editions (n.b. 19th century novels were often first issued in monthly parts; these are more collectable than the first editions in book form)	Dickens (Charles), *Dombey and Son*, first edition, 20 in 19 original parts, 1846–8, original wrappers, worn. Nov. '81, £300. Dickens (Charles), *Dombey and Son*, first edition in book form, 1848, worn. Sept. '81, £26.
	20th-century first editions of the early works and high points from the careers of well-known authors (condition particularly important)	Adams (Richard), *Watership Down*, first edition, Rex Collings, 1972, good condition. Jul. '85, £160. Tolkien (J.R.R.), *The Hobbit*, 1937, torn dust jacket. Dec. '84, £580. Huxley (Aldous), *Brave New World*, 1932, pristine condition. Aug. '84, £220 (No. 2).
Books as Objects	Bindings (fine bindings of any age, but generally more valuable if identifiable as having been bound by a well-known binder and/or for a well-known collector	Tissot (J.J), *The Life of Christ*, 2 vols, folio, 1897–8, vellucent binding by Cedric Chivers. Jul. '85, £800 (No. 1).
	Private Press Books (mostly pre 1950)	Kelmscott Press: Morris (William), *The Earthly Paradise*, 8 vols, limited to 225 copies, 1896-7, good condition. Sept. '84, £545. Doves Press: Shakespeare (William), *Venus and Adonis*, limited to 200 copies, 1912, good condition. Jun. '85, £300. Golden Cockerel Press: Bligh (William), *Voyage in the Resource*, limited to 350 copies, 1937, good condition. Jun. '85, £300.
	Incunabula (i.e. books published prior to 1500)	Boccaccio (Giovanni), *Les Nobles et Chères Dames*, folio, first edition, in French, 143 of 144 leaves, 1493, later fine binding. Nov. '82, £7,000.
	Fine typography: eg Baskerville in England, Bodoni in Italy, early printers, e.g. Estienne of Paris, Aldus Manutius of Venice	Catullus Tibullus & Propertius, *Opera*, 4to, Birmingham, Baskerville, 1772, poor condition. £50.
	Illustrated Books: 16th & 17th century, almost any work with good quality and a reasonable quantity of illustrations	Nuremberg Chronicle: Schedel (Hartmann) *Das Buch der Croniken …*, folio, Nuremberg, 1493, some leaves torn, later binding, average condition. Dec. '84, £7,500. Wither (George), *A Collection of Emblemes, Ancient and Moderne*, folio 1634–5, poor condition. Dec. '81, £110.
	18th century, good quality, illustrations, preferably combined with fine printing and binding (arguably best are French and Italian)	Piazetta (G., illustrator): Tasso (Torquato) *La Gerusalemme Liberata*, folio, 1745, average condition. Feb. '82, £1,600. Picart (Bernard), *Cérémonies Religieuses du Monde*, 8 vols, folio, Amsterdam, 1723–43, incomplete. Dec. '84, £1,000.
	19th century, watch for well-known artists as illustrators (e.g. Blake, Samuel Palmer, D. G. Rosetti, Millais) and High Victorian curiosities	Rosetti (D. G., illustrator): Allingham (William), *The Music Master*, 1855, poor copy. Oct. '84, £170. Moore (Thomas), *The Ferns of Great Britain and Ireland*, folio 1855, 51 nature-printed plates, average condition. Apr. '85, £650.
	20th-century limited editions of works illustrated by e.g. Edmund Dulac, Arthur Rackham, Heath Robinson, George Grosz, Barbier	Dulac (Edmund, illustrator) *Rubaiyat of Omar Khayyam*, limited to 750 copies, 4to, [1904], good condition. June '85, £280. Grosz (George), *Ecce Homo*, Ausgabe D, folio, Berlin, [1923], binding worn. Nov. '80, £155 (No. 3). *Adam Langlands*

Modern First Editions

What is a modern first edition? For the purposes of this article, the term is specifically restricted to the first printing of a book, including the all-important dust jacket, by authors who are, or are likely to become valuable or collectable. The 'first' will have only one date printed on the back and/or the front of the title page. Any indication of a later date, for example, or a reissue, second impression, third edition and so on, and you are buying a 'second-hand' book, not a modern first edition.

Collecting modern first editions has been written about and discussed over the past two or three years more than any other area of book-collecting. Notwithstanding all this recent publicity there are still more misconceptions in this field than in any other. These misconceptions include what a 'modern first edition' is, what is collectable, what is likely to become collectable, ignorance of the effect of fashion on prices, and, most important of all, uncertainty about how and for what reasons a collection should be formed.

There are two apparent motives for starting a collection: financial gain, or admiration for a particular author or genre. Ideally the second reason should be the sole motivation, but in reality, with, for instance, a copy of Tolkien's *The Hobbit* making £1,100 in June 1986 (No. 1), it is not possible to divorce at least some financial consideration, if not the hope of financial gain, from the purer collecting ethic. However, collecting solely for investment purposes requires a great deal of luck and is rather like buying premium bonds: it is always a friend who scoops the pot.

The effect of fashion can be relatively short-term, as in the case of the prices achieved for George Orwell's *Nineteen Eighty-Four* in 1984, or will show only over a period of three or four years, as is beginning to be the case with Ian Fleming's Bond books. The dramatic rise in price of Fleming's *Casino Royale* is a good indicator of what, to a lesser degree, has happened to all his titles—1980 – £420; 1982 – £500; 1983 – £700; 1985 – £1,000. However, there are indications from both the book trade and collectors, that

1

this trend may have peaked, and only a slower, if still steady, increase in price can be expected from now on.

Predicting what will become collectable is a dangerous occupation, but I would like to put in a plea for Mervyn Peake. This artist, illustrator, poet and novelist already has quite a devoted following and his Gormenghast trilogy is widely known (popularized by Radio 4's adaptation of *Gormenghast* including the headline-catching pop star Sting among its cast). Less well-known is some of his poetry, his illustrations of others' work, and his fantastical children's books. There are at least fifty titles that bear his individual stamp. The highlights of any Mervyn Peake collection are the Gormenghast Trilogy, *Titus Groan* published in 1946 (an inscribed copy of which sold for £50 in 1984), *Gormenghast*, 1950, and *Titus Alone*, 1959. Then there are *Captain Slaughterboard Drops Anchor*, first published in 1939 with black and white illustrations, and very scarce as the publisher's stock was destroyed during the war; *Shapes and Sounds*, 1941, Peake's first volume of poetry; *Mr Pye*, 1953, a fable set in the reality of Sark—the island Peake loved so much—recently adapted for television; and finally *The Rhyme of the Flying Bomb*, 1962, which is arguably one

of the best long narrative poems of recent times.

There are also numerous works illustrated by Peake, ranging from the classics *Treasure Island*, 1949, and *The Hunting of the Snark*, 1948, to lesser-known works, such as Christina Hole's *Witchcraft in England*, published in 1946 (No. 2 – see also pp. 218, 219).

With the exception of the prices I have quoted, none of Peake's works should cost more than about £30 in first-class condition, a small price surely for a collection which will reveal the work of a man of great talent in three closely linked yet very different fields.

What is collectable now? Graham Greene's early work is still selling strongly, especially dust-jacketed signed copies. *The End of the Affair*, inscribed, sold for £220; *Loser Takes All*, inscribed, made £220; and *Our Man in Havana*, inscribed, realized £340, all in 1984. To digress briefly, dust jackets are now being auctioned without the books they are supposed to protect, but watch out for forgeries! Evelyn Waugh remains constant as do the majority of the Pantheon of Modern Authors, Fleming being the possible exception.

Adam Langlands

1. *'The Hobbit'*. June '86, £1,100.
   A similar copy sold in Dec. '83 for £780.

2. *Two from a series of 28 Mervyn Peake original illustrations to Christina Hole's 'Witchcraft in England'*. Sept '85, £3,000.

3. *T. S. Eliot, 'The Cocktail Party', first published in 1950.*
   A similar unsigned copy made £78 at California Book Auction Galleries, June '85. The signature on the copy illustrated here should add around £50 to the price.

4. *Malcolm Lowry's 'Ultramarine', first published 1933.* June '86, £85.
   The rare first novel from the author of the recently filmed *Under the Volcano*. Only 1,500 copies were printed and 750 of these were apparently pulped. This was a poor example.

5. *Title page from A. A. Milne's 'Now We Are Six', first published 1927.*
   This dust-jacketed copy, together with a copy of *Winnie the Pooh* in similar condition, made £160 in June '86.

2

THE
COCKTAIL PARTY

a comedy by

~~T. S. ELIOT~~

FABER AND FABER LTD
24 Russell Square
London

3

ULTRAMARINE
A Novel

BY

MALCOLM LOWRY

JONATHAN CAPE
THIRTY BEDFORD SQUARE
LONDON

4

NOW WE ARE SIX
BY A. A. MILNE WITH
DECORATIONS BY
ERNEST H. SHEPARD

METHUEN & CO LTD. 36 ESSEX STREET
LONDON W.C.

5

County Maps

One of the most popular fields of map collecting in Britain has been county maps, and to many people the work of Blaeu, Speed and Saxton have become the archetypal 'old map'. The popularity of this field has been created firstly by the decorative nature of the material, secondly by the large volume of maps printed from 1570 up to the mid-19th century, and in the last decade by the marketing of maps as potential investments. However, since 1980 the market has suffered from an oversupply of material (most county maps were published in atlas form), without a proportionate increase in demand, resulting in a depressed or static market. In general this situation still prevailed in 1985.

One of the greatest strengths in collecting county maps is the depth and diversity of the field. The most sought after county maps are the early editions by Christopher Saxton. Saxton is often thought of as the father of English county mapping; in 1570 he was commissioned by Elizabeth I to survey her realm. This task he finished in 1578, covering the country in 34 maps. The rarity of these in addition to the quality of the workmanship has brought about a great demand for his work. In 1985 examples of his maps varied from £480 for Montgomeryshire to £1,200 for Cheshire. In contrast there has been a declining interest in the later impressions by Web, 1645, and Lea, 1689. None of these maps should be confused with the more common Saxton/Kip/Hole maps which were published in Camden's *Britannia* in 1607, 1610, and 1637. These generally fetch between £40 – £80 depending on county.

The decline in interest in the later Saxton impressions reflects a trend that is apparent among many of the popular decorative maps of the mid-17th century. Good examples of the important counties by mapmakers such as Speed, Blaeu and Jansson have maintained their price levels at auction, but the demand for 'less fashionable' counties, mediocre or poor copies has declined significantly. Whereas early (Sudbury and Humble) editions of Speed's Middlesex regularly sell for between £150 and £220, similar impresions of County Durham rarely exceed £100. The rarer and unusual

maps of the 17th century have not been so affected by changes in fashion; the miniature maps by Bill, Van Langeren and Van den Keere are generally difficult to find. Prices up to £60 are quite usual. Other curiosities such as Drayton's fantasy maps from *Poly-Olbion* have become rarer and sell for up to £70 at auction. Other late 17th-century mapmakers such as Morden and Blome have become less fashionable, and 1695 Morden impressions will only sell for up to £30.

While there has been a decline in interest for many 17th-century cartographers, there has been an increase in popularity in selected 18th-century maps. The work of Emanuel Bowen and Thomas Kitchen has particularly increased in price; these cartographers worked together in the mid 18th century, publishing large, informative and decorative maps. In the past their work has been somewhat undervalued, but today examples of the most popular counties such as Kent or Cornwall fetch £100, Middlesex up to £150.

One of the major cartographical developments in the late 18th and early 19th centuries was the encouragement

and sponsorship of the mapping of the counties of England on a scale of one inch to a mile, and although only 30 such surveys were completed before competition from the Ordnance Survey made them unprofitable, the examples of work by Rocque, Bryant, Greenwood and Davis are of great quality and accuracy. Over the past year some of these early surveys have sold particularly well: Donn's Oxfordshire, 1797, £320; André and Chapman's Essex, 1774, £450; Rocque's London and Westminster, 1747, £750; Rocque's Berkshire, £350.

Other early 19th-century county maps have not improved significantly in price; Teesdale, Cary, Moules, small Greenwoods, Archers, Walkers, Pigots have all been static, although examples published separately in original slipcases have been more buoyant.

By the 1850s and 1860s the competition of a subsidized national survey effectively brought to a close all commercial mapping based on the county unit.

Tom Lamb

1. *John Speed, Middlesex, 1676.* 16 × 21 in. Sept. '85, £180.

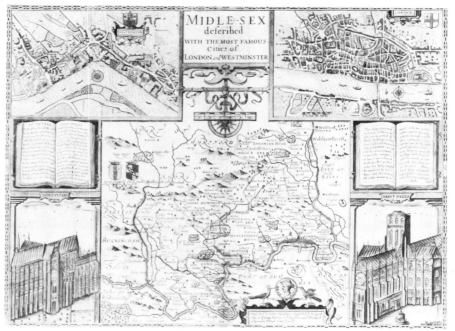

1

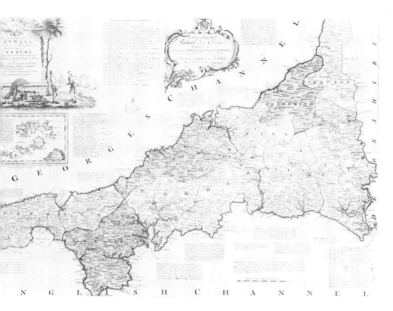

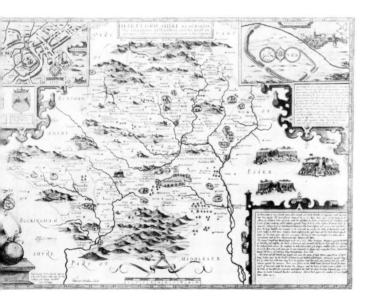

2. *Thomas Kitchen, Cornwall, c.1760.* 21 × 27 in.
   Dec. '85, £100.

3. *Christopher Saxton, Gloucestershire, 1577.*
   15 × 20 in. Sept. '84, £550.

4. *John Speed, Hertfordshire, 1627.* 16 × 20 in.
   Sept. '85, £130.

5. *Pieter Van den Keere, Middlesex (miniature
   Speed), 1627.* 3½ × 5 in. Mar '85, £50.

6. *Johannes Jansson, Somerset, 1646.* 15 × 20 in
   Jul. '84, £60.

Travel Books – Voyages of Discovery and Exploration

An interest in foreign lands, both out of natural curiosity and for commercial gain, is a natural occupation of man, and so down the centuries authors have recounted tales of their voyages and travels and described, sketched and mapped the lands that they found. These published works are termed travel books. Over the past decade this field has become increasingly popular, reflected in rising prices at auction. One category of travel books which has become particularly competitive is accounts of voyages of discovery and exploration. The competition has been especially strong in three areas: the early voyages of the 15th and 16th centuries, the 18th-century voyages in the Pacific, and the 19th-century accounts of the interior explorations of Africa, Asia, Australia and the Americas. As with all book collecting, value is very much conditional on completeness of text and illustrations, and for 18th- and 19th-century works a premium is placed on works in original cloth or boards.

The earliest accounts of 15th- and 16th-century voyages are now rare and very valuable; Vespucci's *Mundus Novus*, 1504, sold for $24,000 in New York in 1985, and even the late 16th-century collections of Hakluyt, Purchas and De Bry – but not, of course, the modern editions – sell for well over £7,000. At the lower end of the market defective copies of the later authors can still be purchased for several hundred pounds, and the later Maclehose editions of Hakluyt, 1903–5, have sold for £150, and Purchas, 1905–7, for £200 (May '86). An offshoot of the demand for these early accounts has been a rise in value of Hakluyt Society publications (a society founded in the mid-19th century, which reprinted accounts of explorations). In May '86 a selection of 165 such publications dating from 1856 to 1982 brought £3,500.

Another area of travel book collecting in which values have improved quite dramatically are voyages in the Pacific during the latter half of the 18th century.

By 1760 the world map was beginning to be completed, and the last great voyages to delineate the extent of the Pacific, Australasia, and the southern continent began. The voyages of Cook, Bligh, Vancouver, Flinders and others opened up vast new territories for European expansion. These voyages have rightly been regarded in this light, and have been particularly sought after: in March 1985 a copy of Cook's *Second Voyage*, 2 vols. 1777, sold for £1,600; Bligh's *Narrative of the Mutiny on board the Bounty*, 1790, made £1,750; and a fine copy of Vancouver's *Voyages*, 4 vols. including atlas, brought £7,500. The offshoot publications from Cook's voyages have also been in demand; Anderson's account of Cook's voyages selling for around £300, Marra's *Journal of the Resolution's Voyage*, 1776, sold for £550 in November '85, and the Hakluyt reprint of *Cook's Journals* edited by Beaglehole, 6 vols. 1968–74, fetched £200.

By the 19th century the outlines of most of the continents were complete, coastal settlements established, and travellers began to explore the interior. Many of these early accounts by Europeans were not published in large numbers, or were published in obscurity, so that some are now very rare. In collecting these 19th-century works condition is all important in relation to price; copies in clean original cloth or boards command premium prices. Similarly different areas of the world become more fashionable.

Against a general increase in price for many 19th-century books in the past year, two particular regions have been in demand, the Middle East and Central Asia. Although Niebuhr wrote about Arabia in the late 18th century, it was not until the 1820s and 1830s, with the travels of Burckhardt, Burton, Buckingham and others, that the area began to be explored. The accounts of these authors have been in demand: in September '85 Burckhardt's *Notes on the Bedouins*, 1830, sold for £750, his *Travels in Syria*, 1822,

for £400, Burton's *Pilgrimage to El-Medinah*, 3 vols., 1855–6, £850 (but see Nos. 1 and 4), and Buckingham's *Travel in Mesopotamia*, 2 vols., 1827, £150.

In the case of Central Asia and Turkestan (now part of USSR), the earliest 'modern' exploration took place in the late 19th century, and it is the scientific reports by explorers such as Hedin and Stein which are popular. Stein's *Serindia*, 5 vols., 1921, sold for £2,275 in May '85, and a copy of Hedin's *Scientific Reports*, 8 vols., 1889–1902, made £1,600 in February '86. Another 20th–century work on this region, Baddeley's *Russia, Mongolia, and China*, 2 vols, 1919, has regularly sold for £1,000.

These examples taken from three different aspects of travel book collecting are indicative of the increased interest in such books, both in Britain and abroad. This is one form of collecting where one can truly say, 'The world is your oyster'!

Tom Lamb

1. *Richard F. Burton*, Explorations of the Highlands of Brazil, *first edition, 2 vols., 1869, original cloth*. May '85, £180. Burton, of *The Arabian Nights*, is of course most in demand for his Middle Eastern works. See also No. 4.

1

A
VOYAGE
TO THE
PACIFIC OCEAN.
UNDERTAKEN,
BY THE COMMAND OF HIS MAJESTY,
FOR MAKING
Discoveries in the Northern Hemisphere.
TO DETERMINE
The POSITION and EXTENT of the WEST SIDE of NORTH AMERICA;
its DISTANCE from ASIA; and the PRACTICABILITY of a
NORTHERN PASSAGE to EUROPE.
PERFORMED UNDER THE DIRECTION OF
Captains COOK, CLERKE, and GORE,
In his Majesty's Ships the RESOLUTION and DISCOVERY.
In the Years 1776, 1777, 1778, 1779, and 1780,
IN THREE VOLUMES.
VOL. I. and II. written by Captain JAMES COOK, F.R.S.
VOL. III. by Captain JAMES KING, LL.D. and F.R.S.
Illustrated with Maps and Charts, from the Original Drawings made by Lieut. HENRY ROBERTS,
under the Directions of Captain Cook; and with a great Variety of Portraits of Persons, Views
of Places, and Historical Representations of Remarkable Incidents, drawn by Mr.
WEBBER during the Voyage, and engraved by the most eminent Artists.

Published by Order of the Lords Commissioners of the Admiralty.

VOL. I.

LONDON:
PRINTED BY W. AND A. STRAHAN;
FOR G. NICOL, BOOKSELLER TO HIS MAJESTY, IN THE STRAND;
AND T. CADELL, IN THE STRAND.
MDCCLXXXIV.

A
VOYAGE
TO
New Holland, &c.
In the Year, 1699.
Wherein are described,
The *Canary*-Islands, the Isles of *Mayo* and
St. *Jago*. The Bay of *All Saints*, with the
Forts and Town of *Bahia* in *Brasil*. Cape
Salvadore. The Winds on the *Brasilian*
Coast. *Abrohlo*-Shoals. A Table of all the
Variations observ'd in this Voyage. Oc-
currences near the Cape of *Good Hope*.
The Course to *New Holland*. *Shark's* Bay.
The Isles and Coast, &c. of *New Holland*.

Their Inhabitants, Manners, Customs, Trade, &c.
Their Harbours, Soil, Beasts, Birds, Fish, &c.
Trees, Plants, Fruits, &c.

Illustrated with several Maps and Draughts; also
divers Birds, Fishes, and Plants, not found in
this part of the World, Curiously Ingraven on
Copper-Plates.

VOL. III.

By Captain *William Dampier*.

LONDON:
Printed for *James Knapton*, at the *Crown* in St. *Paul's*
Church-yard, 1703.

3

THE

LAKE REGIONS OF CENTRAL AFRICA

A PICTURE OF EXPLORATION

BY

RICHARD F. BURTON
Capt. H. M. I. Army ; Fellow and Gold Medallist of the Royal Geographical Society

"Some to discover islands far away"—Shakspere

IN TWO VOLUMES

VOL I

LONDON
LONGMAN, GREEN, LONGMAN, AND ROBERTS
1860

The right of translation is reserved

4

ISTORIA
ò breuissima relatione
DELLA DISTRVTTIONE
dell' Indie Occidentali
DI MONSIG. REVERENDISS.
Don *Bartolomeo dalle Case*, ò *Casaus*, Siuigliano
Vescouo di Chiapa Città Regale nell' Indie .

CONFORME AL SVO VERO ORIGINALE
Spagnuolo, già stampato in Siuiglia.

Con la traduttione in Italiano di Francesco Bersabita .

Dedicata all' AMICITIA.

IN VENETIA Presso Marco Ginammi . M DC XXVI.
Con licenza de' Superiori, & Priuilegio.

A

JOURNEY

FROM

PRINCE OF WALES'S FORT,

IN HUDSON'S BAY,

TO

THE NORTHERN OCEAN.

UNDERTAKEN

BY ORDER OF THE HUDSON'S BAY COMPANY,

FOR THE DISCOVERY OF

COPPER MINES, A NORTH WEST PASSAGE, &c.

In the Years 1769, 1770, 1771, & 1772.

By SAMUEL HEARNE.

DUBLIN:
PRINTED FOR P. BYRNE, No. 108, AND J. RICE, No. 111,
GRAFTON-STREET.
1796.

6

---

2. *Title page, James Cook and James King,* A
    Voyage to the Pacific Ocean *(Cook's third
    voyage), 3 vols. text, 4to, 1748, modern half-
    calf. May '86, £400.*

3. *Title page, William Dampier,* A Collection of
    Voyages, *3 vols., 1697–1705, later half-
    morocco. May '86, £170.*

4. *Title page, Richard Burton,* The Lake Regions
    of Central Africa, *2 vols., 1860, modern
    half-morocco. Sept. '85, £280.*
    *Africa is not yet in such demand as the
    Middle East.*

5. *Title page, Bartolomé de las Casas,* Istoria o
    Brevissima relatione della distruttione dell'
    Indie Occidentali, *4to, Venice, 1626, old half-
    calf. May '85, £300.*

6. *Title page, Samuel Hearne,* A Journey from
    Prince of Wales Fort . . . to the Northern
    Ocean, *first Dublin edition, 1796,
    contemporary calf. May '86, £80.*

Index